D1331355

DE
2 (

2003

2006

The European Office

OFFICE DESIGN AND NATIONAL CONTEXT

Juriaan van Meel

010 PUBLISHERS, ROTTERDAM 2000

Dit proefschrift is goedgekeurd door de promotor:
   Prof. ir. H. de Jonge

Samenstelling promotiecommissie:
   Rector Magnificus, voorzitter
   Prof. ir. H. de Jonge, Technische Universiteit Delft, promotor
   Prof. ir. K.W. Christiaanse, Technische Universität Berlin
   Prof. ir. H.J.M. Ruijssenaars, Technische Universiteit Eindhoven
   Prof. dr. A.A.L.G. Wentink, Katholieke Universiteit Brabant
   Prof. ir. M. Wijk, Technische Universiteit Delft
   Dr. G.P.R.M. Dewulf, Technische Universiteit Delft
   Dr. F. Duffy, DEGW Limited

Credits
   Text editing by Ian Cressie, Oosterbeek
   Design by Sander Boon, Rotterdam
   Printed by Veenman drukkers, Ede

© 2000 The author, Department of Real Estate and Project Management
(www.bk.tudelft.nl/d-bmvb) and 010 Publishers, Rotterdam (www.010publishers.nl)

ISBN 90 6450 382 6

Contents

Preface

Throughout history, architectural styles have been primarily and distinctively regional. Buildings tended to reflect local culture, resources and customs. Today's architecture, however, is global. Cities all over the world are becoming more and more alike with almost identical fast-food outlets, chain stores and hotels.

Office buildings, too, seem to add to an increasing homogeneity. Everywhere we can find similar glass and concrete office blocks. Yet, many of the similarities are superficial. From the outside, offices seem alike. A closer look reveals that they are not. The scale of buildings, their floor plans and their interior layouts vary from country to country. For example, an office that is built in London would not stand a chance of being built in Amsterdam, and vice versa.

These differences are surprising because the office building is supposed to be a very rational building type. Its design is dominated by 'objective' requirements concerning functionality, efficiency and flexibility. International differences, however, show that these requirements are not as clear and universal as is often thought.

This book looks at office design in Europe and explains its variety. It is the result of a four-year explorative study of office design in the UK, Germany, Sweden, Italy and the Netherlands. The study is multi-disciplinary in nature, crossing boundaries of various research fields. It covers topics such as architecture, urban planning, real estate management, economy, labour relations, culture and legislation.

The primary goal of this study is to offer a better understanding of the forces that shape office design: it tries to explain why office buildings are 'the way they are'. In so doing it sheds new light on the relationship between form and function of office buildings. In a more practical sense, it aims to help architects and clients to navigate better in international waters.

Finally the book may be used as a source of inspiration. Design practices in other countries can be used to rethink one's own practices.

Juriaan van Meel | Delft, December 1999

1   Introduction

This book examines office design in the United Kingdom, Germany, Sweden, Italy and the Netherlands. By comparing these countries, it explores how office design is affected by national context, thereby trying to give a better understanding of the forces that shape the office. Our basic idea is that office design is not just the translation of functional needs or technological possibilities, but also a reflection of the society in which it is created. Contextual factors such as culture, labour relations, regulations and market conditions are often taken for granted. Yet they can affect the design of an office building long before an architect or consultant is hired.

This opening chapter describes why and how this study has been conducted. First it describes the research field that is being addressed. From this description, we formulate a research question and describe the focus of this research. Then we explain how we intend to answer the research question. The chapter ends with an outline of this dissertation.

RESEARCH FIELD

Office design

In the past, office design may have been generally regarded as something lucrative but dull. Disdain for the office was common among architects and critics, who believed that the commercial nature of the building was incompatible with the art of architecture.[1] The office building, however, is perhaps the most important building type of the 20th century. Just as factories were the symbol of the industrialisation at the start of the 19th century, offices are emblematic of the current post-industrial era. Offices are all around us. They dominate the contemporary city and accommodate more than half the working population in the Western world.[2] Just take a look at the central business districts of New York, London or Frankfurt, where shiny offices dwarf all other structures. The skylines of these 'global cities' are no longer dominated by cathedrals or palaces, symbolic of society's regard for God and country, but by tall commercial buildings, reflecting the power of the modern corporation.[3] They are today's most visible and tangible index of economic activity, of social, technological and financial progress.

The importance of the office has to be seen in the light of the growing significance of knowledge and information in our society. Drucker has explained that the world is evolving into a knowledge economy.[4] For better or worse, the production of knowledge

1 Church towers have been replaced by secular office buildings

is becoming more important than the production of goods and products. 'Blue-collar' factory workers are being replaced by 'white-collar' office workers. Instead of producing tangible goods they hold meetings, read and write reports, use computer systems, talk to customers and clients or surf the Internet. Sociologist Manuel Castells remarks that 'information becomes the critical raw material of which all social processes and social organisations are made'.[6] Critical in all economic activities is 'the capacity to retrieve, handle, store and generate information and knowledge'. And these are exactly the activities that take place in office buildings.[7]

Because of their significance, offices have recently received much attention in both research and practice. Office design is 'hot'. In only a couple of years, it has become a discipline in itself, with its own magazines, conferences and gurus. Triggered by developments in information technology and management theory, architects, consultants and researchers have developed visionary ideas about how the 'new office',

2 'Work where you want'.

'tomorrow's office' or the 're-invented workplace' should look.[8, 9, 10] New office concepts overwhelm the market. *Shared offices, virtual offices, non-territorial offices, hotel offices, combi-offices, just-in-time offices, free-address offices* and flexible offices are just a few examples from the new dictionary of office design.[11]

These new concepts tell us how offices will become meeting places for 'nomadic' employees equipped with mobile phones and laptops; how the office will become a more diverse and informal environment; or how in the near future offices may no longer be necessary because we can work anywhere and at any time.

All these concepts and ideas are highly normative. Just like architectural theory in general, primarily they tell us how buildings should be, and little about how they actually are.[12] Of course, nothing is wrong with developing new ideas about offices. Radical and visionary ideas are necessary to rethink and question implicit assumptions that underlie often 'tedious' mainstream office design.[13] Nevertheless, it is necessary to understand why today's offices are the way they are. Before you prescribe new solutions, you need to describe and understand the present situation. What are the forces that shape our offices? Is it function, technology, management theory, costs, culture, architectural genius or simply tradition that creates offices? Without a full understanding it is hard to say anything realistic about how the office of the future will or should look. So, what does shape the office?

3 Mobile office

Office design and function

The first thing to do when trying to understand office design is to look at the function that the building fulfils. According to Goldwaithe, function is the most basic tool of analysis to explain building activity.[14] 'People use buildings for specific purposes, and as their needs change so do the demands they make on the places where they do what they have to do, whether it is work, sleep, pray, or play'. This is certainly true for office buildings. In literature on real estate and facility management, office buildings are regarded as a factor of production, just like human resources, technology, finance and information.[15] The main function of these buildings is to facilitate and support the primary processes of the organisation occupying the office. If they are well designed they can play a pivotal role in business successes, and become the means by which the achievement of commercial objectives is accelerated, just as the wrong type of office can stifle them.[16]

The design of offices should, therefore, be based on analysis of organisational objectives and business processes. In line with Louis Sullivan's axiom 'form follows function', one has to know what goes on in the building before any design decisions can be taken.[17] We have to look at variables such as the size and age of the organisation, its organisational structure, and most of all the types of activity performed.[18] Raymond and Cunliffe say: 'What kind of office we need depends on what we do'.[19]

The logic of the above is clear. Good buildings are shaped to a considerable extent by the functions they must satisfy.[20] It explains why lawyers' offices are different from architects' offices, why offices of young businesses are different from those of mature businesses, and why front offices are different from back offices. Yet, function does not tell the whole story. If organisational requirements were the sole determinant of form, one would expect buildings of similar organisations to take the same form. This does not seem to happen. Particularly when looking from an international point of view, we see that similar organisations are accommodated in totally different types of offices.

International differences and office design

In this era of globalisation, one would not expect international differences in office design. Certainly, the world of design is more international than ever. Corporations are expanding into new markets, needing sales offices, research centres, factories, distribution centres or headquarters to support their core business. The requirements for these facilities seem to be fairly similar everywhere, namely that they have to be functional, flexible and cost-efficient. In some cases, organisations use design concepts that have been developed in their home country, expressing a certain corporate image or way of working. For example, when looking at retail stores, hotels and restaurants we see that organisations tend to build completely identical facilities in different countries. There are few cities where one cannot find identical buildings for Toys'R'Us, Benetton, McDonalds, Burger King, The Marriot or The Hilton. Why would office buildings not belong to the same category of global building types?

At first sight, offices do look very similar all over the world. Many writers have observed the similarities between the slick-skinned, air-conditioned, elevator-serviced office towers in cities such as New York, Tokyo, London, Kuala Lumpur and Jakarta. Shiny office towers are regarded as symbols of globalisation. Architectural critics have remarked that 'steel and glass skyscrapers transform urban landscapes everywhere' and that 'where the "flow" of international investment touches the ground, clean and shiny business districts arise'.[21, 22]

4 New York, Tokyo, London or Frankfurt?

Of course, there is some truth in such observations. A closer look, however, reveals that the similarities tend to remain limited to the outside of the building. Literature on office design shows that there are crucial international differences in the shape of buildings, their floor plans and the layout of their workplaces. Lee Polisano, for example, explains that office buildings in Europe tend to be not as high as those in America. Likewise, Richard Saxon describes in his book about atrium buildings that the depth of office buildings differs strongly from country to country.[24] He says that US employees tend to sit within 14-16 m of a window, while British employees are used to sitting within 8-10 m and German employees within 4-6 m of a window. Similar differences can be found in the layout of workplaces. According to Francis Duffy British employees tend to work in open-plan offices while their counterparts in North European countries, such as Germany and Sweden, are used to cellular offices.[25]

International differences in office design are clearly illustrated by the fact that even buildings of the same corporations differ from country to country. Take a look, for example, at the main headquarters of ABN AMRO Bank in Amsterdam and their British headquarters in London (see figures 5 and 6).[26] It takes only one hour to fly from one city to the other but you enter a completely different 'office culture'. In Amsterdam you find a building with corridors and spacious rooms on either side. Inside these rooms you can see people working behind computer screens, next to a window. In London, you will find employees doing similar work, but instead of working in rooms they are working in relatively small cubicles in large open areas. The only rooms you will find are meeting rooms and spare rooms for management.

Office design and national context

International differences in office design indicate that the match between the requirements of an organisation and its office buildings is not a 100% fit. In all countries, architects, consultants and clients try to create efficient and functional offices. In most briefs, one can find the same words saying that the building has to support the company's business processes, that it has to be flexible, that it has to promote employee communication, and that it shouldn't cost too much. Yet, the final outcomes of the design process are different from country to country. This suggests that the interpretation of these requirements is influenced by the national context. One can think of the influence of factors such as culture, regulations, labour relations and market conditions. For example, the term 'efficiency' is likely to have a different meaning in Hong Kong, where rents are sky-high, than in, for example, the Netherlands where rents are relatively low.

Most professionals are probably not aware of the influence of context or are rarely confronted with it. Architects, consultants, and their clients are part of a particular society in a particular period, and usually their ideas simply cannot help but reflect the constraints of their environment. By virtue of living in any given society, they will unconsciously acquire that society's underlying cultural assumptions.[27] Nevertheless, it is relevant to make the relationship between offices and their national context explicit, for three reasons.

The first is that knowledge about the influence of context provides us with a better insight into the complexity of office design. Amos Rapoport emphasises that cross-cultural research is crucial in understanding buildings.[28] Such research touches upon the very basic issue that lies at the core of design theory, namely the source of design. At the beginning of the design process, architects and their clients share a certain collection of

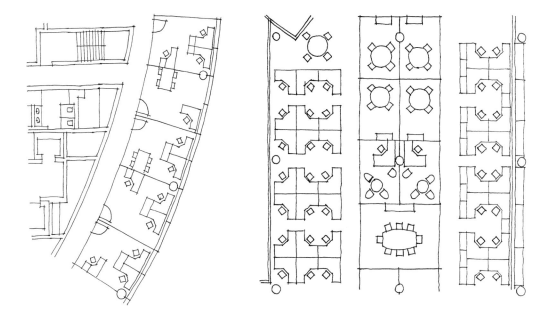

5 Workplace layout
ABN AMRO Bank
Amsterdam

6 Workplace layout
ABN AMRO Bank
London

information, requirements, intentions and assumptions. Then 'suddenly' a design for a
building appears.[29] The design partly derives from the actions of the individual
architect, the consultants and the client. It is, however, partly influenced by the larger
context and conditions in which these parties operate. Normally, the impact of the latter
is hard to study because the context is a given. An international comparison, however,
provides us with the opportunity to vary external factors such as culture, economics and
regulations. It can thereby give us a better understanding of the forces that shape office
design.

A second, related, reason is that an international comparison may shed new light on
the relationship between form and function of office buildings. This is interesting
because the office market is said to have become more demand-driven while it is still
unclear what that actually means. On the demand side organisations are changing
rapidly due to technological and economical developments. But how should the office
market respond to these changes? Is there, for example, still a need for the corporate
superblocks we are building today, or are we all going virtual in the near future? To
answer such questions a fundamental debate is needed about the relations between
supply and demand, and between form and function of offices. By looking at this topic in
a broad perspective – in different times and across different cultures – this study aims to
provide this debate with new input.

A third, more practical reason for making the relationship explicit is that more and
more architects and clients are working on an international level, where they encounter
all kinds of international differences, including differences in office design.[30] Particularly
in Europe, national context seems to have a large impact on design. There may be a
single market, but there is no single European approach to office design – just as there is
no single European business culture or economic system. When, for example, the

American architectural firm Kohn Pedersen Fox started working in Europe they had to 'adapt their design and thinking to meet the challenges of the cultural, civic and legislative differences that occur both in Europe, and between Europe and the US'.[31] Thom McKay of RTKL, another American firm, said that 'Americans tend to believe the myth that the European barriers have broken down and there is a unified European culture, but you have to take into account each country's different ways of practising architecture'.[32]

Similar reactions can be heard from international clients. For example, to many US real estate managers Europe is still 'a great "unknown" fraught with persistent myths'.[33] They are confronted with different expectations and ideas about office design within their own organisations. It seems that business organisations are fed as much by local natural and cultural conditions as by corporate ethos.[34] The same client, therefore, is likely to commission radically different buildings in different locations.[35] For real estate and facility managers, knowledge of the characteristics and background of different 'office cultures' is necessary for developing successful workplace strategies.

RESEARCH QUESTION

From the description of the research field the basic question of this research can be formulated as: what shapes the office, what makes the office the way it is? Our idea is that an important part of the answer lies in the national context in which offices are being designed and produced. This idea is based on international differences that can be observed in office design. They suggest that office design is not only influenced by the function the building performs, but also by the national context in which it takes place. The previous section has shown this notion to be crucial for both a general understanding of office design, as well as for designers and clients who operate on an international level. Therefore a more specific research question should be formulated: **What is the relationship between office design and national context?**

It is clear that the key terms of this research question, *office design* and *national context* can refer to many things. Office design may refer to issues ranging from the architectural style and use of materials to office construction and IT infrastructure. The same is true for the term national context. In the description of the problem area we have already mentioned several contextual factors such as climate, building regulations, culture, tradition, labour relations and costs. Identifying which aspects are dominant is one of the main aims of this study. Yet, a certain pre-selection is still needed in order to know what to look for. For this reason we present a historical analysis and a brief review of the literature of international differences in Chapter 2. The result is a framework that has been used to guide the rest of this study.

FOCUS

To study the relations between office design and national context we have focused on Europe. The main reason being that Europe can be regarded as a cultural mosaic: within a relatively small area, a wide diversity of markets, attitudes, regulations and cultures can be found. These differences enable us to study the influence of context more clearly. Contrasts and extremes can make a research topic more 'transparently observable'.[36] A more practical reason is that, as indicated in the description of the research field, differences in Europe cause a lot of misconceptions among international real estate professionals.

Within Europe, we have selected five countries to study: the United Kingdom, Germany, Sweden, Italy and the Netherlands (see figure 7). These particular countries have been chosen for two reasons. The first being that each represents a different type of national context. They are all economically important countries, with large stocks of offices, but attitudes towards work, human relations, hierarchy and the workplace tend to differ strongly. According to extensive research on national culture by Ronen and Shenkar, all of them come from a different 'country cluster': the UK comes from the Anglo cluster, Italy from the Latin cluster, Germany from the Germanic cluster and Sweden from the Nordic cluster (see figure 8).[37] The Netherlands also belongs to the Nordic cluster and will serve as a reference country.

The second reason for choosing these countries is that they have produced interesting office buildings and concepts. Although the 20th century office is strongly associated with the skyscrapers of New York and Chicago, many of the innovations in office design have taken place in Europe. Unlike North American projects, European buildings have generally tended to reflect architectural or stylistic trends and, in more recent times, managerial fashions quickly and accurately.[38] Germany for example is the country where in the 1960s the Quickborner Team conceived the *office landscape*. Its large open areas with their seemingly random configurations of desks and chairs can be regarded as the first workplace innovation. Likewise, Swedish designers invented the *combi-office* in the late 1970s. This concept consists of private cells grouped around an open common space. The Netherlands is not so much associated with a particular office type, as with a particular building, namely the *Centraal Beheer* building of Herman Hertzberger. With its kasbah-like layout it is regarded as one of the icons of 20th century office design. The United Kingdom has not produced a particular workplace type, but is extremely interesting because it is the only European country that has adopted the US style *open-plan offices* that contrast strongly with the traditional European *cellular offices*. Italy is not known for a specific office building or concept (in fact, there is hardly any accessible literature at all about Italian office buildings). Nevertheless, all together these countries cover the whole range of types and innovations in office design.

RESEARCH APPROACH

The research approach consists of three elements. First, a *research philosophy*, which guides the way data is gathered and analysed and conclusions are drawn. Second, a *research strategy*, which provides an outline of the plan that must be carried out to answer the research question. Third, *research instruments*, for collecting the necessary data.

Research philosophy

Psychologists, physiologists, ergonomists and other specialists have studied the office work environment in great detail.[39, 40] They have studied lighting levels, the need for fresh air, temperature levels and a whole range of other subjects. Most often their research follows what is called a positivist research philosophy, exemplified by precise definition, objective data collection, systematic procedures and replicable findings.[41] In line with the positivist philosophy, they rely on the researcher's objective observations using 'hard' research, instruments such as experiments and surveys.[42]

Unfortunately the positivist approach is difficult to apply in this type of study. The first problem is that a positivist approach assumes that you know what you are looking for. It starts with a predefined, detailed conceptual framework or set of hypotheses to be tested. Our research, however, is much more exploratory in nature. Apart from work by Duffy and Evette, there is hardly any material available on this topic.[43, 44] This makes it difficult to propose a clear hypothesis at the start of our research.

The second problem is that positivism is strongly focused on proving causal and deterministic relations. Using quantitative techniques, it tries to 'nail down' causal factors and identify the exact magnitude of their contributions. Such an approach, however, will not be fruitful for this study. For three reasons, it is almost impossible to prove causal relations between the design of buildings and their context:

  • The first is that buildings are the result of many factors, not one or two alone. Such factors may include climate, natural resources, social structure, legislation and culture, to name a few. It is highly improbable that any of these alone 'caused' one or another set of design characteristics.[45]
  • The second reason is that the contribution of even a single factor may vary from place to place. A factor may be important in one place, but not at all important in another.[46] Climatic circumstances and natural resources may for example be very important in the Sahara or Antarctica, while they may have little explanatory value in Central Europe.
  • The third reason is that causes are not only multiple but also 'conjunctural': they strengthen each other as well as providing a cumulative effect.[47] Because of their complex interplay over time, it is often not possible to do more than say that factors x, y and z may be important: one may not be able to separate out their exact or unique contributions.

Because of these obstacles, this study will follow an alternative, what is called interpretivist research philosophy. Interpretivist research relies much more on the researcher's subjective interpretations and understanding of the phenomena that have to be studied.[49, 50] It focuses on studying phenomena in their natural environment and the importance of qualitative factors such as 'shared norms and values', 'culture' and 'common languages between actors'.[51] Using inductive research, it is more oriented towards theory building than theory testing.

In this study, using an interpretivist philosophy means that we will literally 'interpret' office buildings in their context. Instead of studying them as the logical outcome of some rational decision-making process, they will be studied *as a reflection of*

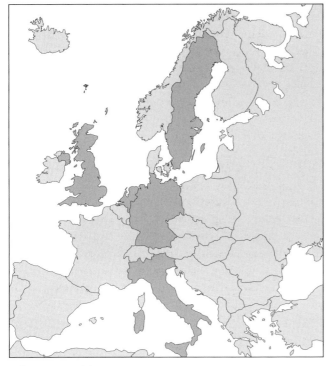

GERMANIC	NORDIC
	Finland
Austria	Denmark
Switzerland	**The Netherlands**
Germany	**Sweden** Norway
United Kingdom	**Italy** Spain
Ireland	France
	Portugal
	Belgium
ANGLO	**LATIN**

7 Selected countries
in Europe

8 Country clusters
in Europe (Ronen and
Shenkar, 1985)

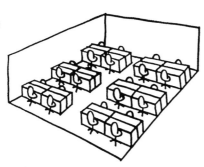
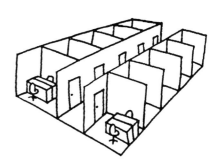

9 Various office
types in Europe:
open-plan office,
cellular office,
combi-office,
office landscape

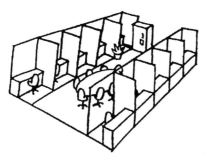

their context. Altman and Chemers used a similar approach when they studied the relationship between houses and culture.[52]

The interpretivist approach can be compared to those used in archaeology and anthropology. In both disciplines, the interpretation of 'physical artefacts' such as buildings plays an important role. In archaeology, material remains are often the only lead. Archaeologists recover them and then try to decipher and interpret them. Likewise anthropologists use 'material culture' as a record of technology, social organisation, cognition, and other aspects of the human condition. Clifford Geertz describes it as 'the art of describing cultural artefacts and interpreting them' and that is exactly what this study tries to do.[53] We describe office buildings – our artefacts – and then try to find 'circumstantial evidence' to explain why those buildings are the way they are.

Another similarity between our study and anthropological studies lies in the problem of interpretation. With cross-cultural research your own cultural background is likely to influence your perception of 'reality'.[54] This notion has to be taken into account when interpreting data. In our research strategy we have tried to deal with this problem by using local experts on office design. An anthropologist would call them *informants*, who have to strip away 'the ballast of expectation and assumption that we take with us from our own cultures into our fieldwork'.[55]

A crucial difference with the anthropological approach is that anthropologists tend to focus on a limited research area, for example a single tribe or village. In contrast, this study encompasses five large countries. For that reason we cannot achieve the same depth and internal validity as studies that focus on a single topic, a single building or a single country. The strength of this study, however, is that it conveys an impression of the otherwise unattainable whole. The technique may be likened to that of a pointillist painting, in which fine details are absent but where the interaction of colour, composition, tones and brightness yields a coherent unity. In line with the interpretivist philosophy, the focus is on 'understanding' rather than 'proving'.

Research strategy
The interpretivist approach is not above criticism. It tends to be less objective, difficult to replicate and therefore it offers fewer possibilities for generalisation. To overcome these shortcomings it is crucial to 'design' a research strategy that shows clearly what has been done, why it has been done, and how conclusions are drawn.

The strategy begins with the development of a research framework. Advocates of what is known as 'grounded theory' suggest the contrary approach: that the inductive researcher needs 'to be open to what the site has to tell us' and 'slowly evolve a coherent framework rather than imposing one from the start'.[57] Yet, the adoption of this suggestion can easily result in 'an incoherent, bulky, irrelevant, and meaningless set of observations', in particular when you are studying five different countries.[58] Therefore, a rough (though not rigorous) research framework needs always to be defined before the field can be entered.[59, 60]

This study makes a historical analysis of European office design to develop the research framework. The analysis has to point out the main differences between offices in the selected countries and indicate when these differences emerged. Analysing whether changes in office design coincide with changes in society gives a first view of the factors that possibly explain international differences. These factors will then be studied in more detail in the rest of the study.

Using this more or less standard framework as a roadmap, the next step is to start the 'fieldwork'. In our research this consists of interviews with experts, literature research and case studies. For each country we try to find out whether there is something like a national office type, or whether we can identify typical design features for that country. After that we try to link these features with traits of the national context.

After each country and its offices are well understood, country-level analyses are compared. Goal is to go beyond initial impressions and to begin to form more general explanations.[61] The comparison has to show whether there are any reoccurring patterns (e.g. in all countries culture plays a dominant role) or striking dissimilarities (e.g. culture is dominant in some countries and not in others).

The overall strategy of this research is summarised graphically in the figure below. In reality, the research process has been more iterative, but the main point is that this study uses a certain framework to perceive reality, and that it uses both single-country analysis and international analysis to come to conclusions.

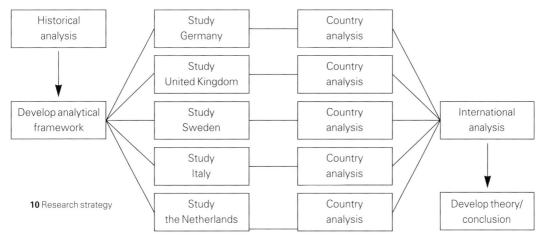

10 Research strategy

Research instruments

With the explorative nature of our research question and the broad selection of countries in mind, we have used three different research instruments: *literature research, interviews with experts* and *case studies*. These different instruments were chosen because countries are too diverse and complex to rely on one source of evidence or one perspective (in particular when studying such diverse topics as architecture, economics, culture, etc). This is what in the literature is called 'triangulation'.[62] The term refers to an iterative process of comparing and checking the results of different sources of information, thus providing valuable feedback. Triangulation increases the reliability of the results, enabling us to get a good view of a complex research subject. Each instrument is described below in more detail.

Literature research The literature study focused on reviews of office buildings in architectural magazines and books, guidelines about office design, and socio-economic studies of the selected countries. One of the limitations of this literature study is that it relies heavily on architectural journals and magazines, which merely focus on prestigious buildings. By definition, these buildings do not represent common office design and often not even the best of office design (at least from a user's point of view). Still, such buildings give a good insight in what is considered as progressive, sophisticated or controversial in a country ('exaggeration is a social scientist's microscope'). Furthermore, they are often described against the background of standard design principles of their time. Thereby the buildings also reveal, indirectly, the characteristics of mainstream office design.

Interviews with experts To get first-hand information about each country, we interviewed local experts on office design, such as architects, researchers, property and facility managers and real estate brokers. For each country we interviewed up to 10 experts (see List of interviewees). The interviews were 'open' and built around two questions: what do you regard as typical characteristics of offices in your country and what is the background of these characteristics. Furthermore, interviewees were asked to comment upon the final country reports afterwards.

Case studies We used case studies to exemplify and clarify the results of the interviews and the literature study. Initially we also wanted to use case studies to investigate in depth the international differences. Five pilot cases, however, showed that the influence of context is hardly traceable at project level.[64, 65] We observed that architects, clients and consultants are seldom aware of the influence of their national context because it is too familiar and too implicit. The differences that we try to explain were seldom the result of clear decisions, but were already embedded in corporate standards or simply taken for granted.

OUTLINE OF THE DISSERTATION

The outline of this book corresponds with the different steps in the research strategy. This first chapter describes the research questions and the 'design' of our research. Chapter 2 describes the historical development of European office design. This results in a research framework that points out the contextual factors that are most interesting and relevant to study. In the following five chapters (3-7) this framework is used to study the UK, Germany, Sweden, Italy and the Netherlands. In Chapter 8 the results of all countries are compared to be able to come to general conclusions. Chapter 8 ends with the practical implications of this study for office design and international real estate management.

Notes

1   Willis, C. (1995), *Form follows finance*, Princeton Architectural Press, New York
2   MacCormac, R. (1992), 'The dignity of office', in: *The Architectural Review*, No. 5,
    pp. 76-82
3   Sassen, S. (1991), *Global Cities*, Princeton University Press, New York
4   Drucker, P.F. (1992), 'The new society of organizations', in: *Harvard Business Review*,
    September/October, pp. 95-104
5   Steward, T.A. (1998), *Intellectual Capital*, Nicholas Brealey Publishing, London
6   Castells, M. (1994) 'European Cities, the information society, and the global economy',
    New Left Review, 204, pp. 18-32
7   Vos, P. G. J. C., Meel, J. J. and Dijcks, A. (1999), *The Office, the whole office and nothing
    but the office version 1.2*, Delft University of Technology, Department of Real Estate and
    Project Management, Delft
8   Duffy, F. (1997), *The New Office*, Conran Octopus, London
9   Raymond, S. and Cunliffe, R. (1997) *Tomorrow's Office: Creating effective and humane
    interiors*, E & FN Spon, London
10 Sims, W., Joroff, M. and Becker, F. (1996), *Managing the Re-invented Workplace*,
    International Development Research Foundation, Atlanta
11 Vos, P. G. J. C., Meel, J. J. van and Dijcks, A. (1999), *The Office, the whole office and
    nothing but the office version 1.2*, Delft University of Technology, Department of Real
    Estate and Project Management, Delft
12 Hiller, B. (1996), *Space is the machine: a configurational theory of architecture*, University
    Press, New York
13 Meel, J. J. van (1999), 'You probably know the slides off by heart!', *Usable Buildings*,
    http://www.usablebuildings.co.uk/Opinion.html
14 Goldwaithe, R.A. (1980), *The building of Renaissance Florence*, John Hopkins University
    Press, Maryland
15 Joroff, M.L., Louargand, M., Lambert, S. and Becker, F. (1993), *Strategic Management of
    the Fifth Resource: Corporate Real Estate*, Industrial Development Research Foundation,
    Atlanta
16 Duffy, F. (1997), *The New Office*, Conran Octopus, London
17 Sullivan, L. (1896), The Tall Building Artistically Considered, in: *Lippincott's*, March,
    pp. 403-409
18 Center for Building Performance & Diagnostics (1995), *flexible grid –flexible density –
    flexible closure officing: the intelligent workplace*, Carnegie Mellon University, Pittsburg
19 Raymond, S. and Cunliffe, R. (1997), *Tomorrow's Office: Creating effective and humane
    interiors*, E& FN Spon, London
20 Gelernter, M. (1995), *Sources of architectural form: a critical history of Western design
    theory*, Manchester University Press, Manchester
21 Çelik, Z. (1998), 'Cultural intersections: re-visioning architecture and the city in the
    twentieth century', in: Koshalek, R., Smith, E.A.T. and Ferguson, R. (1998), *At the end of
    the century: one hundred years of architecture*, Abrams, New York
22 Rodermond, J. (1996), 'Globalisering initieert ook pluraliteit', in: *De Architect*, No. 9,
    pp. 44-45
23 Polisano, L. (1995), 'Complexity and Contrast; American and European High-Rise
    Buildings', in: *Architectural Design*, Vol. 65, No. 7/8, pp. 30-35
24 Saxon, R. (1994), *The atrium comes of age*, Longman, Harlow
25 Duffy, F. (1993), *The Responsible Workplace*, Butterworth Architecture, Oxford
26 Van Meel, J. J. (1998), *Case study ABN AMRO Bank*, Internal report, Delft University of
    Technology, Department of Real Estate and Project Management, Delft
27 Gelernter, M. (1995), *Sources of architectural form: a critical history of Western design
    theory*, Manchester University Press, Manchester
28 Rapoport, A. (1980), 'Vernacular architecture and the cultural determinants of form', in:
    King, A.D. (ed.) (1980), *Architecture and society*, Routledge & Kegan Paul Ltd, London
29 Gelernter, M. (1995), *Sources of architectural form: a critical history of Western design
    theory*, Manchester University Press, Manchester
30 MacInnes, K. (1998), 'The challenge of globalisation', in: *World Architecture*, No. 62,
    pp. 92-93
31 World Architecture (1995), 'KPF International', in: *World Architecture*, No. 34, pp. 26-65
32 EuroProperty (1995), 'Cross-Border Business', special issue *Europroperty*
33 Searing, J.E. and Goldstein, J.C. (1992), '10 Myths and realities American real estate
    managers need to know', in: *National Real Estate Investor*, Vol. 34, No. 2, pp. 17-21
34 Melvin, J. (1996), 'I want one like that', in: *World Architecture*, No. 52, pp. 62-67
35 Wislocki, P. (1998), 'Old-fashioned boy', in: *World Architecture*, No. 64, pp. 86-87
36 Eisenhardt, K.M. (1989), 'Building Theories from Case Study Research', in: *Academy of
    Management Review*, No.14, pp. 532-550
37 Ronen, S. and Shenkar, O. (1985), 'Clustering Countries on Attitudinal Dimensions: A
    Review and Synthesis', in: *Academy of Management Review*, Vol. 10, No. 3, pp. 435-454
38 Duffy, F. (1980), 'Office buildings and organisational change', in: King, A.D. (ed.), *Buildings
    and Society*, Routledge, London

39   Sundstrom, E. (1986), *Workplaces*, Cambridge University Press, New York
40   Wineman, J.D. (1982), 'Office Design and Evaluation: An Overview', in: *Environment and Behavior*, Vol. 14, No. 3, pp. 271-299
41   Daft, R.L. (1983), 'Learning the Craft of Organisational Research', in: *Academy of Management Review*, Vol. 8, No. 4, pp. 539-546
42   Meel, J.W. van (1994), *The Dynamics of Business Engineering: Reflections on two case studies within the Amsterdam Municipal Police Force*, Van Meel, Dordrecht
43   Evette, T., Bonnet, C., Fencker, M., Michel, P. and Philipon, B. (1992), *L'architecture tertiaire en Europe et aux Etats-Unis*, CSTB, Paris
44   Duffy, F. (1997), *The New Office*, Conran Octopus, London
45   Altman, I. and Chemers, M. (1980), *Culture and environment*, Brooks/Cole, Monterey
46   ibid.
47   Miles, M.B. and Huberman, A.M. (1994), *Qualitative data analysis*, Sage publications, London
48   Altman, I. and Chemers, M. (1980), *Culture and environment*, Brooks/Cole, Monterey
49   Checkland, P. (1981), *Systems Thinking, Systems Practice*, Wiley, Chichester
50   Lee, A.S. (1991), 'Integrating positivist and interpretative approaches to organizational research', in: *Organization Science*, Vol. 2, No. 4, pp. 342-365
51   Meel, J.W. van (1994), *The Dynamics of Business Engineering: Reflections on two case studies within the Amsterdam Municipal Police Force*, Van Meel, Dordrecht
52   Altman, I. and Chemers, M. (1980), *Culture and environment*, Brooks/Cole, Monterey
53   Geertz, C. (1973), *The Interpretation of Cultures*, Basic Books, New York
54   Ellen, R.F. (1984), *A Guide to the general conduct of ethnographic research*, Academic Press, London
55   ibid
56   Yin, R.K. (1989), *Case study research: design and methods*, Sage publications, London
57   Miles, M. (1979), 'Qualitative data as an attractive nuisance: The problem of analysis', in: *Administrative Science Quarterly*, Vol. 24, December, pp. 590-601
58   ibid.
59   Yin, R.K. (1989), *Case study research: design and methods*, Sage publications, London
60   Mintzberg, H. (1979), 'An emerging strategy of "direct" research', in: *Administrative Science Quarterly*, Vol. 24, December, pp. 582-589
61   Eisenhardt, K.M. (1989), 'Building Theories from Case Study Research', in: *Academy of Management Review*, No.14, pp. 532-550
62   Jick, T. (1979), 'Mixing qualitative and quantitative methods: Triangulation in action', in: *Administrative Science Quarterly*, Vol. 24, December, pp. 602-611
63   Brand, S. (1994), *How buildings learn: what happens after they're built*, Phoenix Illustrated, London
64   Meel, J. J. (1998), *Businesses globalise, buildings don't*, Internal report, Delft University of Technology, Department of Real Estate and Project Management, Delft
65   Meel, J. J. van, Blakstad, S., Dewulf, G. P. M. R. and Duffy, F. (1997), *Power-relations in office design*, Internal report, Delft University of Technology, Department of Real Estate and Project Management, Delft

2   History

To understand international differences in office design today, it is useful to look at their origins. From an analysis of the differences and the context in which they emerge, it is possible to develop a research framework that can be used in the rest of the book.

The historical description of office design focuses on the 20th century. This does not imply that offices have no earlier history. There are, for example, illustrations of 15th century merchants working behind what now may be called workstations. There is even a 9th century image of St Matthew doing 'office work' at his desk. It is clear, however, that such images have little to do with modern office design. It was only at the start of the 20th century that the office as we know it today was created with its own style, layout and technology.

We divide the history of the office in the 20th century into seven periods: the early 20th century, the 1950s, the 1960s, the 1970s, the 1980s and the 1990s. This division is based on the varying themes that have dominated European office design. We also pay attention to American office design because it has strongly influenced European office design, particularly during the first half of the century.

12 Early office: 9th century painting of St Matthew working at a desk

EARLY 20TH CENTURY: WHITE-COLLAR FACTORIES

The early 20th century is the starting point of a huge growth in the number of office workers in Europe. In the UK, for example, the number of office workers grew from 0.8% of the working population in 1851 to 7.2% in 1921.[1] This 'administrative revolution' was caused by the concentration of enterprise and finance.[2] Mergers and techniques of mass production created large professional corporations which required more co-ordination and administration, resulting in an increase in the scale of office work.

13 19th century high status office work

The new office jobs differed greatly from those in preceding ages. Before, office work had had a certain prestige as it was performed by educated men (rarely women) who could read and write. In the early 20th century office work became widespread and routine. Moreover, women entered the work environment. Sociologists referred to this as the 'proletarisation' of office work, to indicate it's increasing similarity to factory work.[3]

The growth and changing nature of office work had a huge impact on the design of office buildings. Whereas offices had previously been small residential buildings, now

14 20th century low status office work

they became 'white-collar factories' with flexible floor plans and anonymous workrooms with noisy office machines.[4] The main inspiration for both the organisational and physical design of offices came from America.

AMERICA

In the 1920s, the American office environment was strongly influenced by the ideas of the American engineer Frederick Taylor – probably the first management guru. Taylor took a 'scientific' look at work processes to find ways to maximise efficiency by dividing the process into a series of repeatable steps.[5] This way of working had first been applied to industry, but it also seemed suitable for office work, especially when 'information technology' such as typewriters, calculators and telephones invaded the office environment.

Taylor's ideas were translated into office design by the concept of large open floor spaces with an orthogonal arrangement of desks, all facing the same direction (that of the supervisor).[6] The openness had to facilitate the flow of work from one desk to another and maximised the potential for visual supervision of clerical staff. An American handbook on business administration says 'No longer are clerical staff separated from each other by partitioned spaces which obstruct the flow of work'.[7] Only managers were provided with cellular offices, often with windows to aid supervision.

15 Interior Larkin Building (p. 24)

The icon for the open plan is the Larkin Building (1904) in Buffalo, designed by Frank Lloyd Wright (see figure 15). The size, layout and technology of this building marked the coming of the modern corporate office. The building housed over 1,000 women of the Larkin Soap Company, a mail order business, who sat in an open office processing huge volumes of paper. To bring daylight and fresh air into the building, it was equipped with a primitive form of air-conditioning and skylights. In 1907, an article in *Business Man's Magazine* referred to it as 'a model administration building' in which 'no outlay was spared to make the lighting, ventilating, plumbing and every feature that means comfort for the daily worker, the best in the world'.[8]

EUROPE

American office design and its underlying Tayloristic ideology left a strong mark on European offices. Just as today, new ideas spread internationally through magazines, books, trade shows and courses on 'scientific office management'. In the Netherlands, for example, there was a large exhibition called 'Modern Office Interiors' where people could see the latest, mainly American, developments in office design.[9]

Despite all the attention given to the American office, European office buildings were not just copies of their trans-atlantic counterparts. The open-plan arrangement spread much more slowly and office spaces tended to be smaller and less anonymous.[10] In fact, European 'ink pools' were little more than large rooms (although in Sweden they were still referred to as 'seas of slaves').[11]

16 Dutch exhibition on modern office design

One reason for the differences in design was that in Europe Taylor's ideas were taken up with less enthusiasm and faced more resistance rooted in tradition than in the US.[12] European business culture seemed to be less 'modern' and rationalised than in America. Another crucial factor was that the European office market was also less well developed and less professionalised than in American. This can be explained by the fact that in America the administrative revolution had taken place several decades earlier.[13]

A good example of a European 'Tayloristic' office is the headquarters of Thule, a Swedish insurance company (G. Clason, 1942). In line with Taylor's ideas, the design was based on a close study of work processes in the organisation and how they could be improved.[14] Standardised workplaces, classroom-like layouts and glazed partitions were the result of this study. Another characteristic feature was a mechanical conveyor belt to transport paper from desk to desk, emphasising the idea of a 'white-collar factory'. Typically European was the building's moderate depth (16.5 m) and the use of a central corridor with rooms on both sides. (see figures 17 - 19)

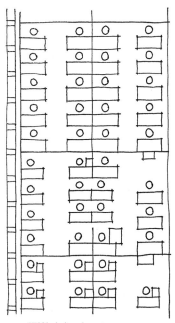
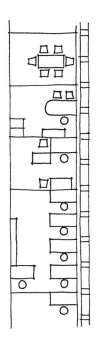

17 Workplace layout
Thule Huset,
Stockholm

18 Floor plan Thule
Huset, Stockholm

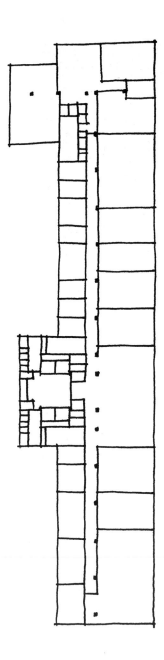

19 Interior
Thule Huset,
Stockholm

20 The 1950s were the years of reconstruction with the US as example (*Les constructeurs*, Fernand Lèger, 1950)

1950S: GLASS BOXES

After the Second World War, the growth of office work accelerated due to economic expansion. With assistance of the USA, Western Europe emerged rapidly from its post-war ruins and set out a course for unrivalled prosperity.[15] Most striking was Germany's 'Wirtshaft Wunder', but Italy's 'miracolo' and Sweden's 'record-breaking years' were hardly less spectacular (see table 2.1). This success went hand in hand with growing faith in progress and technology.

Table 2.1 The average yearly growth of GDP 1948-1963[16]

West Germany	7.6 %
Italy	6.0 %
UK	2.5 %

The optimism that was characteristic of these years was reflected in the introduction of a new type of office building: the glass box – a rectangular high-rise office block with glazed facades. This type of building would become strongly associated with commercial and international architecture for the next fifty years. And, once again, America was the country to emulate.

AMERICA

America had already established a tradition of high-rise buildings in the early 20th century (e.g. the Chrysler and the Empire State Building in the 1930s), but in the 1950s it received new impetus from improved construction techniques and new ideas about architecture. The innovations were embodied in the Lever House (see figure 21) and the Seagram Building (paradoxically the latter had been created by an immigrant architect from Europe, Mies van der Rohe). The most visually striking feature of these buildings was their glass facade. This type of facade was cherished by 'Modernists' for their 'continuous' and 'light' appearance. Later on it became clear that such facades could cause major heating and cooling problems. Nevertheless, they became the most copied feature of the Modernists' high rises.

Inside the American office, another change had taken place. With the introduction of air-conditioning in the 1930s, and fluorescent lighting in the 1940s, the floor depth of these buildings was no longer limited by the need for daylight and natural ventilation.[17] It was now possible to create high-rise buildings with deep and open floors, the type of universal spaces that the Modern architects valued so much (exemplified by Mies van der Rohe who placed a high intellectual value on the concept of 'universal space').

More important than the aesthetic value of deep and uninterrupted floors were their economic benefits. Deep floors were 'economical', 'easy to subdivide' and they 'contained no awkward corners that were difficult to let'.[18] For the employees, however, little changed. Rank-and-file employees still spent their days in open plans, while their supervisors occupied glazed rooms along the perimeter. In 1958, the American sociologist Wright Mills described the Modern American office as 'a big stretch of office space, with rows of identical desks'.[19]

21 Lever House

22 Union Carbide
Building

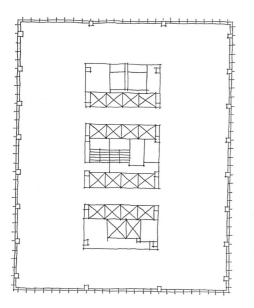

23 Floor plan Union
Carbide Building

24 Interior Union
Carbide Building

A good example of an American 'glass box' is the Union Carbide Building in New York, which was designed by Skidmore Owings and Merrill (SOM) in 1960 (see figures 22 - 24). From the outside, the building was characterised by a refined glass-and-steel curtain wall. Inside, the building demonstrates how air-conditioning and artificial lighting facilitate the creation of deeper, more compact offices. One of its technological novelties was a suspended ceiling that integrated the lighting and air-distribution, to satisfy the client's demand for a flexible ceiling capable of functioning perfectly no matter how interior partitions were arranged.[20]

EUROPE

In Europe, American glass boxes like the Union Carbide Building attracted a lot of publicity. Absorption of the new ideas was aided by wartime devastation that provided unprecedented opportunities to rebuild many cities in the new Modern style.[21] Yet, the scale of European office buildings remained smaller than in America.

First of all, European buildings tended to be not as high as the American prototypes. Prior to the Second World War, commercial high rises were unknown in Europe. There had been none of the intermediate stages in high-rise design as in the US, so standards on what was regarded as 'high' were totally different. The difference becomes clear when we compare the tallest buildings in New York in 1950 and the tallest buildings in London in 1965 (see table 2.2).

Table 2.2 Five tallest buildings in New York and London

New York tallest office buildings in 1950		London tallest office buildings in 1965	
Empire State Building (1931)	373.5 m	Shell Centre (1961)	107 m
Chrysler Building (1930)	314 m	Portland House (1963)	100 m
American International Building (1932)	285 m	Moore House (1963)	67 m
40 Wall Tower (1929)	278 m	Royex House (1963)	67 m
RCA Building (1933)	255 m	St Alphage (1961)	64.5 m

One reason for this difference was that the urban setting in Europe was completely different from that in the US, with its grid-like city structures. The urban setting of European cities was much older and more complex. Furthermore, European architects and clients had to deal with regulations regarding the height of buildings, which were meant to preserve the historical character of cities.[24] In London, for example, the *London Building Act* of 1894 limited the building height to 24 m at the cornice and 30 m in total height. In Berlin the height limit was related to the street width, but the maximum was 22 m.

After the Second World War, European regulations on building heights were eased, but still planners were not fond of tall buildings that were meant to reflect the power of large corporations. In London, local planners were clearly suspicious of tall commercial buildings.[25] Cowan even suggests that there was a tendency among British planners to view property developers as enemies of the welfare state.[26] A report from 1956 stated that 'it should be made clear to developers that the council does not recognise any right to erect high buildings'.[27]

25 Pirelli Tower

Apart from differences in height, the scale of European glass boxes was also smaller in terms of floor plans. Artificial lighting and air-conditioning became widely available on the European market, but this did not result in deeper plan forms as in the US. The British architect Hugh Krall said: 'None of the air-conditioned office buildings in central London is of anything but the traditional pattern, though all have full supplementary artificial lighting and are not perimeter dependent'.[28] One reason for this may be that the deep, American open plans still did not match European business culture. Another is that architects were simply not interested in the internal layout of office buildings.

When European architects studied US skyscrapers they focused on their technical properties, the thickness of the skin and the dimensions of the window module rather than on their work environment.[29] In particular, the window module seemed to be extremely important. The main question was which module size was most efficient and flexible for creating rooms of different sizes. The British magazine *Architectural Design* wrote in 1958: 'In planning an office the first consideration is the module to be adopted'.[30]

The Pirelli Tower (Gio Ponti, 1958) in Milan is an excellent example of a post-war high-rise building (see figures 25 - 27). It is a typical product of the 'faith in the country, in industry and in the imagination' of that time.[31] Behind its impressive facade, the building consists of a central corridor with 'freely divisible office space' on either side.[32] This space is divided into cells for management and group rooms for the clerical staff that are based on a window module of 95 cm.

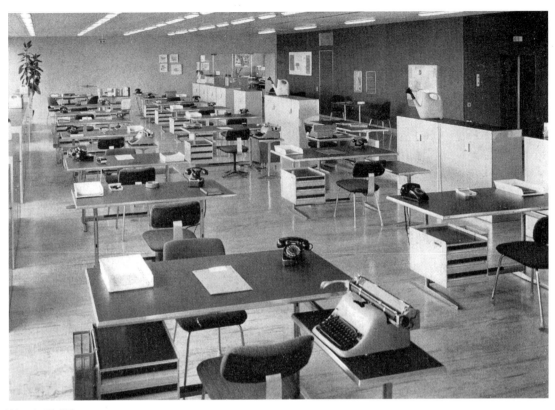

26 Interior Pirelli Tower

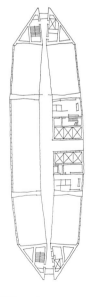

27 Floor plan
Pirelli Tower

When comparing this floor plan with that of the Union Carbide building (see page 30) the difference in scale becomes clear. The floors of the Pirelli building have a depth of 18.5 m, while the Union Carbide building has a depth of over 40 m. A similar tale can be told for other European high-rises of that time such as the Portland House in London (1963), the Unilever building in Hamburg (1963) and the Folksamhuset in Stockholm (1959).

1960S: OFFICE LANDSCAPES

It was in the 1960s that Europe replaced America as the forerunner in office design. While shiny high rises were being erected everywhere, a German consultancy group, the Quickborner Team, was working on a radically new office concept. According to the leaders of the group, Wolfgang and Eberhard Schnelle, conventional office buildings no longer met the needs of modern office work.[33]

The arguments the Quickborner Team used were strikingly similar to those that are being used to promote new solutions today. First of all, they stressed the importance of communication. Following the ideas of (American) organisational thinkers such as Mayo and McGregor, they stressed the importance of 'human relations' at work.[34, 35] Exchange of information no longer had to take place in a vertical direction, downward from boss to worker, but along functional lines, ignoring departmental or hierarchical barriers.[36] Secondly, the Quickborner Team stressed the need for flexibility. Office

28 Literal
interpretation of the
office landscape

buildings had to be able to accommodate 'rapid organisational change' without too much disruption of on-going activities. Thirdly, they mentioned the growing importance of information technology (at that time, large main frame computers), which they predicted would take over routine activities.

Their ideas about communication, flexibility and new technologies were encapsulated in a concept called the *Bürolandschaft*, literally meaning office landscape. In terms of size and technology, this concept was clearly inspired by American offices: office areas were large and open, using air-conditioning to make their deep spaces habitable. The interior design, however, was governed by ideas that stood far apart from 'the cold and hard efficiency of the American open-plan office'.[37] The office building was regarded as a shell for the interactive processes that take place within.[38] Inside, communication had to be able to flow freely without being hindered by walls or doors. Therefore, there were no private offices, no rooms at all, and desks and other equipment seemed to be strewn about, totally without pattern.[39] Employees, regardless of their rank or position, had to be accommodated in the same space, thereby 'eliminating the hierarchical order and uniting the entire staff from its head down to the last typist'.[40]

The first office landscape project was an office for Bertelsmann, a large German publishing house located in Guttersloh (see figures 29 - 31). It was a project for 270 employees that served as a 'study object' for a new headquarters with 2,000 employees. The building consisted of a rectangular open floor with removable screens and

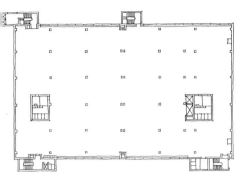

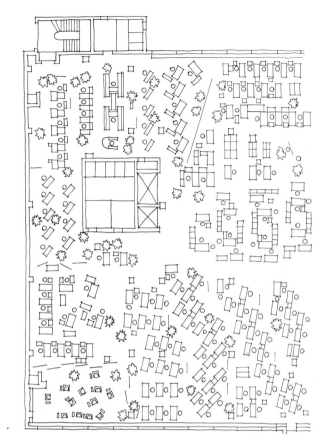

29 Floor plan
Bertelsmann

30 Workplace
layout Bertelsmann

31 Interior
Bertelsmann

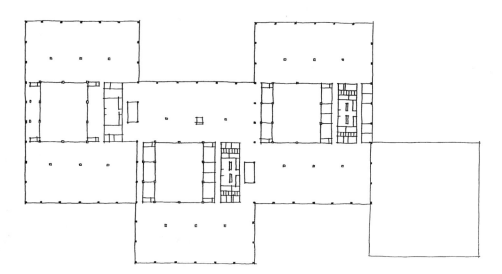

32 Floor plan Volvo

lightweight furniture as the main structuring elements. Wall-to-wall carpets, ceiling treatment and screens with acoustical surfaces had to control the noise. Workplace arrangements were based on the detailed study of communication patterns between the different groups of the organisation.

When the first projects had been completed, awareness of what the Quickborner Team was doing spread rapidly as a result of visits by architects and clients, articles in architectural magazines, and books about office design (the Schnelles had their own publishing house). The concept soon became fashionable all over Europe.

The office landscape seemed to capture the spirit of the period, with society becoming more open and receptive to 'progressive ideas'.[41] All parties involved in office design reacted enthusiastically. For architects it presented a formal solution that was radically different from conventional office types. The business community in its turn was charmed by the fact that the landscape was cost-efficient and progressive at the same time. German authority Professor Siegel said that 'low building costs beside the advantage of easy organisation are the most important arguments in favour of the landscape'.[42] From the user's point of view too, the office landscape seemed to be a good solution. With its spacious workplace layouts, wall-to-wall carpets and the rest areas it provided, it was a welcome deviation from the austere white-collar factories of previous decades.[43, 44]

One of the first large-scale projects outside Germany was Volvo's headquarters in Torslanda, Sweden, designed by Lund and Valentin, 1967 (see figures 32 - 34). At the start of the project, a study group of representatives from the Volvo Company (from different departments and different levels) made trips to study office buildings (both cellular and open-plan offices) in Sweden and the rest of Europe. Based on the experience of these study tours the board of directors decided to build an office landscape.[45] Extensive studies of communication processes and interviews with employees preceded the design of the building. Nevertheless, ten years later the landscape worked out differently than had been expected.

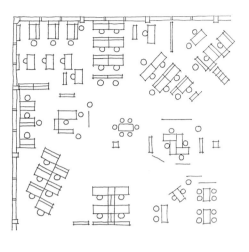

33 Workplace layout
Volvo

34 Interior Volvo

1970S: EXPERIMENTAL OFFICES

During the 1970s, the popularity of the office landscape faded all over Europe. This
change took place in the context of an economic downturn that was triggered by the
oil crisis of 1973. The consequent hike in the costs of space heating and lighting made
the corporate showcases of the 1960s suddenly expensive.[46] Furthermore, the crisis
contributed to a questioning of the seemingly limitless optimism regarding technological
developments and economic progress of the previous two decades.

At this particular point in time, office design in Europe began to diverge: a split
emerged between the UK and Continental Europe. As office landscapes fell out of fashion
both British and Continental European architects started experimenting with new types
of offices, but for different reasons and in different directions.

CONTINENTAL EUROPE

In Continental Europe, the loss of popularity of office landscapes was driven by
employee complaints. Employees made it clear that the office landscape was not such
a perfect solution after all. Surveys indicated that employees disliked it because of
'unpleasant temperature variations, draughts, low humidity, unacceptable noise levels,
poor natural lighting, lack of visual contact with the outside, and lack of natural
ventilation'.[47] Apart from these mostly practical problems, the office landscape may
also have clashed with the office culture of that time. Professor Carl Christiansson,
who had been one of the protagonists of the office landscape in Sweden, said: 'I reached
the conclusion that there was no functioning culture on which to build here in Sweden.
We were not accustomed to so much openness and tight contact'.[48]

The complaints of employees had a direct effect on office design because in the 1970s
employees in Continental Europe became more and more influential in organisational

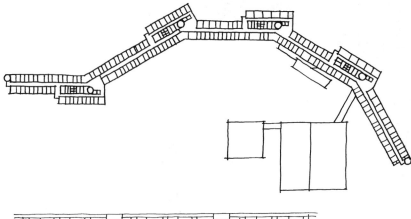

35 Floor plan IBM
headquarters

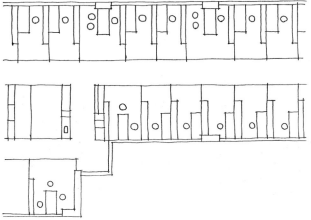

36 Workplace layout
IBM

decision-making. In Germany, for example, the law on *Mitbestimmung* (1976) gave employees' representatives the right to sit on the supervisory board of a company. Similar legislation was being adopted in the Netherlands (1979), Sweden (1977) and also Italy (1975). Using their newly acquired rights, employees' representatives took a firm stand against the landscape. One effect was that some countries adopted extensive regulations that governed the use of space per employee, and secured access to daylight and an outside view.

As a result of the changing role of users and their rejection of office landscapes, preference was given to cellular offices. The most radical reaction took place in Sweden, where it became common practice to give every employee a private office with individual climate control, daylight and an outside view. The project for the construction of IBM's headquarters near Stockholm is a good example. In 1970, at the start of the project, IBM had planned to build a large office landscape. The economic depression, however, put a temporary stop to these plans. When they were resumed in 1974, a new building committee was formed and this new committee recommended that the company build a cellular type of office with individual rooms for all employees (see figures 35 - 38).[49] Within the space of only a few years, a radical shift in thinking about office design had taken place.

37 Exterior IBM

38 Interior IBM

A similar tale can be told for the rest of Northern Europe: cellularisation and standards for space increased. In the Netherlands, for example, the use of office space per worker rose from 17.5 GEA m² in 1950 to 25.2 GEA m² in 1977.[50]

Yet, not all architects and clients were willing to return to the conventional corridor-type office building. Herman Hertzberger's Centraal Beheer Building in the Netherlands (1972) can be regarded as an early example of this tendency (see figures 39 - 41). For both Hertzberger and his client Centraal Beheer – a large and successful insurance company – 'human scale' was a key word. The brief stated that 'they (the employees) must have the feeling of being part of a working community without being lost in the crowd'.[51] One idea for achieving this goal was to transform the office into a small village. Small office units for only 8-10 people were linked by raised walkways, atria and common spaces, creating a kasbah-like office. Another crucial idea was that users had to play an important role in finishing the building. Hertzberger intended to design a structure that the employees themselves had to make 'their own' by, for example, adding decorations or bringing furniture from their homes.

Another decisive experiment, a couple of years later, was Canon's Swedish headquarters (1978). The building was designed by Tengbom Architects, who had been the first Swedish advocates of office landscaping. Åke Beijne, the project architect,

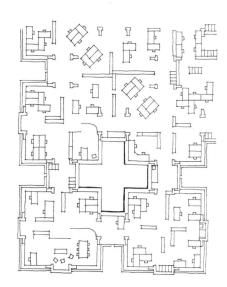

39 Centraal Beheer
Building from the air

40 Workplace layout
Centraal Beheer
Building

41 Interior Centraal
Beheer building

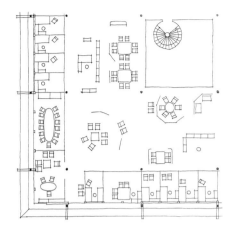

42 Workplace layout Canon headquarters

43 Interior Canon headquarters

created a hybrid solution that was referred to as a 'combi-office'. As the name implies, it was a combination of cellular offices and open spaces (see figures 42 - 43). The cellular offices were small rooms with glazed partitions that were located along the perimeter of the building. In these spaces, employees had to be able to work privately without much hindrance from their colleagues. The open space was located in the middle of the building and accommodated common facilities such as photocopiers and archives. This space was the 'living room', which had to promote employee interaction.

UNITED KINGDOM

In the UK, the office landscape never really took off as it had in Northern Europe. By the end of the 1970s, after several promising experiments, it was clear that the office landscape would not become a success. This had, however, little to do with the opinion of users. British users had the same complaints as their Continental European counterparts, but they had few possibilities to express these complaints effectively.

Unlike their European counterparts, British employees had no formal right to be involved in decisions concerning their working environment. At the end of the 1970s, the proposal to give employees and their union representatives more power met virtually unanimous opposition from British employers.[52] Also, the regulations concerning the design of the working environment remained largely unchanged as the British continued to use their *Offices, Shops and Railway Premises Act* of 1963, which gave relatively general requirements for the design of work spaces.

The adverse attitude towards employee participation was probably typical of the British office culture of that time. The British seemed to be more hierarchical and rigid than on the Continent. This is also likely to be one of the main reasons why the office landscape, with its egalitarian ideology, did not become a success in the UK. Hugh Krall suggests that one of the major difficulties of the office landscape was the differing responses from junior and senior staff.[53] Senior staff in particular objected to their loss

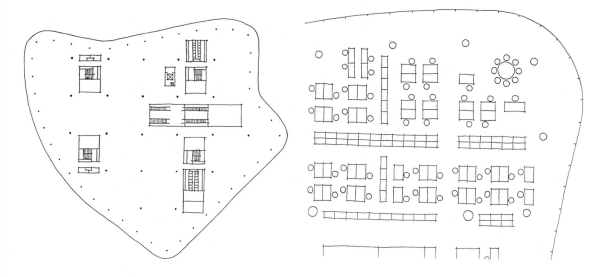

44 Floor plan Willis
Faber & Dumas

45 Workplace layout
Willis Faber & Dumas

of acoustic and visual privacy. In several projects this resulted in some cellular
subdivision which undermined the 'ideological purity' of the concept.[54]

Another crucial reason was British market conditions at that time. The British office
market was dominated by developers. British organisations leased offices rather than
building their own facilities, as most German, Swedish and Dutch companies did. In the
UK less than one-fifth of office space was owner-occupied, while in the Netherlands, for
example, almost two-thirds of the office buildings were owner-occupied.[55, 56] Because
British managers rarely commissioned their own building projects, they had fewer
opportunities to translate fashionable organisational theories into building design,
assuming they had been willing to do so.

Taking into account the power relations in the British office market and the attitude
of British employers, it is logical that office design in the UK took another direction than
in Northern Europe. Just as in Continental Europe, British organisations began to use
private cellular offices again, but in combination with open-plan offices.[57] With these
open-plan offices, the idealistic concept of the office landscape was replaced by a focus on
efficiency and flexibility.[58] Basically, British open plans were very much like those of the
1920s, just more sophisticated. One major innovation in the open plan was the
introduction of systems furniture. Most influential was Herman Miller's Action Office
that reduced the problems with privacy and noise in open space in a very flexible way.

One of the most innovative British open plans of that time was Norman Foster's
Willis Faber & Dumas building in Ipswich (1975). This project is of particular interest
because it was the headquarters of an insurance company, like the Centraal Beheer
building in the Netherlands. Despite their similarity in function, the two buildings could
not have been more different. The Centraal Beheer building was very much user-driven;
it had to be finished by the employees themselves. In contrast, the Willis Faber & Dumas

46 Interior Willis Faber & Dumas

building was a very 'controlled' and 'clean' work environment with a rigid and orthogonal arrangement of workplaces (see figures 44 - 46). Furthermore, it was much more technology-driven than the Centraal Beheer building. One of its many technical innovations was a raised floor with integrated service trenches. Without knowing it, the designers had anticipated the growing importance of information technology, at a time when typewriters and telephones were the only office equipment visible.

1980S: ELECTRONIC OFFICES

In the 1980s, business picked up as the energy crisis drew to a close. Driven by economic growth, European corporations were able to manifest their strength in a series of remarkable buildings that reflected the confidence and panache of the business sector in Europe. One of the main issues in office design was the advent of personal computers. Whereas computers had previously been bulky machines, accommodated in the cellar of a building, now computers came to the employee's desktop. By the mid-1980s, personal computers had become common equipment in offices.

The general expectation was that these computers would radically change office design. British office expert Frank Duffy stated in 1984 that 'many buildings quite suddenly are becoming obsolete'.[59] Even more radical were books such as Toffler's *Third Wave* or Naisbett's *Megatrends*, which predicted that in the near future it would no longer be necessary to build offices because computers would enable people to work anywhere they wanted.[60, 61]

In reality, computers affected the design of offices only at a very practical level. Buildings had to deal with the data cabling and extra cooling loads that came along with

47, 48 Personal computers of the 1980s

the personal computer. Furthermore, computers were used to create so-called 'intelligent' or 'smart' buildings in which HVAC (Heating, Ventilation and Air Conditioning) systems, security and maintenance were regulated automatically.

The 'computerisation' of the office was a global development. Cabling and cooling problems had to be solved in every office. All over Europe, magazines and conferences addressed the issue of information technology and intelligent buildings. Yet, this did not mean that offices in Europe were becoming more alike. In fact, the gap between British and Northern European office design only widened.

UNITED KINGDOM

In the UK, information technology had become extremely important because in London – the financial capital of Europe – financial services were rapidly expanding at the same time as the use of computers was changing the conditions of their business. Computerised trading created a demand for large open trading floors that were air-conditioned and had the capacity to accommodate the IT infrastructure.[62]

In response to this need for 'modern' office space, British developers started to study American practice. Simultaneously, American developers and architects were attracted by the construction boom in the UK and started working there. The American influence was widespread because the development boom in London was huge. It produced the most sweeping and most rapid physical transformation London had ever seen since the Great Fire of 1666. In the City alone, one year saw as much office space completed as in the previous decades.[63]

A clear example of the American influence in the UK is Canary Wharf in London. The project's landmark, One Canada Square Tower (Pelli, 1991), was designed and developed by Americans. It is a full-size copy of a Manhattan skyscraper (see figures 49 - 50). At the time it was the tallest building in Europe. Inside, the building followed the classic American plan with a central core, large uncomplicated floor slabs, increased floor-to-floor heights and high levels of servicing. This project was a sign of the faith and fortune that was fuelling the property business (although later it would contribute to the bankruptcy of its developer).[64]

Another characteristic building was Richard Rogers' building for Lloyd's of London (1986). With its expressive high-tech appearance it was unmistakably a statement of corporate vanity. One of its most striking features was that all secondary functions, such as lifts, stairs and toilets, were located outside, around the perimeter of the building (see figures 51 - 54). Inside, a large atrium brought daylight into the deep plan form. The office areas were equipped with raised floors and suspended ceilings that could accommodate vast quantities of cabling and services. The building was regarded as the first European representation of how information technology could change architecture.[65]

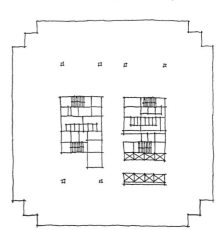

49 One Canada
Square Tower

50 Floor plan One
Canada Square Tower

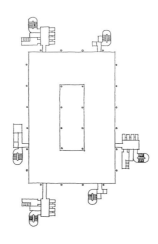

51 Exterior Lloyd's
of London

52 Floor plan Lloyd's of
London

53 Atrium Lloyd's of
London

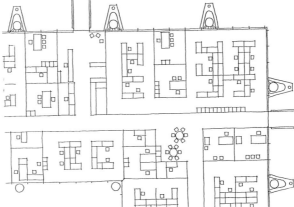

54 Workplace layout
Lloyd's of London

NORTHERN EUROPE

In Northern Europe, buildings such as Lloyd's of London or One Canada Square Tower could not have been built at that time. Instead of information technology, user satisfaction was the main driving force in office design. Following the rejection of office landscapes in the 1970s, office design continued to move towards cellular workplace layouts. Privacy, individual climate control, daylight, openable windows and an outside view were thought to be crucial for the well-being of employees. One of the many handbooks on office design called for 'more natural surroundings, including daylight as opposed to artificial light, contact with nature, and a view of the world outside'.[66]

Information technology hardly seemed to affect office design in Continental Europe. Air-conditioning became more popular, but raised floors were rare. They were simply not necessary because of the narrow floor depths of the building. Workplaces were invariably located next to the windows, so computers could be served by trunking running along the building's perimeter.

The primary focus on user comfort, rather than information technology, resulted in buildings that were radically different from those in the UK. The most striking examples were the Colonia building in Germany (1984), the NMB building in the Netherlands (1987) (see figures 55 - 56) and the SAS building in Sweden (1988) (see figure 57). What these buildings have in common is that they were designed like small 'cities', but on a human scale. The buildings were cut into separate 'houses' that were united by internal 'streets' or 'squares'. The main purpose of these atria was not to bring daylight into the building (as in Lloyd's of London) but to function as a 'social heart'.

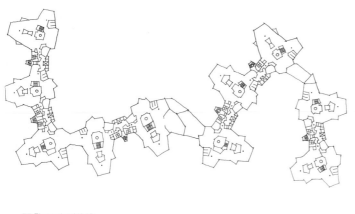

55 Floor plan NMB headquarters

56 Interior NMB headquarters

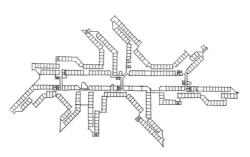

57 Floor plan SAS headquarters

1990S: VIRTUAL OFFICES

In the early 1990s, the demand for new buildings slackened due to a downturn in business activity. Simultaneously, radical ideas emerged about what office buildings should be like. These new ideas were triggered by changes in information technology and related to organisational developments. Whereas in the 1980s office design had mainly focused on accommodating information technology, now information technology brought so-called 'virtuality' to the office. With hardware such as mobile phones and laptops, and software such as Internet browsers and e-mail, office employees actually became 'footloose' – free of place and time.

Furthermore, information technology changed ideas about work and organisation. According to the new organisational theories, all conventions regarding work and organisation were open to question. One of the keywords was 'business process re-engineering', which was used to denote organisational transformation focusing on integral design of both information technology (IT) and organisational processes.[67] Basically it meant 'working smarter' with the use of information technology.[68]

Re-engineering, however, was not the only new idea. In the predominantly American business literature, one could read about learning organisations, virtual organisations, lean organisations, and so on. These developments seemed to provide unprecedented possibilities in office design. Utopian ideas of the 1980s about people working in 'telecottages' finally became a realistic option. Articles about workplace design showed pictures of people working in cafés, at home, or at the side of the pool.[69, 70] In the office itself, employees are supposed to share workplaces, using intranets and electronic archives to give every workplace the same functionality.

The actual adoption and interpretation of the 'alternative office solutions' varies from country to country. Again, major differences can be seen between the UK and Northern Europe.

UNITED KINGDOM

In the UK the changes in office design seem to be largely cost-driven. Open plans remain the standard and in particular the desk-sharing aspect of 'alternative officing' has become popular. A good example is British Telecom (see figures 58 - 60). Their building in Stockley Park is an efficient 'business park' building, designed by Foster and Partners. Its interior is almost completely open plan, with both personal and non-territorial workplaces (DEGW, 1996). A flexible infrastructure takes voice, data, and video connections to each workstation. British Telecom presents it as an example of its 'Workstyle 2000'.[71]

At the same time, there is also a tendency to move away from large US-style office floors. Since the mid-eighties, when the first studies of the Sick Building Syndrome were under way in the USA and the UK, public perception of buildings had undergone considerable changes.[72] Just as in Northern Europe, air-conditioned offices without an outside view or daylight entrance have become associated with absenteeism and dissatisfied employees. This has resulted in a tendency to build shallower-plan, lower-rise buildings, often with windows that may be opened.[73] Also, amenities such as

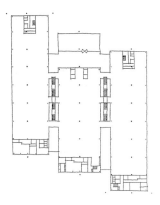

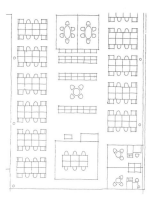

58 Floor plan
British Telecom

59 Workplace layout
British Telecom

60 Interior British
Telecom

break areas are being given more attention in order to create a more 'human' or 'user friendly atmosphere'.

NORTHERN EUROPE

In Northern Europe, costs also seem to have become more important. In this decade of harsh 'global competition', expensive and tailor-made offices such as the NMB and SAS buildings no longer appear to be valid models. Furthermore, it seems that highly cellularised workplace layouts no longer match with so-called 'new ways of working' in which teamwork and interaction are central themes. In response to these ideas, there is a tendency to create more open work areas. Yet the office layouts remain less deep and of a smaller scale than in the UK.

Scandinavia is setting the example in new office design in Continental Europe. One major project is the headquarters of SOL, a Finnish cleaning company, in which 75 employees share 26 workstations in an unconventionally decorated former film studio (see figure 61). In the Netherlands and Germany, this project has received a lot of attention: Scandinavia is regarded as the place where the workplace of the future has already been implemented. Also, the Swedish combi-office has become increasingly popular in Germany and the Netherlands.

An interesting example of a Northern European forerunner is the Dynamic Office of the Dutch government (Uytenhaak, 1997). This building combines the combi-office concept with desk sharing. The underlying idea is that employees move around the building, using different purpose-designed workplaces for different activities: 'cockpits' for solo activities, open spaces for group work, and relaxation areas for informal conversation (see figures 62 - 64).

It is difficult to assess these developments accurately and determine which ideas will have a lasting influence, and which will quietly disappear in a few years time. Therefore our analysis will focus on historical development up until the late 1980s. Today's trends will be more closely studied in the chapters to follow.

61 Interior SOL

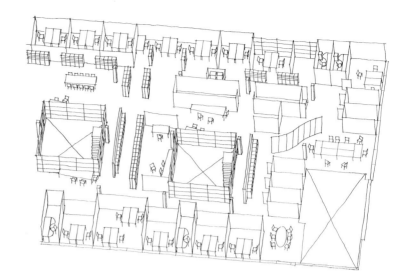

62 Workplace layout
Dynamic Office

63 Interior Dynamic
Office

64 Interior Dynamic
Office

HISTORIC DIFFERENCES

We have outlined the history of 20th century European office design. The early 20th century saw the rise of administrative work and of Taylor's ideas about management, creating 'white-collar factories'. In the decades that followed, the Tayloristic office was further developed by the use of air conditioning, which made it possible to build deeper spaces. In the 1950s, improvements in construction technology resulted in higher and higher buildings, with thinly glazed facades. In the 1960s, new ideas about communication and flexibility were translated by the Quickborner Team into the office landscape. And in the 1980s, the rise of the personal computer resulted in the 'electrification' of the office. Further developments in information technology have brought us today's ideas about the virtual office.

At first sight, this succession of changes in office design seems to be very international. New ideas and concepts emerge and spread quickly – 'diffuse' as anthropologists say – to other countries. The main vehicles for international diffusion are architectural magazines and books about office design. We have seen that major projects, such as the Centraal Beheer building or the SAS building, have been discussed in almost every architectural magazine or book on office design.

Other crucial impulses for the international spread of design concepts are visits by architects and clients to such buildings. For example, in the 1960s, Volvo made a tour of European office buildings to find inspiration for the design of its new headquarters. Furthermore, clients and architects visit conferences and exhibitions, where they learn about new ideas in office design. Already in the 1920s, there were large-scale exhibitions about 'modern', American, offices. Such exhibitions were little different from today's trade fairs, such as, for example, the Orgatech in Cologne.

The international spread of ideas does not mean that new concepts are immediately copied everywhere. Indeed the interpretation, acceptance and actual adoption of new concepts differs from country to country. The first differences could be seen in the 1920s and the 1950s. In those periods the US was the forerunner in modern office design. Europe copied American-style offices, but only on a smaller scale. In the 1960s, with the invention of the office landscape in Germany, strong differences within Europe arose. In Continental Europe, the office landscape was a short-term success. In the 1970s, cellular offices replaced landscape offices. In the UK the office landscape never really took off, and the ideological concept was soon transformed into an updated version of the Tayloristic open plan. From the 1980s on, the differences between the UK and the rest of Europe became even stronger. British office design is, once more, heavily influenced by American office design. In contrast, Continental Europe has taken its own user-oriented course, which, for example, has resulted in the combi-office in Sweden.

Analysis of these differences shows that they are related to different aspects of buildings. These aspects vary from their height, to the arrangement of desks and chairs inside the building. Going from a macro to a micro level we see three basic types of differences: differences at building, floor plan and workplace level.

Building level

Differences at building level concern the overall mass and shape of buildings. In the 1950s, European architects copied American high-rises with their glazed exteriors, but on a much smaller scale. Today such differences seem to persist. American buildings still seem to be much higher than those in Europe. And within Europe we see that Rotterdam, London and Frankfurt have high rises (by European standards) while other European cities do not.

Floor plan level

Differences at floor plan level concern the size and shape of office floors inside the building. At this level there are crucial differences between British and Continental European offices. We have seen that since the 1970s European buildings tend to have narrow and linear floor plans. British buildings on the other hand are modelled after American ones, with deep and compact floors.

Workplace

Differences at workplace level mainly concern the way office floors have been subdivided into open or enclosed work areas. At this level differences can be seen in the adoption of Tayloristic open plans in the 1920s, office landscapes in the 1960s and, more recently, new workplace concepts such as combi-offices and non-territorial offices.

In the rest of the book this division will be used to describe differences in office design in more detail.

Building level   **Floorplan level**   **Workplace level**

65 Building level,
Floorplan level,
Workplace level

EXPLANATORY FRAMEWORK

Besides a view of differences in design, the historical analysis also gives a first insight into why these differences exist. For example, in the 1970s the emergence of differences in office design between the UK and Continental European countries coincided with the emergence of a crucial difference in labour relations. The combination of such observations with a literature review on international differences points to five explanatory aspects of particular interest: urban setting, market conditions, labour relations, culture and regulations.

Urban setting

International differences in urban setting are one of the major explanations of why Europe has been much more hesitant in building high-rise than the US. The urban setting of European cities is much older and more complex than that of American cities, with their grid-like structures. In the 1950s this complicated the construction and acceptance of large-scale office buildings. Another crucial issue related to urban setting is city planning. Even at the beginning of the 20th century, European cities had regulations that restricted the height of buildings. Today, too, city planning is likely to affect office development. The literature shows that planning systems vary within Europe.[74, 75] Public participation, for example, is an issue that differs from country to country. This will affect the acceptance and realisation of large-scale office developments.

Market conditions

Differences in market conditions also explain international differences in design. One explanation for the early differences in scale between the US and Europe is that the American market was larger and more professional than in Europe. In the 1960s, market conditions were also an important explanation for differences in the adoption of the office landscape. At that time developers dominated the British market. For British organisations this made it much more difficult to experiment with new concepts than for their Continental counterparts. By contrast, Continental European organisations typically tended to build owner-occupied projects, with little attention to developer interests such as gross-to-net ratios, flexibility and marketability. Another crucial difference in market conditions is rent level. Studies of international real estate agents make clear that rent levels differ from country to country.[76] Research by Hakfoort and Lie suggest that such differences affect the use of space per employee.[77]

Labour relations

The influence of labour relations on office design was most obvious in the 1970s: employees in Continental Europe became more and more powerful while in the UK the business community adopted a more 'harsh', American style of management. This difference was formalised when Germany, Sweden, the Netherlands and Italy adopted labour legislation that gave employees the right to participate in organisational decision making, while the UK did not. Office buildings of that time seem to be physical evidence of that difference. Recent literature shows that such major differences in labour relations still exist.[78, 79] American and British labour relations are dominated by what is called shareholder capitalism. Shareholders and their profits are the main interests of organisations. On the Continent, stakeholder capitalism prevails. Organisations explicitly regard the well-being of their employees and society in general as part of their interests.

Culture

We use the term culture to refer to the norms and values of employees and managers about work and workplaces. Cultural differences are one reason why in the 1920s, Taylor's ideas about scientific office management were less easily adopted in Europe than in the US. European business culture still seemed to be rooted in the high-status-

high-trust of the male clerks of the 19th century. Cultural differences are also an
explanation for different responses in the 1960s to the office landscape. In the UK,
egalitarian ideas underlying the concept seemed to clash with the hierarchical culture of
British organisations. In Continental Europe similar problems occurred, but there was
also strong emphasis on the notion that employees were not used to the openness of the
landscape. The idea that norms and values have an impact on the design of the physical
working environment is supported by studies that regard buildings as symbols or
artefacts of culture. Furthermore, studies of cultural researchers such as Hofstede and
Trompenaars make clear that international differences are still strong today and
therefore likely to affect the working environment.[80, 81]

Regulations

The last factor that may explain international differences is regulations. Historically the
influence of regulations was most obvious in the 1970s. At that time, Continental
European countries adopted extensive labour regulations due to pressure from employee
representatives and unions. By contrast, the British continued to use the *Offices, Shops
and Railway Premises Act* of 1963, which lays down rather general requirements for the
design of workspaces. Now, with the formation of the European Union such differences
seem to be fading. Literature, however, suggests that the impact of regulation is still
important. First of all, not all European countries have implemented the European
legislation yet. More fundamentally, however, the EU accepts that there may be
differences in the application of regulations due to differences in climate, or in ways of
life, or different degrees of protection that may prevail.[82]

These five factors give a first indication of why office design differs internationally.
Together with the differences in design they comprise the framework given in table 2.3.
In the following five chapters, this framework has been used as a map for studying each
of the selected countries.

Table 2.3 Research framework

Office	Context
Building level	Urban setting
Floor plan level	Market conditions
Workplace level	Labour relations
	Culture
	Regulations

Notes

1   Lockwood, D. (1958), *The Blackcoated Worker*, Allen and Unwin, London
2   Crouzier, M. (1965), *The world of the office worker*, The University of Chicago Press, Chicago
3   ibid.
4   Bedoire, F. (1979), 'Open plan offices, landscape offices and celltype office', in: *Arkitektur*, No. 1, pp. 16-26
5   Taylor, F. (1975), *Scientific Management*, Greenwood Press, Westport, Conn. (originally published by Harper Row, New York, 1911)
6   Leffingwell, W. H. (1925), *Office Management: Principles and Practice*, A.W. Shaw, Chicago
7   Hopf, H.A. (1931), 'Physical factors', in: Donald, W.J. (ed.), *Handbook of Business Administration*, McGraw-Hill, New York
8   Quinan, J. (1987), *Frank Lloyd Wright's Larkin building; myth and fact*, MIT Press, Cambridge
9   De Wit, O. and Ende, J. van den (1998), 'Het gemechaniseerde kantoor 1914-1940', in: Lintsen, H.W., Rip, A., Schot, J.W. and Albert de la Bruhèze, A. A. (eds.), *Techniek in Nederland in de twintigste eeuw*, Walburg Pers, Zutphen
10 Baldry, C. (1997), 'The social construction of office space', in: *International Labour Review*, Vol. 136, No. 3, pp. 365-378
11 Doxtater, D. (1994), *Architecture, Ritual Practice and Co-determination in the Swedish Office*, Ashgate Publishing, Aldershot
12 Duffy, F. (1997), *The New Office*, Conran Octopus, London
13 Crouzier, M. (1965), *The world of the office worker*, The University of Chicago Press, Chicago
14 Blakstad, S. (1997), *The Scandinavian Office Building 1900-1980*, Trondheim University
15 Davies, N. (1996), *Europe: A History*, Oxford University Press, New York
16 ibid.
17 Sundstrom, E. (1986), *Workplaces*, Cambridge University Press, New York
18 Banham, R. (1969), *The Architecture of the Well-Tempered Environment*, Architectural Press, London
19 Mills, C. W. (1958), *White Collar; the American middle classes*, Oxford University Press, New York
20 Krinsky, C. H. (1988), *Gordon Bunshaft of Skidmore, Owings & Merill*, Architectural History Foundation, New York
21 Polisano, L. (1995), 'Complexity and Contrast; American and European High-Rise Buildings', in: *Architectural Design*, Vol. 65, No. 7/8, pp. 30-35
22 Gerometta, M. (1999), *The World's Tallest Buildings On-Line*, http://www.worldstallest.com/hot500/tall50.html
23 Simon, R. D. (1996), 'Skyscrapers and the new London Skyline: 1945-1991', in: *Architronic*, Vol. 5, Nr. 2, http://www.saed.kent.edu/Architronic/v5n2.06html
24 Polisano, L. (1995), 'Complexity and Contrast; American and European High-Rise Buildings', in: *Architectural Design*, Vol. 65, No. 7/8, pp. 30-35
25 Simon, R. D. (1996), 'Skyscrapers and the new London Skyline: 1945-1991', in: *Architronic*, Vol. 5, No. 2, http://www.saed.kent.edu/Architronic/v5n2.06html
26 Cowan, P. (1969), *The office: a facet of urban growth*, Heineman, London
27 London County Council (1956), *High Buildings in London*, 28 Town Planning Report, No. 2
28 Krall, H. (1972), 'Offices: the issues related', in: *Built Environment*, vol. 1, No. 7, pp. 468-469.
29 Duffy, F. and Cave, C. (1976), 'Bürolandschaft: an appraisal', in: Duffy, F., Cave, C. and Worthington, J. (eds.), *Planning office space*, The Architectural Press, London
30 Bennett, P. H. (1958), 'Offices for rent', in: *Architectural Design*, Vol. 28, No. 7, pp. 256-258
31 Branzi, A. (1984), *The Hot House; Italian New Wave Design*, MIT Press, Cambridge
32 Hohl, R. (1968), *International Office Buildings*, Verlag Gerd Hatje, Stuttgart
33 Schnelle, E. (1963), Preface, in: Gottschalk (1963), *Flexiebele Verwaltungsbauten; Entwürfe, Ausbau, Einrichtung, Kosten, Beispiele*, Verlag Schnelle, Quickborn
34 Mayo, E. (1933), *The Human Problems of an Industrial Civilization*, MacMillan, New York
35 McGregor, D. (1960), *The Human Side of the Enterprise*, McGraw-Hill, New York
36 Pile, J. (1978), *Open office planning*, The Architectural Press, London
37 Krall H. (1972), 'Offices: the issues related', in: *Built Environment*, Vol. 1, No. 7, pp. 468-469
38 Gottschalk, O. (1984), 'Zur Entwicklug des Verwaltungshaus', in: *Bauwelt*, No. 43, pp. 1836-50
39 Pile, J. (1978), *Open office planning*, The Architectural Press, London
40 Henn, W. (1962), 'Large-size Office and the Architect', in: *Baumeister*, July, pp. 655-660
41 Bedford, M. and Tong, D. (1997), 'Planning for diversity: new structures that reflect the past', in: Worthington, J. (ed.), *Re-inventing the Workplace*, Architectural Press, Oxford
42 Siegel, C. (1962), 'What does a large-size office cost?', in: *Baumeister*, July, pp. 667-672
43 Sundstrom, E. (1986), *Workplaces*, Cambridge University Press, New York
44 Baldry, C. (1997), 'The social construction of office space', in: *International Labour Review*, Vol. 136, No. 3, pp. 365-378
45 Blenner, H. and Mannervik, S.C. (1967), 'How information was organized', in: *Arkitektur*, No. 12, pp. 696-699

46 Baldry, C. (1997), 'The social construction of office space', in: *International Labour Review*, Vol. 136, No. 3, pp. 365-378
47 Kammerer, H., (1985), 'From Open Plan to Individual Offices', in: *Baumeister*, Vol. 82, No. 10, pp. 17-27
48 Sommar, I. (1995), 'The Lean Office', in: *Arkitektur*, No. 1, pp. 28-35
49 Doxtater, D. (1994), *Architecture, Ritual Practice and Co-determination in the Swedish Office*, Ashgate Publishing, Aldershot
50 Bak, L. (1980), *Kantoorprofiel; struktuur en ontwikkeling van de kantorensektor*, Van Loghum Slaterus, Deventer
51 Staal, G. (1987), *Between Dictate and Design: the architecture of office buildings*, Uitgeverij 010, Rotterdam
52 Roberts, B.C. (1985), *Industrial Relations in Europe: The Imperatives of Change*, Croom Helm, London
53 Krall, H. (1972), 'Offices: the issues related', in: *Built Environment*, vol. 1, No. 7, pp. 468-469.
54 Duffy, F. and Cave, C. (1976), 'Bürolandschaft: an appraisal', in: Duffy, F., Cave, C. and Worthington, J. (eds.), *Planning office space*, The Architectural Press, London
55 Krall, H. (1972), 'Offices: the issues related', in: *Built Environment*, vol. 1, nr. 7, pp. 468-469.
56 Bak, L. (1980), *Kantoorprofiel; struktuur en ontwikkeling van de kantorensektor*, Van Loghum Slaterus, Deventer
57 Sundstrom, E. (1986), *Workplaces*, Cambridge University Press, New York
58 Baldry, C. (1997), 'The social construction of office space', in: *International Labour Review*, Vol. 136, No. 3, pp. 365-378
59 Duffy, F. (1983), 'Taming the beast from the wild', in: *Computer Weekly*, January 19
60 Toffler, A. (1981), *The Third Wave*, Pan Books, London
61 Naisbett, J. (1984), *Megatrends*, Warner, New York
62 Simon, R. D. (1996), 'Skyscrapers and the new London Skyline: 1945-1991', in: *Architronic*, Vol. 5, No. 2, http://www.saed.kent.edu/Architronic/v5n2.06html (internet site)
63 Powell, K. (1993), *World Cities: London*, Academy Editions, London
64 Foster, P. (1993), *Towers of Depth: Rise and Fall of the Reichmanns*, Hodder & Stoughton, London
65 Wagener, W. (1997), 'Officing: The Office in the Age of Information', in: *Arch+*, No. 136, pp. 90-92
66 Dichmann, D. W. (1984), *Ein freundliche Welt für jedes Büro, Handbuch Moderne Burogestaltung, Verlag Moderne Bürogestaltung*, Detmold
67 Meel, J. W. van (1993), *The Dynamics of Business Engineering*, Doctoral dissertation, Delft University of Technology
68 Drucker, P. F. (1991), 'The New Productivity Challenge', in: *Harvard Business Review*, Vol. 69, No. 6, pp. 109-118
69 Apgar IV, M. (1998), 'The Alternative Workplace: Changing Where and How People Work', in: *Harvard Business Review*, May-June, pp. 121-136
70 Arch+ (1997), 'Your Office is Where You Are', *Arch +*, No. 136
71 Jenkin, D. (1997), 'Emerging building forms', in: Worthington, J. (ed.), *Re-inventing the Workplace*, Architectural Press, Oxford
72 Leaman, A. (1994), *Complexity and manageability: pointers from a decade of research on building occupancy*, paper, National Conference of the Facility Management Association of Australia, Sidney, 30 November - 2 December
73 Leaman, A. and Bordass, B. (1996), *Buildings in the Age of Paradox*, paper, Institute of Advanced Architectural Studies, University of York
74 Newman, P. and Thornley, A. (1996), *Urban planning in Europe: International Competition, National Systems and Planning Projects*, Routledge, London
75 Barlow, J. (1995), *Public Participation in Urban Development: The European Experience*, Brookings Institute, Washington D.C.
76 CB Richard Ellis (1999), *Global Market Rents*, http://www.cbcommercial.com/corp/markets.htm
77 Hakfoort, J. and Lie, R. (1996), 'Office Space per Work: Evidence from Four European Markets', in: *The Journal of Real Estate Research*, Vol. 11, No. 2, pp. 183-196
78 Charkham, J. P. (1998), *Keeping Good Company: A Study of Corporate Governance in Five Countries*, Oxford University Press, Oxford
79 Ferner, A. and Hyman, R. (1999), *Changing Industrial Relations in Europe*, Blackwell, London
80 Hofstede, G. (1991), *Cultures and organisations: software of the mind*, McGraw-Hill, London
81 Trompenaars, F. (1993), *Riding the waves of culture: understanding cultural diversity in business*, The Economist Books, London
82 Gier, H. G. de (1991), *Arbeidsomstandigheden in Europees perspectief, implementatie van EG-richtlijnen op het vlak van arbeidsomstandigheden en produktveiligheid*, Kluwer, Deventer

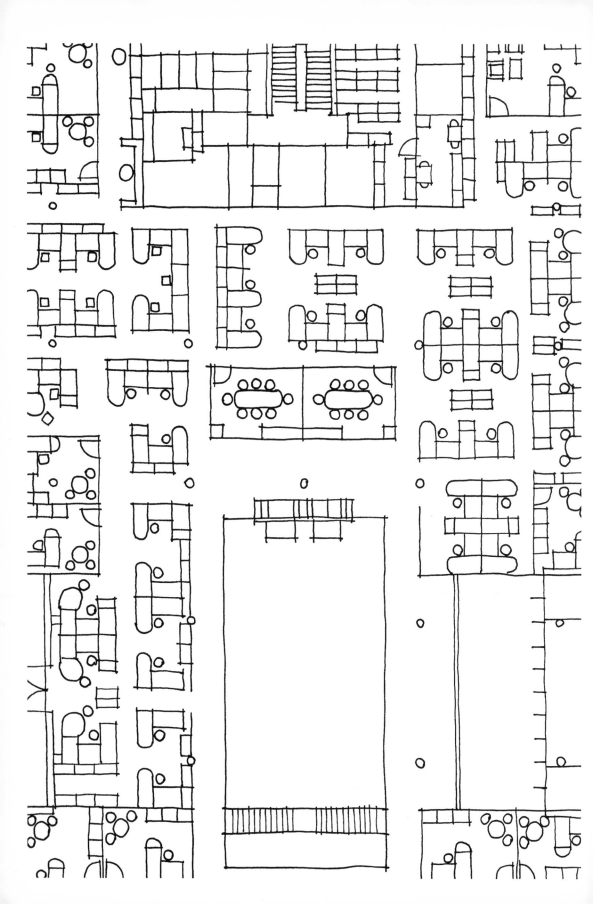

3   United Kingdom

The fact that Europe is a continent of highly diverse cultures, beliefs and customs is most clearly demonstrated through a comparison of the UK with the rest of Europe. The UK is not only physically disconnected from the European continent, but it has always viewed itself as being quite 'distinct' from its neighbours. Also in terms of office buildings, it is clear that the British office situation bears little resemblance to that of the rest of Europe. British buildings have more in common with their counterparts across the Atlantic than with those across the Channel.

The American influence on British office design is to be expected, as a large number of American architects, space planners and developers are working in the UK. It is not without reason, however, that Americans and their ways of working are so easily accepted in the UK. American concepts would not have achieved success if the market and clients had not found them so attractive. It seems that the British context is suited to the American way of working.

In our analysis of British office design – presented in this chapter – we focus on London, the UK's main office centre (see table 3.1). For this analysis we will use the framework introduced in Chapter 2. First, we give an overview of the characteristics typical of British office design. Then we will describe how these characteristics can be explained by the context in which they are produced. And finally we will present our conclusions about the relationship between British office design and its national context.

Table 3.1 Regional spread of office space in England and Wales (British Government, Department of Environment, 1995)

Region	Percentage of office stock
North	3.3 %
Yorkshire & Humberside	6.6 %
North West	9.9 %
East Midlands	4.7 %
West Midlands	7.5 %
East Anglia	3.1 %
South East	54.9 %
(which includes Greater London)	(Greater London = 33 %)
South West	7.2 %
Wales	2.8 %

BRITISH OFFICES

Building

London is a 'global city'.[1] It accommodates a large number of headquarters of international corporations, institutions and related trades and professions. In particular, London's financial role is important. For bankers and investors, London is in the same league as New York and Hong Kong.

The fact that London is a global city cannot be read from its skyline. In London the skyline is not completely dominated by high-rise office buildings like in New York or Hong Kong. In fact, many office developments seem to be relatively modest in comparison. For example, the Broadgate project, one of London's largest post-war office developments, is by no means characterised by tall buildings (see figure 67).[2] Instead the floor area spreads horizontally, divided over fourteen buildings, none higher than ten floors.

At the same time, it is clear that the skyline of London's City has changed dramatically during this century (see figures 68 - 69). It is no longer like Canaletto's version of the London skyline, with low brown houses doffing their caps to the spires of church and state; St Paul's presiding over everything. What we see is a low skyline punctuated by high-rise buildings. Several high rises are 'dotted' around London: Centre Point, the British Telecom Tower and The Euston Tower, separated by respectful distances.

Real British skyscrapers can be found at Canary Wharf, which used to be a dock outside the City of London (see figure 70). In the 1980s it was

67 Broadgate

68 18th century
London skyline by
Canaletto

69 20th century
skyline, City of London

70 One Canada
Square Tower at
Canary Wharf

71 Millennium Tower
in the City

redeveloped into a modern office centre by the Canadian developers Olympia and York.
The project's landmark is the One Canada Square Tower, a pure copy of an American
skyscraper (Pelli, 1991). Just like the buildings that surround it, it is the type of building
that could also have been built in Chicago, Dallas or New York. Shannon Cairns, a
geographer, described her acquaintance with Canary Wharf as follows 'It felt to me as
though I stepped from London into a life-sized architect's model of a North American
city'.[3]

Initially Canary Wharf seemed to be an anomaly in London. From an architectural
point of view there was much criticism that the buildings had no relationship with the
British context whatsoever. At the time such criticism seemed to be supported by the
fact that the project was not the success it was intended to be. Now, however, the project
fulfils all initial expectations. Due to an improved rail connection with the City and the
recovery of the office market, many new projects are currently under way at Canary
Wharf. Some 220,000 m² of commercial property is being developed, 200,000 m² of
which has already been pre-let.[4]

As a result of the successful high-rise developments in Canary Wharf, the City of
London is also considering plans for high-rise developments. Sir Norman Foster came
up with a plan for a 386 m high Millennium Tower (see figure 71). This project was turned
down in 1997, but since then the debate over building skyscrapers in the City has been
raging.[5] Some experts are convinced that without more skyscrapers, London could lose
its status as Europe's leading financial centre. More particularly they refer to Frankfurt,
the location of the European Central Bank.[6]

Floor plan

With the coming of American skyscrapers in the 1980s, the British office market adopted
American-style deep office floors with air-conditioning and raised floors. British
guidelines and handbooks on office design give a good impression of common floor
depths. The British Council for Offices, for example, recommends a depth of 18 m.[7]
Likewise, Raymond and Cunliffe mention building depths of 15-18 m.[8] Air-
conditioning and raised floors are needed to bring fresh air and cabling into the deep
spaces.

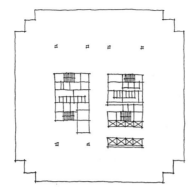

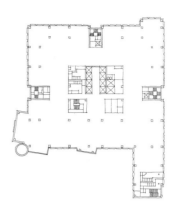

72 Floor plan One
Canada Square Tower

73 Floor plan
Goldman Sachs
headquarters

It is characteristic of the deep plans that they tend to have central cores. Some of them resemble the classic floor plan of the American skyscraper. All secondary functions (toilets, stairs, lifts, ducts and so on) are concentrated in a single core with vast areas of office space wrapped around it. Not surprisingly these are often projects designed by US architects for US clients. The One Canada Square Tower at Canary Wharf (Pelli, 1991) is an obvious example (see figure 72). But low- and medium-rise offices, such as Goldman Sachs' headquarters in London (Kohn Pedersen Fox, 1992), also have such floorplans (see figure 73).[9]

A hallmark of British office design is the use of atria. Atria are often designed as grand and glamorous spaces that bring daylight into deep building spaces. Furthermore they give employees working next to them a view, called 'outside awareness' in trade jargon.[10] From the point of view of construction, atria are popular because of their economy. Walls around atria are cheap to build as they do not have to be fully weatherproofed or soundproofed, and atria often lack fully conditioned environments.[11]

An example of a building that was certainly not economical but famous for its atrium, is the Lloyd's of London building. Richard Rogers, its designer, located all secondary functions such as lifts, stairs, toilets and ducts around the building perimeter. In the centre of the building he created a huge atrium. In doing so, he turned the conventional plan of the central core, high-rise office building inside out (see figure 74).

Although it is common to build deep offices, there is also a tendency to build shallower-plan buildings (15 m or less), providing daylight, the ability to open windows, and outside view.[12, 13] The PowerGen building (Bennetts Associates, 1995) is a good example (see figure 75). As an electricity company, PowerGen wanted a naturally ventilated building that would maximise energy efficiency and improve staff conditions.[14] The PowerGen building is, however, an exception because most 'spec' offices remain faithful to the American archetype of deep, air-conditioned buildings.

Workplace

Deep floor plans are very suitable for open solutions. Unlike offices in the rest of Europe, British offices tend to have open-plan workplace layouts. Just as in the US, an increasing number of employees work in cubicles or behind desks arranged in groups of four or six. In Europe such open layouts are often associated with the German office landscape of the 1960s. British open plans, however, do not have an 'organic' layout like the

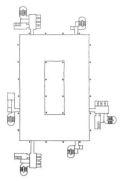

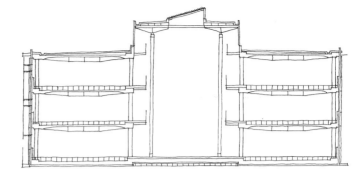

74 Floor plan Lloyd's of London

75 Cross-section of the PowerGen building showing two narrow bays of office space with an atrium in the middle

landscape, but use a strictly orthogonal planning grid. It seems to be aimed at accommodating as many people as possible in the space available.[15, 16]

To unaccustomed continental Europeans, British offices may have the look and feel of a trading room in a bank: open and intensive, with everyone knowing what everyone else is doing. The difference becomes clear from an anecdote of a Dutch employee working in the UK: 'At my previous Dutch employer, I had a spacious room. In the heart of London you can forget about that. Most employees are accommodated in a cubicle, a small space with medium-height partitions. Fans of the Dilbert comic know exactly what I mean. Such a roofless office pen is small and noisy, and it does not have much of a view'.[17]

A case that exemplifies the difference in workplace layouts between the UK and Continental Europe is the Ark building in London, designed by Swedish-British architect Ralph Erskine and developed by the Swedish developer Åke Larsson. The workplace layouts proposed by Erskine show several Swedish combi-like solutions, consisting of an individual cellular office for everyone and open common areas in the centre of the floor (see figure 76). The combi-office, however, is virtually unknown in the UK. Not surprisingly, Seagram, the occupant of the building, chose an open-plan layout, which was very difficult to implement because of the many curves in the building.[18]

In the UK, cellular offices are usually reserved for management (see table 3.1). In classic open plans, their offices occupy the outer walls of the building ('tell me how many windows you have and I know your power'). Their offices enclose work areas for junior staff and secretaries in the dark middle of the building. The use of glazed partitions brings light to these normally dark areas. An example of a classic layout is the space planning arrangement from the letting brochure of Terry Farrell's Embankment Place (see figure 77).[19]

Table 3.1 Typical space standards in the UK[20]

Function	Type of space	m² per person
Senior manager/director	Private office	20-30
Manager/head of department	Private office	15-20
Manager professional	Private office	10-15
Professional	Group room/open plan	9
Secretarial/Administration	Open plan	9
Clerical	Open plan	7-9
Dealer	Group room/open plan	6-9

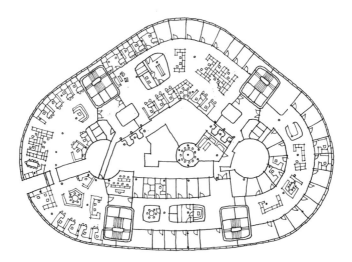

76 Erskine's layout for the Ark

One current trend in space planning is to invert the classic open plan that we have just described. In the inverted open plan, managers occupy the artificially lit interior while their staff is located near the windows, so that a maximum number of people have the benefit of the view and daylight. An inverted plan can be seen in the Citibank headquarters at Canary Wharf, (see figure 78) (Swanke Hayden Connell, 1997).

Another more radical trend is to use a totally open plan layout in which neither staff nor management have cellular offices. This radical solution can be seen at the British Telecom building in Stockley Park where all workplaces are open (see figures 79 - 80).[21] According to the designers (DEGW, 1996) the project shows how 'simple' and 'straightforward' the layouts for new ways of working have become.[22]

A crucial aspect of the British Telecom building is that many of its workplaces are non-territorial. Practising what they 'preach', British telecom strongly promotes teleworking among its employees. As a result employees spend less time in the office, which makes it possible to share workplaces. In the building 3000 employees have 1300 workplaces at their disposal. This manner of saving space is becoming increasingly popular in the UK. Many organisations, ranging from the Ministry of Defence to Ernst & Young, are using such concepts on a large scale.

The result of the British approach to workplace design is a very efficient use of space. The popularity of the open plan may very well explain why the average number of m² per employee in London tends to be half of that in Amsterdam or Frankfurt (see table 3.2).[23] The use of space per employee may decrease even further if desk sharing becomes more popular.

Table 3.2 Average use of lettable space per employee in Europe (Hakfoort and Lie, 1996)

City	m² per employee
Central London	16.8
Frankfurt	25.5
Amsterdam	24.0
Brussels	24.0

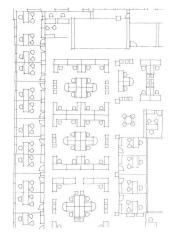

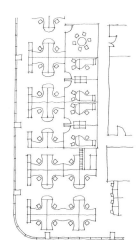

77 'Classic' open plan layout for Embankment place

78 Inverted open plan at Citibank

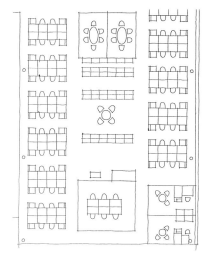

79 Totally open plan at British Telecom

80 Interior British Telecom

BRITISH CONTEXT

British offices tend to be low- and medium-rise buildings, with major exceptions to be found in the City of London and the London Docklands. Floor plans tend to be deep and air-conditioned, while workplace layouts tend to be open plan. In this section we will try to explain these features.

Urban setting

In London, office designers and developers are operating in a historical urban setting, which is typical of most European cities. This is one of the main reasons why London has less high-rise buildings than one would expect. The tight city structure, with its narrow streets, limits the possibilities for large-scale development. In the case of the 90-storey Millennium Tower, planners were concerned that the medieval streets would become heavily congested. Another problem is the acquisition of large plots upon which to build high rises, because the land has been cut up into small parcels that limit the bulk they can accommodate.[24] In addition, there are a large number of protected monuments, which constrain the style and size of new buildings.

At the same time, there is a huge demand for modern office space in the City. Financial institutions have always been eager to be located in the prestigious 'square mile' in the City, in close proximity to the Bank of England. Technological developments such as glass-fibre cabling and Internet have hardly affected this tendency. Recently a major Dutch bank, for example, decided it definitely wanted to be located in the City. The general opinion among the bank's business heads was that if they wanted to be seen as a 'world player', then being located in the City was desirable, if not essential.[25]

British planners have to deal with the struggle between the desire to preserve the historical city and commercial pressures. The UK has one of the most sophisticated and comprehensive planning systems in the world. Yet its post-war construction has largely been dominated by developers, who did not always concern themselves that much about the effect on the quality of urban life. If we look at the conservation of historic areas, London does not compare favourably with many other European cities. British critics talk of a drastic decline in the quality of the urban environment since the mid-1950s.[26]

Each side has its protagonists. On the one hand there are conservationists, who do not want the historical skyline of the city to change. Great Britain's royal architectural critic, Prince Charles, is one of them. He has said 'I try very hard to appreciate the sort of skyline that has been imposed on the City but I can't'.[27] Of the One Canada Square Tower, he said that he would go mad if he had to work in a building like that. Although most British architects do not share the Prince's views, his ideas are well received by the general public.[28] Furthermore, he seems to be supported by planning officials. The London Planning Advisory Committee (LPAC), for example, designates 'strategic views', which are to be protected from 'inappropriate development'.[29] This means that there are large areas of London in which high-rise development is prohibited.

On the other hand, there are politicians, designers and developers who want to change the skyline of London drastically. In particular, the City Corporation is currently propagating the development of skyscrapers. Archie Galloway, deputy chairman of the City Corporation says of the LPAC's policy to protect historical views: 'We have enough views of St Paul's already, thank you very much, and new ones might preclude development'.[30] Their main argument is that high-rise buildings are necessary to satisfy the demand for large areas of office space. There is a certain fear that Frankfurt, with its high-rise plans, may take over London's position as Europe's financial capital. Norman Foster says that London needs a prominent 'symbol of optimism, confidence and prosperity… a sign that London occupies a world league position'.[31] He also thinks that high-rise buildings are necessary to meet pressing commercial needs. If they are not met, 'The City will go into decline'.

London's current intermediate skyline, neither low nor very high, seems to be a product of this wrestling match between business and conservationists. Unable to decide whether it is a city of tourism or of business, of heritage or of dynamic change, London tries to be them all.[32] In that sense, London is different from many other European cities. It is no high rise-city, but nor is it a relative backwater like Stockholm or Rome, whose conservation policies British planners admire. The reason is that London is subject to far more vigorous market forces than any other European city.

Market conditions

The British office market it is dominated by developers rather than users. One of the underlying reasons for this is the UK's so-called 'shareholder capitalism'. In the UK, 'the City' is one of the main sources of capital for corporations. British corporations tend to be owned by investors who, above all, seek a quick return on their investment. This puts managers under pressure to go for the 'quick buck'.[33] They are reluctant to invest in long-term resources, such as office buildings, which do not yield direct profits for shareholders. As a result, British organisations traditionally lease 'speculative' buildings rather than building their own, which, for example, the Germans tend to do.

The domination of developers partly explains the strong American influence on British office design. Much of the development capital that fuelled office-building booms in the UK after 1945 was influenced and even provided by Americans. The style to which they had grown accustomed across the Atlantic was replicated in the UK.[34] Canary Wharf in London is probably the best example of this. In the words of Colin Davies: 'it was as if a fragment of Manhattan had floated across the Atlantic and dropped anchor at the West India Docks'.[35]

As a result of American influence, British developers have adopted 'international' – i.e. American – standards for office design. This means designing air-conditioned, compact office blocks with relatively large floor-to-floor heights and raised floors. Some British architects criticise this idea of universalism. Ian Pollard says: 'The design was exported with the assumption that the requirements for space are identical wherever you are over the world. In point of fact this is not the case … If you are working in Phoenix or Houston and the temperature outside is 120 degrees, of course you need the air conditioning going, but you only need it about three days a year in the UK.'[36]

Although the value of air-conditioning may be questioned, there are aspects of American office design that clearly do fit the British context. In particular the efficiency and flexibility of American office design are welcome because the London office market is driven by high rent levels.

Due to London's role as a 'global city', rent levels are more than twice those in other European cities, such as Amsterdam, Brussels or Frankfurt (see table 3.3). This puts an enormous pressure on the accommodation budgets of British organisations. This pressure is further strengthened by the economic circumstances in which British firms operate (see table 3.4). In the decade between the early 1980s and the early 1990s, recession hit British firms twice. More over, the government's open-door policies have subjected these firms to fierce competition from Japanese, German and American rivals, among others.

City	Prime rent levels (US Dollars per m² per annum)
Stockholm	479
Frankfurt	548
Amsterdam	386
London City	1117
Milan	381

Table 3.3 European rent levels (Richard Ellis, 1999)

Country	GDP per head (US Dollars)
Sweden	25 720
Germany	25 632
Netherlands	23 094
UK	21 848
Italy	19 919

Table 3.4 European GDPs per head (The Economist Group, 1997)

At building level, the high rents and the crucial role of developers explain the desire for, and in some cases realisation of, high-rise buildings in London. Nevertheless, the number of high rises is not as great as one would expect. As Simon puts it: 'considering London's central role in world financial markets, and the enormous value placed on proximity to the Bank of England, the question could be asked why London does not have more skyscrapers or why they are not taller, particularly in the historical financial core known as the City'.[37] Apparently, the financial pressures are not so high that they 'overrule' the influence of the urban setting. As said before, the City's intricate medieval street pattern, protected views and complicated landownership structures mean that it has been difficult to assemble large plots of land upon which to build skyscrapers.

At floor plan level, the influence of financial forces is clearer. The importance of cost efficiency explains the deep floors. Deep floors are believed to be relatively cheaper to build than narrow ones because they have a lower facade-to-space ratio. This means that you have to build relatively little (expensive) frontage. More important, however, is that deep floors can achieve higher gross-to-net ratios than narrow ones.[38] Frank Duffy estimates that the gross-to-net ratios of modern buildings in London are about 85% against about 70% in northern Europe.[39] These ratios are of crucial importance because developers want to 'squeeze' as much rentable space out of a building as possible.[40] End-user desires for daylight or outside views are simply not their main concern.

At the workplace level, the craving for cost-efficient design probably explains the popularity of the open plan. Open plans are very efficient. Eley and Marmot point out that in open plan the average space usage per worker can be as low as 7 m².[41] If people are bunched in groups of four or six, this figure decreases even further. Moreover, open plans facilitate change. When people move, you don't have to move any walls, making change easier as well as cheaper.[42]

High costs also propel workplace innovation. Already for some years now organisations have been experimenting with new workplace concepts such as teleworking, non-territorial offices and club offices. Generally these innovations are driven by technological and organisational change. It is clear, however, that particularly in London cost savings are equally important. Because of high rents, desk-sharing solutions result in higher savings than in the rest of Europe. The savings add up to a lot more than the extra investments in technology, office management and adjustable furniture.

Cost, however, cannot be the only explanation for the way British workplaces are designed. If costs were the main driving force in office design, one would expect that offices outside London would be different. This is certainly not the case. The Lloyds TSB bank, for example, moved an important part of its operation from London's City to a new building in Bristol (Arup Associates, 1997). In Bristol, accommodation costs are a fraction of those in London. This did not mean, however, that the bank used a more spacious layout. In fact, many employees had to trade their cellular office in London for an open plan-office in Bristol (see figure 81).[43]

One of the reasons why cost-efficient layouts like open plans are popular all over the country is that London office design leads the market. It stamps its mark on office design for the rest of the country. Another explanation is that British offices do not only reflect high costs, but also British labour relations.

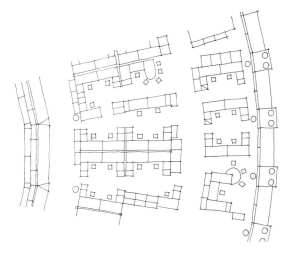

81 Workplace layout
Lloyds TSB Bank

Labour relations

British labour relations are very much like those in America. Because of the UK's
shareholder capitalism, British managers, just like American ones, are strongly focused
on the capital market and have relatively little concern for their own organisation.[44]
Traditionally they have one overriding goal: to maximise returns to shareholders.[45]
As a result employees have relatively little influence on the decision-making (see table 3.5).
Structural and formal employee participation in organisational decision-making as is
practiced in Continental Europe is relatively rare. According to Hampden-Turner and
Trompenaars the idea of works councils strikes fear into British managers.[46]

Table 3.5 Characteristics of large European corporations (De Jong, 1996)

	Anglo-Saxon	Germanic
Orientation to capital markets	++	-
Orientation to Banks	-	++
Employee influence	-	+

++ very important; + important; - unimportant, absent or indirect

The minor role of employees in decision-making can also be seen in building projects.
The majority of decisions are being taken by real estate managers close to the 'corporate'
core of the organisation. Historically, British real estate departments are much more
financially oriented than their continental European counterparts.[47] Their major
performance ratio is the extent to which corporate real estate can add value to the
corporate economics of the company as a whole. Cost control, increasing return on real
estate investments, and improving the balance sheet are the key energisers of Anglo-
Saxon corporate real estate managers. Not that user satisfaction is neglected, but it does
have to fit within the overall corporate framework.

These power relations seem to be another important explanation for the popularity of
deep and open office floors in the UK. This type of office reflects corporate interests of
efficiency and flexibility. Deep and open plans can accommodate larger groups and allow
easier communication between groups.[48] It has, however, little to do with the desires of
the individual employee. Extensive research by Adrian Leaman and Bill Bordass has
shown that the deeper buildings get, the more overall worker satisfaction tends to

decline.[49] Among other things, they showed that individual climate control is crucial for an employee's well-being, something that is difficult to achieve in an open plan. Nevertheless open plans are becoming more and more popular among employers in the UK.

At the same time, however, there are also several examples of British projects that explicitly focus on user satisfaction. In particular owner-occupiers tend to erect buildings that deviate from standardised 'spec' offices. This trend may have to do with changes in British labour relations. Due to the increasing scarcity of skilled labour, the relative power employees have is changing. Furthermore, a change in politics is likely to have played a role. Since Tony Blair's New Labour has been in government, the UK's 'shareholder model' seems to be losing its sharp edges. The idea that employees are important stakeholders in an organisation is becoming more and more popular. It is logical, therefore, to provide them with workplaces of a higher standard.

According to the popular press, the new headquarters of British Airways (BA), designed by Swedish architect Niels Torp, is an embodiment of the new situation. 'Welcome to a vision of Tony Blair's New Britain' says architectural critic Rowan Moore.[50] 'Very New Labour' writes the *The Telegraph*.[51] The building is regarded as very user-friendly. It is built like a village with a central street and office blocks along it (see figures 82 - 83). Status symbols such as big private offices have been stripped away and most employees work in sunlit, spacious open-plan workplaces. This openness is not regarded as a problem. According to the press it is the best place in which to work in the UK: 'For all-too-many people BA headquarters would probably be an ideal place to work', writes *The Telegraph*.[52]

It is interesting to compare the headquarters of BA with the headquarters of its Scandinavian competitor, SAS, in Sweden. The SAS building was built ten years earlier by the same architect. In that sense the two buildings reflect how ideas about work have changed in that time. But, they also reflect differences in labour relations between the UK and Sweden. The SAS building clearly reflects that Swedish employees are much more powerful than their British counterparts. At floor plan level this difference is not yet very clear. Both buildings look very similar with a large internal street as their main feature. At the workplace level, however, large differences can be observed. In the British Airways buildings employees are accommodated in open plans. In contrast their Scandinavian counterparts all have their own private office, however similar their activities may be (see figures 84 - 86).

Culture

To the naive anthropologist, the difference in workplace layouts between the British Airways and SAS buildings might indicate that British employees have a more communicative culture than their Swedish counterparts. One might deduce from the absence of walls and doors that British employees value interaction highly and care little about privacy. Such a conclusion is, however, not very likely to be true. Several cultural studies have pointed out that British culture is highly individualistic and neutral in nature. This means that the British tend to be reserved, and share a love of privacy and self-control.[53, 54, 55] From that point of view, British employees are much more likely to prefer cellular offices than open plans.

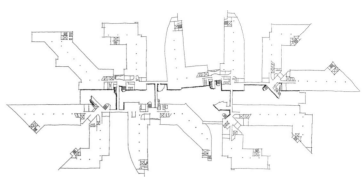

82 Interior street
British Airways

83 Floor plan British
Airways

A more plausible cultural explanation for the popularity of open plans is the hierarchic character of British culture. The stereotypical image of the British is that they are very class-conscious. Class-consciousness may be reflected in the culture of their organisations. According to Moran's *Cultural guide to doing business in Europe*, British employees tend to be deferential towards their superiors and this requires keeping one's appropriate distance, both figuratively and literally.[56] This may explain why managers are accommodated in cellular offices and their employees in open plans.

Another cultural issue is that private offices in open-plan layouts tend to have glazed partitions. Several cultural explanations can be given for this. One is that the glazed partitions are used for visual control, to give managers the ability to see their employees working. This would indicate a very hierarchical culture indeed. The opposite explanation would be that it reflects a very open management style (in which employees can see what their supervisors do). The underlying reasons, however, are quite practical. First, the glass reduces the claustrophobic effect of enclosed offices (which tend to be smaller than on the Continent). Second, glazed partitions allow 'borrowed' light to reach interior spaces, which is necessary because of the large floor depths.[57]

It is questionable to what extent the open-plan office will retain its symbolic function. Some British businesses are still quite rigid, but there is a clear trend towards diminishing class distinctions. Many firms have got rid of such status symbols as corporate dining rooms and reserved car parking, 'where bosses were less likely than workers to get their hair wet in a rainstorm'.[58] Commensurately, organisations are changing their corporate standards for workplace design. According to Eley and Marmot, a hierarchical approach to space standards is still common in traditional UK organisations, but they also say that in a modern context such status symbols make a poor impression.[59]

Changes in British organisational culture may explain the creation of 'inverted' layouts, in which private offices are located in the darker inner areas of the building, and the fully open plan layouts in which private offices have been totally done away with. The new 'headquarters' of British Airways is again a good example (British Airways does not want to refer to the building as its headquarters: 'We don't like the word too much.

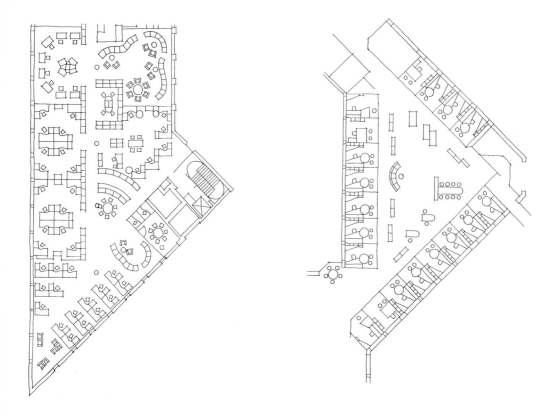

84 Workplace layout
British Airways

85 Workplace layout
SAS

86 Interior British
Airways

It's too hierarchical and elitist'[60]). To promote the idea of a non-hierarchical
organisation, managers have had to give up their large private offices and join their
subordinates in the open plan.

Regulations

Regulations are said to be a reflection of a country's culture.[61] Even building regulations,
which appear to be sensible, rational devices, are always impregnated with cultural
meaning.[62] They reflect the cultural condition of the society in which they are
formulated. From that perspective it may be typical that British health and safety
regulations place relatively few constraints on workplace design. *The British Workplace
(health, safety and welfare) Regulations 1992* are rather general, with little detailed
technical specifications.

When trying to explain British office design it is interesting to note that regulations
say relatively little about the size of workplaces. They say that 'every room where
persons work shall have sufficient floor area, height and unoccupied space for purposes
of health, safety and welfare'. It is clear that this does not have a major effect on office
design.

Guidance from the Health and Safety Executive seems to be more detailed.[63] It says
'the total volume of the room when empty divided by the number of people normally
working in it should be at least 11 cubic metres'. For typical offices this would imply an
average floor area of about 4.6 m². This figure is based on considerations of hazards to
life; it is to ensure adequate ventilation, to provide room to escape in case of fire, and to
create space that is not too stressful. But it is certainly not based on a concept of the
amount of space needed for the job.

Eley and Marmot say with regard to these requirements that 'any sensible
organisation provides adequate space for doing the job'.[64] They suggest that a typical
open-plan workplace should be approximately 6 m². Interestingly enough, such a
workplace would be forbidden in the Netherlands and Germany. According to Dutch
regulations, office workplaces should be at least 7 m² (excluding space for a filing cabinet
or circulation).[65] German regulations even prescribe 8 m² per workplace in open-plan
settings.[66]

Another crucial aspect is that, in contrast to Continental European legislation,
British regulations say nothing about the access of daylight and an outside view. This
explains why British buildings can be deeper than those in Continental Europe.

SUMMARY AND CONCLUSIONS

A summary of the characteristics of British offices and their national context is given in
table 3.6.

To sum up, the British skyline is a mixture of low- and medium-rise buildings,
punctuated by an occasional high rise. The skyline reflects the struggle between two
forces: on the one hand the historical city, with its tight street patterns, protected views
and complicated ownership structures; on the other hand, strong business pressure to
meet demands for modern office space and a desire to compete with other cities, such as
Frankfurt.

Table 3.6 Summary of results

Office	Context
Building	*Urban setting*
Low- and medium-rise buildings	Historical urban structure
Major exception: Canary Wharf, with occasional	Restrictive planning policies
high-rises in the City	Struggle between conservationists and business
Floor plan	*Market conditions*
Deep floor plans	Strong developers
Compact shapes with central cores or atria	High rents
Air-conditioning and raised floors	Relatively low GDP
Workplace	*Labour relations*
Open plans with cellular offices for management	Strong shareholders
Low use of space per employee	
Trends: more open, non-territorial offices and	*Culture*
teleworking	Hierarchic
	Strongly individualistic
	Neutral way of interaction
	Regulations
	No specific workplace size given
	No requirements for daylight/outside view

At floor plan level British offices tend to have US style, deep and air-conditioned buildings with raised floors. This is mainly due to a market that is driven by high rents and developers that are strongly influenced by American practice. It also reflects the relatively small role that employees play in organisational decision-making.

At the workplace level British offices tend to have open plans with cellular offices set aside for management. The efficient open plans reflect the high rents in London. These rents are also an important incentive for experiments in teleworking in combination with desk sharing. Furthermore, British layouts reflect British labour relations in which corporate interests are more important than employee desires for privacy and space.

The open workplace layouts may also be a product of the hierarchical culture of British organisations. The importance of hierarchy, however, is fading; this is mirrored in the increasing popularity of 'inverted' open plans and totally open workplace layouts.

In respect to the research question (What is the relationship between office design and national context?), it is clear that the British situation has strongly been influenced by American office design. Yet, American practices have not been copied uncritically. Despite extremely high rents and London's role as a global city, the number of high-rise buildings has remained limited. Furthermore British architects have interpreted the deep American floors in their own way, as, for example, Richard Rogers did in the Lloyd's building. In that sense British office design is still British. More importantly, however, is that American design practices would never have been so successful if the British market had not been willing to adopt them. They have been successful because they fit within the British context of a developer-dominated market, high rent levels, and shareholder capitalism. Clearly, there is a strong fit between the national context and office design.

Notes

1   Sassen, S. (1991), *The Global City: New York, London, Tokyo*, Princeton University Press, Princeton

2   Simon, R.D. (1996), 'Skyscrapers and the new London skyline: 1945-1991', in: *Architronic*, Vol. 5, No. 2, http://www.saed.kent.edu/Architronic/v5n2.06html

3   Cairns, S. (1996), *The North American Influence on the London Docklands*, http://www.macalstr.edu/~geograph/world-urbanization/scairns/noam.html

4   Richard Ellis St Quintin, *News*, http://www.richardellis.co.uk/news

5   Bar-hillel, M. (1999), 'City anger at bid to protect London sights', in: *This is London*, May 10, http://www.thisislondon.com

6   Grimston, J. (1999), 'City builds itself up to be second Manhattan', in: *The Sunday Times*, April 18, http://www.sunday-times.co.uk

7   British Council for Offices (1997), *Best Practice in the Specification of Offices*, British Council for Offices

8   Raymond, S. and Cunliffe, R. (1997) *Tomorrow's Office: Creating effective and humane interiors*, E & FN Spon, London

9   Bussel, A. (1992), '(In)visible Giant', in: *Progressive Architecture*, No. 3, pp. 96-100

10 Eley, J. and Marmot, A. (1995), *Understanding offices*, Penguin, London

11 ibid.

12 Leaman, A. and Bordass, B. (1997), *Productivity in Buildings: the 'killer' variables*, paper presented to the Workplace Comfort Forum, Central Hall, Westminster, London 29-30 October

13 Burland, J. (1997), 'Building study: Stockley Park updated: Architect's account', in: *Architects' journal*, March 20, pp. 30-31.

14 Bennetts, R.(1995), 'Building study:The choice of a new generation: Architect's account', in: *Architects' journal*, March 2, pp. 44-48

15 Fenker, M. (1995), 'The influence of culture on the design and use of office space', in: *InterVIEWS*, No 1., pp. 2-12

16 Evette, T., Bonnet, C., Fencker, M., Michel, P. and Philipon, B. (1992), *L'architecture tertiaire en Europe et aux Etats-Unis*, CSTB, Paris

17 Carp (1999), 'Carp International: Marc Straat, business development manager bij ICO Global Communication in London', in: *Carp*, No. 12, p. 7

18 Singmaster, D.(1996), 'Peopling the Ark', in: *Architects' journal*, Vol. 204, October 31, pp. 47-51

19 Farrell, T. (1991), 'Response Farrell', in: *Architects' journal*, Vol. 193, May 22, pp. 38-39

20 Bailey, S.(1990), *Offices: a briefing and design guide*, Butterworth Architecture, Oxford

21 Gascoine, C. (1996), 'The office lines are open at Stockley Park', in: *Architects' journal*, April 11, p. 38

22 Jenkin, D. (1997), 'Emerging building forms', in: Worthington, J.(ed.), *Reinventing the Workplace*, Architectural Press, Oxford

23 Hakfoort, J. and Lie, R. (1996), 'Office Space per Work: Evidence from Four European Markets', in: *The Journal of Real Estate Research*, Vol. 11, No. 2, pp. 183-196

24 Simon, R.D. (1996), 'Skyscrapers and the new London skyline: 1945-1991', in: *Architronic*, Vol. 5, No. 2, http://www.saed.kent.edu/Architronic/v5n2.06html

25 Meel, J.J. (1998), *Case study of a Dutch Bank*, Internal report, Delft University of Technology

26 Bor, W. (1995), 'A meeting of minds', in: *Architects' journal*, March 2, pp. 60-61

27 Charles, Prince of Wales (1989), *A vision of Britain; a personal view of architecture*, Doubleday, London

28 Simon, R.D. (1996), 'Skyscrapers and the new London skyline: 1945-1991', in: *Architronic*, Vol. 5, No. 2, http://www.saed.kent.edu/Architronic/v5n2.06html

29 London Planning Advisory Committee (1998), *High Buildings and Strategic Views: A Guide to Draft Strategic Planning Advice*, http://lpac.gov.uk/hbguide.html

30 Bar-hillel, M. (1999), 'City anger at bid to protect London sights', in: *This is London*, May 10, http://www.thisislondon.com

31 Moore, R. (1996), 'Record-breaking tower "would lift City"', in: *Electronic Telegraph*, September 10, http://www.telegraph.co.uk

32 Moore, R. (1998), 'High and low really can line together', in: *This is London*, April 7, http://www.thisislondon.com

33 Tayeb, M. (1993), 'English Culture and Business Organizations', in: Hickson, D.J. (ed.), *Management in Western Europe: Society, Culture and Organization in Twelve Nations*, Walter de Gruyter, New York

34 Eley, J. and Marmot, A. (1995), *Understanding offices*, Penguin, London

35 Davies, C. (1992), 'Critique: On the Waterfront', in: *Progressive Architecture*, No. 4, pp.122-124

36 Pollard, I. (1993), 'Academy international forum: learning from London', in: Powell, K. (ed.), *World Cities: London*, Academy Editions, London

37 Simon, R.D. (1996), 'Skyscrapers and the new London skyline: 1945-1991', in: *Architronic*, Vol. 5, No. 2, http://www.saed.kent.edu/Architronic/v5n2.06html

38 Eley, J. and Marmot, A. (1995), *Understanding offices*, Penguin, London

39 Duffy, F. A. and Crisp, V. (1993), *The Responsible Workplace, The redesign of work and office*, Butterworth Architecture, Oxford
40 Duffy, F. (1997), *The New Office*, Conran Octopus, London
41 Eley, J. and Marmot, A. (1995), *Understanding offices*, Penguin, London
42 ibid.
43 Meel, J.J. van (1998), *Case study Lloyd's TSB Bank Bristol*, Internal report, Delft University of Technology, Department of real estate and project management, Delft
44 Jong, H.W. de (1996), 'Rijnlandse ondernemingen presteren beter', *Economisch Statistische Berichten*, vol. 81, No. 4049, pp. 228-232.
45 The Economist (1996), 'Unhappy families', in: *The Economist*, February 10, http:www.economist.co.uk
46 Hampden-Turner, C. and A. Trompenaars (1993), *The Seven Cultures of Capitalism*, Doubleday, New York
47 Meel, J.J. van, Blakstad, S., Dewulf, G. and Duffy, F. (1997), *Power-relations in office design*, Internal report, Delft University of Technology, Department of real estate and project management, Delft
48 Eley, J. and Marmot, A. (1995), *Understanding offices*, Penguin, London
49 Leaman, A. and Bordass, B. (1997), *Productivity in Buildings: the 'killer' variables*, Paper presented to the Workplace Comfort Forum, Central Hall, Westminster, October 29-30, London
50 Moore, R. (1998), 'The future office has landed', in: *This is London*, July 21, http://www.thisislondon.com
51 Worsley, G. (1998), 'A perfect place for work?', in: *Electronic Telegraph*, August 15, http:www.telegraph.co.uk
52 ibid.
53 Hampden-Turner, C. and A. Trompenaars (1993), *The Seven Cultures of Capitalism*, Doubleday, New York
54 Hofstede, G.(1991), *Cultures and Organisations, Software of the Mind*, McGraw-Hill, London
55 Tayeb, M. (1993), 'English Culture and Business Organizations', in: Hickson, D.J. (ed.), *Management in Western Europe: Society, Culture and Organization in Twelve Nations*, Walter de Gruyter, New York
56 Moran, R.T. (1992), *Cultural Guide to Doing Business in Europe*, Butterworth-Heinemann, Oxford
57 Eley, J. and Marmot, A. (1995), *Understanding offices*, Penguin, London
58 Tayeb, M. (1993), 'English Culture and Business Organizations', in: Hickson, D.J. (ed.), *Management in Western Europe: Society, Culture and Organization in Twelve Nations*, Walter de Gruyter, New York
59 Eley, J. and Marmot, A. (1995), *Understanding offices*, Penguin, London
60 North, R. (1999), 'flights of future fancy?', in: *Electronic Telegraph*, October 22, http:www.telegraph.co.uk
61 Hofstede, G.(1991), *Cultures and Organisations, Software of the Mind*, McGraw-Hill, London
62 Coleman, C. (1997), 'Going Global', in: *Perspective*, Winter, http://www.iida.com/communications/publications/perspective/winter97/GoingGlobal/index.htm
63 Health & Safety Executive (1992), *Approved Code of Practice and Guidance. Workplace health, safety and welfare*, London
64 Eley, J. and Marmot, A. (1995), *Understanding offices*, Penguin, London
65 Ministery of Social Affairs and Labour (1998), Arbo-Informatieblad '*Kantoren*', Sdu Publishers, The Hague
66 ZH 1/168 *Sicherheitsregeln für Bildschirmarbeitsplätze im Bürobereich* 10.80

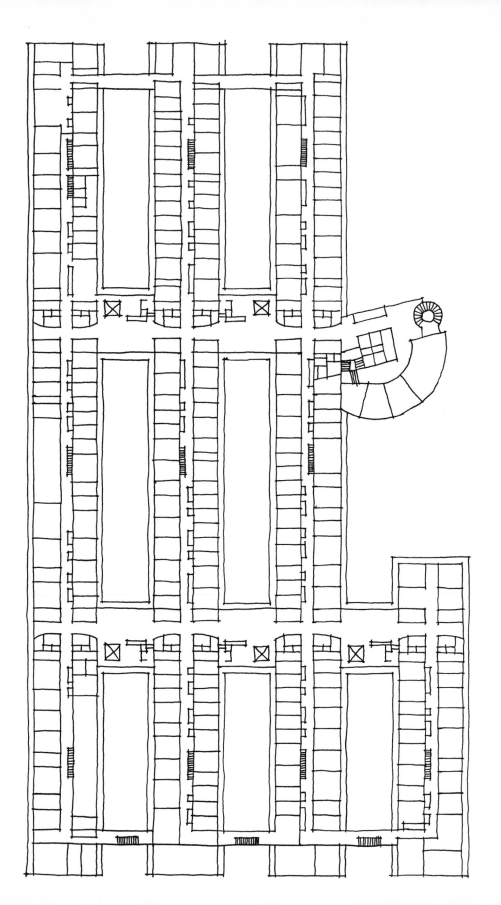

4 Germany

The phrase 'Made in Germany' stands for quality, durability and reliability. These virtues are commonly ascribed to German products such as cars, but they can be applied just as well to office buildings. German office buildings are among the most luxurious workplaces in Europe. They are spacious and cellularised, and they provide every employee with an outside view, daylight and the ability to open windows.

'Made in Germany' also stands for a certain kind of conservatism. German offices tend to be rather conventional, even those in the architectural hotspot, Berlin. The globalisation of the economy, reunification and the need for liberalisation seem not to have affected office design – yet. New 'alternative' office concepts, such as the combi-office, the shared office or teleworking, presented at conferences and in magazines, are much written about, but still little used in practice.

This chapter discusses German office design. First, we give an overview of the characteristics typical of German office design. Then we describe how the characteristics can be explained by the context in which they are produced. Conclusions about the relationship between German office design and its national context are presented in the last section.

GERMAN OFFICES

Building

In Germany most office buildings are low- or medium-rise. *World Architecture* writes in its report on Germany, 'skyscrapers are unwelcome in cities like Hamburg, Munich and Berlin, all of which are conscious of retaining traditional urban design, and allow tall buildings only in suburban business parks or limited locations'.[1]

Berlin is the clearest example of German resistance to building high-rises. It is currently Europe's largest building site, with approximately 1.2 million m² of commercial offices currently under construction.[2] The buildings are being designed by such foreign 'starchitects' as Sir Norman Foster, Jean Nouvel, Renzo Piano and Cesar Pelli. Contradicting the desire for gleaming new buildings, most of them remain true to the spirit of the historical past of Berlin.[3] New buildings seldom exceed the traditional Berlin building height of 22 m. Only at Alexanderplatz and Potzdamerplatz can office towers reaching up to 150 m be found (see figure 88). The local newspaper *Berliner Morgenpost* refers to them as 'high-rises' and 'skyscrapers' but they are relatively small by world standards.[4]

88 Debis Tower at
Potsdamerplatz.

89 Frankfurt skyline

A good example is the Debis Tower at Potsdamerplatz. This 85 m high tower, designed by Renzo Piano, clearly differs from the traditional 'American' skyscraper. Its aim is to reconcile the tower building with the city: make it into something human and not just a brochure image. Typically German is the tower's roof that has been landscaped to conform with German regulations that impose green areas to compensate for high-rise construction. It is one of the reasons why Peter Davey – editor of *The Architectural Review* – seriously doubts whether this building could have been built in the US.[5]

The only real German high rises can be found in Frankfurt-am-Main, often referred to as 'Mainhattan'. Frankfurt is the financial centre of Germany (see figure 89). Its importance seems to be reflected in its skyline, the only one in Europe that is really dominated by skyscrapers. At this moment Frankfurt has seven buildings, almost all bank headquarters, which exceed the height of 150 m. The main landmark is the headquarters of the Commerzbank.[6, 7] With a height of 259 m it is currently the tallest building in Europe.

The Commerzbank building was designed by the British architect Norman Forster. Yet it is typically a German office in the sense that all its inhabitants have an outside view and that they are able to open the windows. Furthermore, it is a very environmentally sound building. These are typical features of German office design.

Floor plan

The most typical characteristic of German floor plans is their limited depth, ranging from about 12 to 14 m. The narrow floor plans have to do with the fact that German employees generally sit within 6.5 m of a window, making it impossible to build deep buildings.[8] This limited depth comes from the desire to give every employee the ability to open windows and have direct access to daylight and an outside view.

The narrow floor depth produces buildings of a linear shape, consisting of office

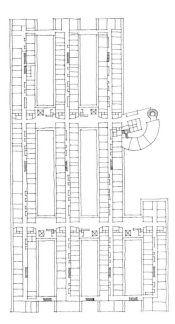

90 Floor plan
Gruner + Jahr

91 Interior
Gruner + Jahr

'wings' in different configurations, x-shaped, l-shaped, u-shaped, and so on. A typical characteristic of these 'non-compact' shapes is that distances from one end of the building to the other can be long. The headquarters of the publishing house Gruner + Jahr in Hamburg is a good example (Steidle and Kiessler, 1991). In this large low-rise building, some staff members complain about its 'endless' corridors (see figures 90 - 91). As an employee remarks: 'still can't get used to the endless walks along seemingly never-ending passageways just to use the Xerox, get a cup of coffee, or go to the rest room'.[9]

Another crucial effect of this type of narrow floor plan is that construction costs tend to be relatively high. Because of the limited depth one has to build more frontage than in similarly sized deep buildings. This is the price you have to pay for daylight and an outside view. The British *Architects' journal* says of the Gruner + Jahr building: 'the high building costs, caused by the large surface area and the complexity of the external envelope have given positive benefits in the light, comfortable interior spaces'.[10]

Similar problems occur in high-rise buildings. Because of the limited floor depth, German high-rises tend to be very slender. A good example is the Kastor & Pollux project in Frankfurt, two commercial high-rise towers designed by the American architects Kohn Pedersen Fox (KPF). Both buildings have a large core with relatively little office space around it (see figure 92). As a result the ratio between the total space of the building and the space that can actually be used for work is relatively inefficient when compared to the much 'thicker' American skyscrapers, which KPF usually builds back home. By comparison, the floor plan is also rather inflexible (less layout options) and inefficient in terms of the ratio of external wall-to-floor area (more expensive facade).

A more efficient way to build narrow spaces is to wrap the office space around a courtyard or atrium, creating a compact building and still providing employees with a view. The most radical example of such a solution is the Commerzbank in Frankfurt, which has an atrium 160 m high. Davies says in his book on the project that 'one of the

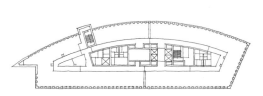

92 Floor plan Kastor Tower (depth from core to facade: 7.5 m)

93 The towers of the Kastor & Pollux project

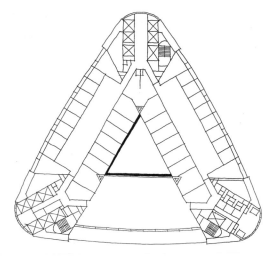

94 Floor plan Commerzbank

95 Skygardens Commerzbank

major factors influencing the design was not specific to the Commerzbank brief, but applied generally to all office buildings in Germany'.[11] This was the requirement that every workstation should be close to a window with a view out. This limitation had a profound effect on the form and structure of the new building. A monolithic New York-style skyscraper, with large floor slabs was effectively ruled out'. For these reasons the architects designed a triangular floor plan with a full-height atrium, which brings light and a view in to the middle of the building. Another special feature is that each floor has three wings, two of which serve as office space and a third wing that forms part of one of the four-storey high gardens (see figures 94 - 95). These gardens give the employees who are located on the inside of the building, and who would normally just have a view of the atrium, an outside view also.

The limited depth of German office floors is also related to climate control in buildings. The advantage of narrow floors is that they open up the possibility of using

natural ventilation. In Germany, natural ventilation is almost a standard feature of
buildings. One of the main reasons is that it saves energy, which seems to be very
important to German architects and clients. Both seem to have a particular obsession
with environmentally sound design.[12, 13] Furthermore, the ability to open windows is
thought to be important for the satisfaction of employees. It restores 'direct contact
between employees and nature' and is believed to enhance the quality of the
workplace.[14]

It is characteristic that even a high-rise building like the Commerzbank has openable
windows. Like most other modern German offices it is a 'mixed-mode' building. It has
an expensive climate facade (a *Klima Façade* as the Germans say), which enables
employees to open windows right up to the fiftieth floor, despite cold and windy
conditions outside. At the same time, the building is equipped with air conditioning for
hot weather and special areas, such as rooms for photocopying. Such a double solution is
relatively expensive, but 'apparently it is worth it', comments the British critic Davies.[15]

Workplace

When looking at German workplaces the first striking observation may be the relatively
ample use of office space per employee. Compared to other countries, German
employees have rather spacious workplaces: 25.3 m² lettable space per employee in
Frankfurt and 28.9 m² space (GEA) in the whole of Germany.[16, 17]

In part, the liberal use of space has to do with the ample provision of secondary
spaces in German offices, for example the large atria and gardens described in the
previous subsection. Another crucial reason, however, lies in the German preference for
cellular offices, which take up more space than open plans.[18,19] The average German
office floor consists of a corridor flanked by small rooms or group rooms for employees
and larger, private rooms for management. A good example is Norman Foster's lens-
shaped Business Centre in Duisburg (see figure 96).

Open office layouts are scarce in Germany. If offices do have open plan layouts, these
tend to be smaller and less deep than those in the US. The outlandishness of the
American-style open plan becomes clear from the description that a German employee
gave from his American work-environment: 'Working conditions were surprisingly
similar in the US, with a few exceptions. One is that the environment tends to be simpler.
I worked for a long time in a cubicle before I got my own windowless office. A cubicle is
a small compartment built from movable plastic walls. Normally large rooms are
subdivided into countless little cubicles, almost all of which have no natural light.
Windows are for management and other non-technical people, regardless of job
status'.[20]

The scarcity of open plan-offices in Germany may be surprising because Germany is
the *Heimat* of the Schnelle brothers, who invented the office landscape in the 1960s. The
office landscape was, however, only a short-term success in Germany. Ten years after its
creation German organisations had rejected the concept with the same force as it had
been welcomed, recoiling in favour of cellular offices (see Chapter 2).

Today, some of the more progressive German organisations and architects regard the
cellular office as conventional and outdated again. One trend is to replace cellular offices
with combi-offices – a Swedish concept consisting of individual cells situated around

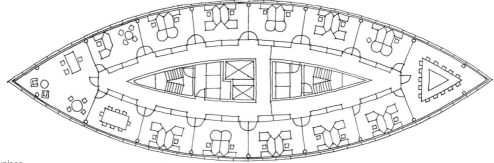

96 Workplace
layout business
centre Duisburg

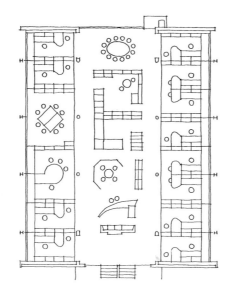

97 Workplace layout
Edding headquarters

98 Interior Edding
headquarters

99 Interior
Commerzbank

common group spaces (see Chapters 2 and 5). This concept has been the 'big idea' in German office planning during the last decade.[21] It is typical that the standard book about this Swedish concept is German.[22]

The first combi-office completed in Germany was the headquarters of Edding in Ahrensburg (see figures 97 - 98). It was designed by Hans Struhk, a German advocate of the combi-office. A striking detail is its depth of 14 m, which is relatively deep by German standards. This depth allows both enclosed offices and shared open-plan areas in the central floor area. It was intended that this layout would encourage more communication, interaction and teamwork. In practice, however, the shared areas were not used that often because staff could not easily get used to the open space.[23, 24]

Despite the initial excitement about the combi-office, the predicted breakthrough of the concept has failed to occur. German developers and real estate brokers say that all potential users have declared their love for it, but no one really wants to move in.[25] Nevertheless, the publicity about the concept did stimulate client and architects to re-think their work environment. Nowadays, the main trend seems to be to use some sort of 'mix' of office concepts, a *Misch Struktur* as the Germans say (the Commerzbank headquarters has also been fitted out in a mix of layouts, see figure 99). This mix may consist of cellular offices, combi-offices, open-plan layouts and group offices, depending on the activities of the organisation.

In some cases experiments with new workplace layouts are combined with the concepts of teleworking and desk-sharing. With a call for flexibility in German organisations and increasing economic pressure,[26] corporations have started to wonder whether their office buildings are being used efficiently, and whether they still need them. In response to these developments, IT companies such as IBM Germany and Siemens Nixdorf are experimenting with groups of employees working at home in combination with desk-sharing solutions for those who are seldom at the office. A realistic forecast for the general adoption of these innovative workplace concepts is absent. German corporations are still rather hesitant.[27, 28] For the moment, they seem to be sticking to traditional methods to cut down their property costs, such as limiting the ample use of space per workplace.

GERMAN CONTEXT

We have seen that with the exception of Frankfurt German offices tend to be low- or medium-rise. Buildings are characterised by limited floor depths and cellular layouts. Organisations are experimenting with new office types, but only on a limited scale. In this section we will try to explain these characteristics.

Urban setting
Just as in most other European cities, German cities tend to have a historical urban structure, which can limit the possibilities of developing high-rise buildings in inner cities. Plot sizes may be too small and streets too narrow to deal with the large number of cars, deliveries and people that such large buildings bring with them. Furthermore, high rises may obstruct the view of monuments such as churches or rob neighbouring buildings of their view and sunlight.

100 Redeveloping Berlin

Restrictive planning policies seem to be even more important than these practical concerns. German urban planners tend to have a rather negative attitude towards large-scale office buildings. Particularly in Berlin, development is strongly influenced by local planners' ideas about how cities should be. Like many other German cities, Berlin was heavily damaged during the war. Today planners are trying to restore its pre-war atmosphere. One of their means is to restrict the height of buildings.

Hans Stimmann, Berlin State Secretary for Planning and Ecology, has described the method for the redevelopment of Berlin as 'critical reconstruction', which entails erecting new buildings on exactly the same sites and of the same height as before, in order to save or renew the idea of the European city. Stimmann states that 'the aim of planning policy... seeks to strengthen the identity of Berlin by insisting that architecture must relate to the city, to the historical and built context, to architectural tradition'.[29] More bluntly, he says in *World Architecture* 'If an investor gives me a plan for a building higher than the traditional 22 m plus roof, I don't look at the plan at all' (22 m was the maximum length of the ladders of Prussian firemen).[30]

One of the characteristics of German planning is that it tends to be fairly democratic. Radical building plans can meet a lot of resistance from the public. This complicates the planning process. A proposal for a record-height building for the German Post Office in Bonn outraged local citizens. In choosing the skyscraper design of the American-German firm Murphy/Jahn, the Post Office ignored the wishes of local residents, who had previously chosen a low-rise design by the German architect Peter Böhm. Many locals regard the decision to build a high-rise building as rank hypocrisy on the part of the planning authorities, as for many years the city had refrained from developing the left bank of the Rhine, home to the heritage-protected parliament building.[31]

In Frankfurt high-rise office development has been less of a problem. First of all, because it does not really have a large historical urban structure. During bombing by allied aircraft in World War II, downtown Frankfurt was the worst hit of all German cities. More than 95% of downtown was destroyed.[32] Another reason is the predominant position of banks in Frankfurt. The fact that other financial centres such as New York, Hong Kong and London also have many high-rises indicates that high-rise buildings and financial services are closely related. It seems that in the financial world, skyscrapers play an important role in positioning cities as economic powers. Recently, Frankfurt unveiled a ten-year plan for up to 35 skyscrapers. According to London's *Sunday Times* this plan is part of its bid to overtake London as Europe's financial powerhouse.[33]

But even in Frankfurt, planning regulations and politics play an important role. For example, when Commerzbank started thinking about a new headquarters, it seemed unlikely that the bank would be allowed to build such a tall building. In response to popular sentiment, local government policy during the early 1980s aimed to limit development and effectively outlaw new high-rise buildings. By 1989, however, public opposition to tall structures had relaxed.[34] Instead of putting restrictions on the height of buildings, local planners demanded that the bank addressed a wide range of ecological issues before planning permission was granted. This trend can now also be seen in other German cities where planning regulations impose green areas to compensate for high-rise construction.

Market conditions

The creation of offices with as much concern for employee desires and ecology as there is in Germany, would not have been possible without a prosperous economy (see table 4.1). Whatever the question marks that still surround the effects of reunification and more recently the adoption of the Euro, Germany's economic dominance in post-war Europe is unquestioned. The German economy achieved extraordinary success in the space of two generations.[35] As a result German corporations could usually spend more money on property than their counterparts in other countries. This luxury was, and still is, strengthened by the fact that German real estate managers are dealing with relatively low rent levels. For example, top-rate office rents in Frankfurt or Berlin are still about half those in London (see table 4.2).

Another crucial market characteristic is that users rather than suppliers of office space dominate the market. German corporations tend to build their own buildings rather than leasing or renting them.[36] Although the commercial market for office space is currently very large, German organisations traditionally borrow money from their bank to erect custom-built offices.[37] The fact that German corporations are bank-funded rather than stock-financed enables them to invest in resources such as buildings that do not result in immediate profit.[38]

These market conditions have affected the design of office buildings in several ways. At the building level, low rent levels may explain the hesitance to build high-rise in Germany. Rent levels do not seem high enough to justify the high rises, which are basically a means to multiplying the value of a piece of land. Only Frankfurt has a

Table 4.1 European GDPs per head (The Economist Group, 1997)

Country	GDP per head (US Dollars)
Sweden	25 720
Germany	25 632
Netherlands	23 094
UK	21 848
Italy	19 919

Table 4.2 European rent levels (Richard Ellis, 1999)

City	Prime rent levels (US Dollars per m² per annum)
Stockholm	479
Frankfurt	548
Amsterdam	386
London City	1117
Milan	381

reputation for high rises, which may be helped by the fact that its rents are the highest in Germany. But in Frankfurt too, rents have remained far behind those in cities such as New York and Hong Kong. Therefore, it is more likely that Frankfurt's skyscrapers are built to show the economic success of its financial institutions.

At floor plan level, the combination of a liberal budget and low costs explains how German organisations can afford to build such narrow floors. They can focus on their own specific interests rather than those of developers, who are mainly geared to ease of construction and short-term profit. It also explains why costly 'green' solutions, such as climate facades and mixed-mode systems, are more popular in Germany than in most other countries.

At the workplace level, the low cost and prosperity of the Germany economy explain why employees are accommodated in rather spacious cellular offices. Simply, German organisations can afford it and they are willing to invest money in such long-term advantages as employee satisfaction. It also explains the popularity of a concept such as the combi-office, a concept that is driven by organisational ideas rather than cost savings.

Labour relations

The fact that German organisations are willing to invest their money in high-standard offices says something about German labour relations. In Germany, relations between employers and employees tend to be based on mutual trust and consensus rather than on control and opposition.[39] German workers feel a strong bond with the corporation they work for. Likewise, German employers have traditionally shown a degree of paternalistic concern for worker interests. Good labour relations encourage consensus among big social groups (workers, managers, unions and so forth) and put a premium on stability. As a result the interests of German corporations tend to go beyond economic profits, to the interests of society as a whole. In a survey done by Trompenaars and Hampden-Turner in 1993, German managers rejected significantly more often than Americans did the notion that profit was the only real goal of the company.[40]

On an organisational level consensus-oriented labour relations are reflected in the relatively powerful position of employees within corporations. Over the last few years, power structures in German organisations have been changing, but the concept of *Mitbestimmung* or co-determination remains a powerful force.[41] The major element of their power is formed by a system under which labour representatives sit on the supervisory board of the companies they work for. They have access to corporate information and a real, if limited, participation in governance.[42] Furthermore, organisations have works councils, which have the statutory right to participate in an employer's plans to change anything as fundamental as the working environment.[43]

The result of the powerful position of employees is that working conditions in Germany are relatively luxurious. Over the years German unions and employee representatives have been able to bargain for favourable terms of employment. The last few years, things are changing. But still, for example, Germany's wage levels are among the highest in the world (see table 4.3). In such a context it is not surprising that the standards of accommodation are high also.

Table 4.3 European Labour costs (The Economist Group, 1997)

Country	Labour costs per hour (US Dollars)
Germany	28.4
Sweden	22.6
Netherlands	20.6
Italy	16.6
UK	15.3

At a project level, the relatively powerful position of German employees can be seen in the design and briefing process. According to Jockush, workers want to be an active component in the work process and require every possible control over working conditions.[44] The Gruner + Jahr case is a good example (see p. 79). Over a period of seven years, project groups, architects and specialist engineers worked together with the works council and 22 internal work groups.[45] The chairman of the Gruner + Jahr board, Gerd Schulte-Hillen remarked that 'one of the principles of modern management is, as far as possible, to consider the needs and wishes of individual workers in the design of their workplaces'.[46]

Over the years, the involvement of employees has resulted in fairly user-friendly working conditions. It explains the narrow depth of German office floors, which provide all employees with an outside view, daylight and the ability to open a window, despite the extra costs these bring. It also explains the popularity of cellular offices and combi-office-like solutions, which are in line with employees' desires for privacy and space. More generally, the notion that German managers are not just focusing on profits but also on the role of their organisations in society probably, explains why ecological issues are so important in German office design.

Culture

Because German employees are involved in the briefing and design processes, they are able to leave their cultural imprint on the building. The cliché about German culture is that the people are industrious, hierarchic and orderly, and that they appreciate punctuality, privacy and skill. In today's global village, it is hard to make such general statements about people, but there seems to be some truth in these characteristics. Several are reflected in German office design. In particular privacy and hierarchy are issues that leave their mark on German office design.

Kurt Lewin, a famous psychologist of the 1930s, has said that the German psyche has a large private space and a small outer public space, which is also relatively inaccessible (see figure 101). Although these observations were pre-war, they retain a certain validity.[47] Germans still like to keep to themselves. Their casual discourse will be rather

101 Kurt Lewin presented human personality as a series of concentric circles with certain 'living spaces'.[50] The most private areas are located in the centre of the circle and the more public spaces on the outside. According to him there was a difference between the living spaces of a U-type (United States) and a G-type (German). This difference can also be seen in the perception of physical space by Germans and Americans.

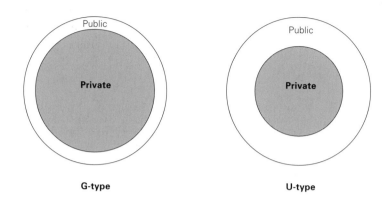

G-type   U-type

formal and distinctly unrevealing.[48] These characteristics also seem to work spatially. To Germans space seems to be sacred. Residences are protected by a variety of barriers, fences, walls, hedges, solid doors, shutters and screens to prevent visual or auditory intrusion.[49]

A similar influence can be seen in German offices, where employees have their own, rather spacious, territory and are likely to leave their office doors closed.[51] So the importance of privacy and personal space in German culture may explain the popularity of the cellular office in Germany. It may also explain why the combi-office has not yet become the success many think it ought to be, despite many experiments with the concept. One of the premises underlying the combi-office concept is that shared open space is used for interaction. Employees, however, may not feel that comfortable using the open space, which was the case in the combi-office in the Edding headquarters. Another issue is that the combi-office uses glazed partitions to let sunlight penetrate the inner areas of the building. The lack of visual privacy may also have contributed to the failure of the concept to break through.

The desire for privacy and personal space seems to be especially important to those in the higher ranks of German corporations. In cultural studies, Germany has not proved to be that much more hierarchical than other European countries.[52] Yet Germany has a tradition of somewhat formal interaction between managers and their subordinates. Up until the 1970s, it was, for example, usual for office buildings to have a *Chef Etage* (management floor). Furthermore, the managers' office spaces were likely to have a *Vorzimmer* – a room, often with secretary, which had to be passed before you got to the manager's office. Nowadays such differences are no longer obligatory, but visible status symbols are still expected and regarded as normal. The use of formal titles such as *Herr Doktor* or *Chef* is, for instance, still very common.

In buildings, the differences may be reflected in the layout. A good example is Opel's headquarters in Rüsselheim, just outside Frankfurt. The brief for the building stated that it had to be a non-hierarchical workplace. The British *Architects' journal*, however, commented wryly that 'the resulting building achieves this within the limitations of common German office practice. The fact that the office suites of top management are only slightly larger than those of middle management is seen as pretty revolutionary. And there is no question that those top managers should have to follow the circulation route of the rest of the staff. Their private car parking is underneath the building from where lifts whizz straight to the management floors'.[53]

Another example of the impact of culture on office design can be seen at Mercedes Benz, also a German car manufacturer. When Mercedes Benz decided to transfer a group of its employees to Alabama (USA), the company gave this group special preparation to get used to American ideas about status and privacy. To begin the necessary acculturation, the employees were accommodated in a building that was much more intimate than is common in German businesses: 'work spaces are open, doors left ajar. Privacy, a cherished commodity in densely populated Germany, is being eradicated'.[54, 55]

Regulations

Another often heard cliché about German culture is that Germans have a tendency to regulate everything in great detail. Michael Porter says in his study of national competitiveness that German product standards are consistently among the most stringent of any nations.[56] Also in architecture, Germany has very detailed and stringent legislation. Neven Sindor of the British architectural firm Nicholas Grimshaw has said: 'we are working in a much more highly regulated climate than we are used to. I sometimes think that Germany is the fountain of all regulations, and it has been a bit of a shock to us'.[57]

For office design, you can find several different types of regulations and guidelines ranging from the *Deutsche Industrie Normen* (DIN) via the *Arbeitsstätttenverordnung* to the *Sicherheitsregeln*.[58] The different standards set specific requirements for both the design and furnishing of office buildings. They control a wide range of issues, such as the use of space per employee, the minimum floor-to-ceiling height, the dimensions of desks and chairs, provision of fresh air, temperature, lighting, the number and size of break areas and washrooms, and so on.

One crucial requirement is that all workplaces that are intended for permanent use must have visual contact with the outside world. This requirement is one explanation of why German floor plans are so narrow. Regulations give no specific distance from workplace to window, but in practice it means that every workplace is located within 6 m of a window.

Furthermore, German law states that the minimum size for a workplace is 8 m². The *Sicherheitsregeln* prescribe that the minimum use of space per workplace is 8-10 m² or more (including the transportation space within the same room). In open-plan offices, however, the minimum space per workplace should be at least 12-15 m².[58] When including space for stairs, corridors and toilets, this easily adds up to a high use of space per employee, explaining the relatively ample use of space by German organisations (see table 4.4).

Table 4.4 Area per workplace in Germany (DTZ Zadelhoff, 1995)

Function	m²
Standard office space	10.4
Guest workers	0.3
Administration	0.5
Conference and meeting space	0.9
Technical service	1.1
Storage	3.3
Archive and library	0.6
Lobby, reception	0.4
Telephone, LAN	0.4
Post, delivery	0.2
Security and facility areas	0.3
Medical officer	0.1
Works council	0.1
Canteen, kitchen	1.8
Marketing	0.5
Corridors	4.7
Lifts and ducs	3.3
Total	**28.9**

SUMMARY AND CONCLUSIONS

Table 4.5 summarises the characteristics of German offices and the factors influencing them.

Most German offices are of low or medium height, except those in Frankfurt. The reason is that most German cities have a historical structure and use restrictive planning policies to retain traditional urban design. Frankfurt is an exception because heavy bombing during World War II destroyed many of the city's historical buildings.

Floor plans of German office buildings are narrow (12-14 m), resulting in linear floor shapes and buildings with atria or courtyards. This can be explained by the relatively powerful position of employees who have been able to realise their desire for an outside view and daylight (which is formalised in German workplace regulations). Furthermore, German organisations have the financial means to realise such buildings.

Workplace layouts tend to be spacious and cellular. This clearly matches German workplace culture, in which privacy and personal space are important. Layouts reflect the relatively powerful position of employees. German employers are in turn able to afford it, and they are willing to invest in good working conditions.

German organisations have only recently begun to question the high and costly standards of German office design. This has resulted in experiments with desk-sharing and teleworking. Up until now, however, these concepts have had little impact on the size and design of mainstream office buildings.

In terms of the research question of this study ('what is the relationship between office design and national context), these observations show that Germany's urban setting, labour relations, market conditions, culture and regulations have left a clear mark on the design of offices. Basically, German offices are user friendly because German employees want them to be that way and because German employers are able and willing to build them so that they are so. External forces such as developers and investors have had little influence on German office design.

Table 4.5 Summary of results

Offices	Context
Building	*Urban setting*
Low- and medium-rise buildings	Historical urban structure
Major exception: Frankfurt	Major exception: Frankfurt
	Restrictive planning policies
Floor plan	*Market conditions*
Narrow floor plans	Strong owner-occupiers
Linear shapes	Low rents
Natural ventilation/mixed mode systems, attention to	High GDP
ecological issues	
Workplace	*Labour relations*
Cellular layouts	Strong employee representatives
High use of space per employee	*Culture*
Trends: combination of open and cellular offices,	Hierarchic/formal
relatively few experiments with non-territorial offices	Strong emphasis on privacy and personal space
and teleworking	Neutral way of interaction
	Regulations
	Minimum workplace size: 8 m^2
	Stipulates access to daylight/outside view

When reflecting upon the German situation, it is interesting to ask the question whether the involvement of employees has also resulted in more productive buildings. Research shows that large German organisations are more productive than organisations in the UK or the US, where working conditions are radically different.[60] It is tempting to say that the working conditions have contributed to this situation. The material presented in this chapter indicates, however, that the high standards of German office design are the result rather than the cause of the economic success. Even more important is the impression that in Germany, investments in the physical work environment are not rational decisions aimed at financial gain. Instead, they are more a matter of course, an outcome of the relatively harmonious relations between employers and employees. They belong in the general German picture of high wages and excellent secondary working conditions.

Notes

1   Stimpel, R. (1997), 'Country Focus: Germany', in : *World Architecture*, No. 60, pp. 53-58
2   DTZ Zadelhoff (1996) *European Commercial Property Markets Overview* 1996, DTZ Zadelhoff
3   World Architecture (1995), 'Country Report Germany', in: *World Architecture*, No. 54, pp. 89-111
4   Kannenberg, S. (1997), 'The Alexander-platz of the future', in: *Berliner Morgenpost*, http://www.berliner-morgenpost.de/bm/international/
5   Davey, P. (1999), 'Critique: Could Piano's Debis Tower in Berlin have been built in the US? The answer reveals the flaws affecting American architecture', in: *The Architectural Record*, No. 4, pp. 35-36
6   http://www.commerzbank.com/navigate/zent_frm
7   http://www.fosterandpartners.com/projects/1991/80
8   Hanscomb (1998), 'USA/Europe comparisons', in: *World Architecture*, No. 64, p. 82
9   Gruner + Jahr (1994), T*he Gruner + Jahr Media Building*, Gruner + Jahr, Hamburg
10   Dawson, L. (1991), 'Hamburg Headquarters', in: *Architects' journal*, June, pp.34-39
11   Davies, C. and Lambot, I. (1997), *Commerzbank Frankfurt, Prototype for an Ecological High-Rise*, Watermark/Birkhäuser, Surrey
12   Stimpel, R. (1997), 'Country Focus: Germany', in : *World Architecture*, No. 60, pp. 53-58
13   Dawson, L. (1997), 'Architecture for the people', in: *World Architecture*, No. 60, p. 85
14   AiT (1999), Auf sendung, AiT, http://www.quickborner-team.de/english/newspresse/index.htm
15   Davies, C. and Lambot, I. (1997), *Commerzbank Frankfurt, Prototype for an Ecological High-Rise*, Watermark/Birkhäuser, Surrey
16   Hakfoort, J. and Lie, R. (1996), 'Office Space per Worker: Evidence from Four European Markets', in: *The Journal of Real Estate Research*, Vol. 11, No. 2, pp. 183-196
17   DTZ Zadelhoff (1995) flächen pro Arbeitsplatz, *internal report DTZ Zadelhoff*, Frankfurt
18   Hanscomb (1998), 'USA/Europe comparisons', in: *World Architecture*, No. 64, p. 82
19   Eley, J. and Marmot, A. (1995), *Understanding Offices*, Penguin, London
20   Driemeyer, T. (1998), *Working in the USA: Experiences of a European*, http://www.bitrot.de/workinusa.html
21   Duffy, F. (1997), *The New Office*, Conran Octopus, London
22   Congena (1994), *Zukunftsstrategie Kombi-Büro*, Callway/FBO, Munich
23   Gottschalk, O. (1992) *Use and appropriation in office buildings*, Proceedings of the international symposium Corporate space and Architecture, Lille, Lyons, Nantes, Paris, June 30 - July 3
24   Duffy, F., A. and Crisp, V. (1993), *The Responsible Workplace, The redesign of work and office*, Butterworth Architecture, Oxford
25   Jockusch, P. R. A (1992) *Recent German experience with changes of existing administrative organizations in the public sector*, Proceedings of the international symposium Corporate space and Architecture, Lille, Lyons, Nantes, Paris, June 30 - July 3, 1992
26   The Economist (1996), 'Divided still, A survey of Germany', in: *The Economist*, November 9th-15th
27   AiT (1998), 'Nonterritoriale Bürowelt', in: *AiT*, September, http://www.quickborner-team.de/english/newspresse/index.htm
28   Econy (1998), 'Büros in bewegung', in: *Econy*, January, http://www.quickborner-team.de/english/newspresse/index.htm
29   Balfour, A. (1995), *World Cities Berlin*, Academy Editions, London
30   Stimpel, R. (1997), 'Country Focus: Germany', in : *World Architecture*, No. 60, pp. 53-58
31   World Architecture (1999), 'Jahn tower offends, Bonn residents' wishes ignored', in: *World Architecture*, No. 75, p. 22
32   http://www.boomtown-frankfurt.com/wolkenkratzer/reportagen/skyline/bericht-03/e_index.shtml
33   Grimston, J. (1999), 'City builds itself up to be second Manhattan', in: *Sunday Times of London*, April 18, http://www.sunday-times.co.uk
34   Davies, C. and Lambot, I. (1997), *Commerzbank Frankfurt, Prototype for an Ecological High-Rise*, Watermark/Birkhäuser, Surrey
35   Fukuyama, F. (1995), *Trust: the Social Virtues and Creation of Prosperity*, Hamish Hamilton, London
36   Nathanson, N. and A. Andersen (1993), *Real Estate financing in Europe*, Arthur Andersen
37   Duffy, F. (1992) *The Changing Workplace*, Phaidon Press, London
38   Warner, M. and Campbell, A. (1993), 'German management', in: Hickson, D. (ed.), *Management in Western Europe, Society, Culture, and Organization in Twelve Nations*, De Gruyter, New York
39   Max Planck Institute for the study of societies (1998), *The development of co-determination as an institution*, http://www.mpi-fg-koeln.mpg.de/bericht/endbericht/
40   Hampden-Turner, C. and Trompenaars, F. (1993), T*he seven cultures of capitalism*, Doubleday, New York

41 The Economist (1999), 'The sick man of the euro', in: *The Economist*,
    http://www.economist.com./editorial/freeforall/current/sf4100.html
42 Charkham, J. P. (1995), *Keeping good company; a study of corporate governance in five countries*, Clarendon, Oxford
43 Duffy, F. (1992) *The Changing Workplace*, Phaidon Press, London
44 Jockusch, P. R. A (1992) *Recent German experience with changes of existing administrative organizations in the public sector*, Proceedings of the international symposium Corporate space and Architecture, Lille, Lyons, Nantes, Paris, June 30 - July 3, 1992
45 Gruner + Jahr (1994), *The Gruner + Jahr Media Building*, Gruner + Jahr, Hamburg
46 Dawson, L. (1991), 'Hamburg Headquarters', in: *Architects' journal*, June, pp.34-39
47 Trompenaars, F. (1993), *Riding the Waves of Culture*, London, Nicholas Brealey Publishing Limited, 1993
48 Hampden-Turner C. and Trompenaars, F. (1993), T*he seven cultures of capitalism*, Doubleday, New York
49 Hall, E.T. and M.R. Hall (1990) *Understanding Cultural Differences, Germans, French and Americans*. Yarmouth, Intercultural Press Inc
50 Lewin, K. (1936), *Principles of Topological Psychology*, McGraw-Hill, New York
51 ibid.
52 Hofstede, G. (1991), *Cultures and Organisations, Software of the mind*, McGraw-Hill, London
53 Slavid, R. (1998), 'Opel HQ in Russelheim, Germany, by BDP', in: *Architects' journal*, August 13, No. 6, pp. 32-28
54 Atkinson, T. (1994), 'Mercedes immerses executives in 'Bama drawl', in: *International Herald Tribute*, No.1, p. 4
55 Schneider, S.C. and Barsoux, J. (1997), *Managing Across Cultures*, Prentice Hall, London
56 Porter, M.E. (1990), *The Competitive Advantage of Nations*, Free Press, New York
57 EuroProperty (1995), Cross-Border Business, *Europroperty*, special issue
58 Gottschalk (1994), *Verwaltungsbauten, flexibel, Kommunikatief, Nutzorientiert*, Wiesbaden, Bauverlag, pp. 94-99
59 Segelken, S. (1994), 'Vorschriften für den Bürobetrieb', in Gottschalk (ed.) *Verwaltungsbauten, flexibel, Kommunikatief, Nutzorientiert*, Wiesbaden, Bauverlag, pp. 94-99
60 Jong, H.W. de (1996), 'Rijnlandse ondernemingen presteren beter', in: *Economisch Statistische Berichten*, vol. 81, nr. 4049, pp. 228-232

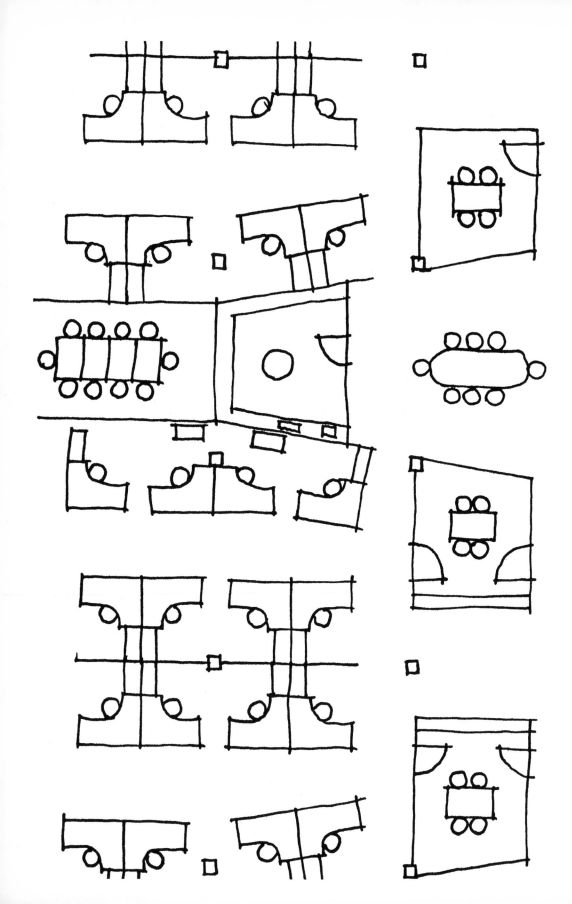

5 Sweden

Swedish design is a byword for safety and quality. Swedish cars, furniture and tools are cherished for their functionality, their simplicity and their user-friendliness. The same characteristics can be ascribed to Swedish office buildings. Among foreign architects and their clients, Sweden is a popular destination for finding inspiration for new office buildings. Franklin Becker, an American guru on office innovation, refers to Swedish offices as the most beautiful and functional in the world.[1]

But what exactly are those 'beautiful' and 'functional' characteristics of Swedish office design? And why do Swedes create such office buildings while others do not? Our purpose in this chapter is to describe and explain Swedish office design. First it will describe Swedish offices. Then it describes key factors that make Swedish offices the way they are. Conclusions about the relationship between Swedish office design and its national context are presented in the final section.

SWEDISH OFFICES

Building

Mainstream offices in Sweden tend to be low- or medium-rise. There are no reliable statistics of the number of floors in office buildings, but Scandinavian office buildings tend to be 3-4 storey high.[2] Tall buildings are even more an exception than in the rest of Europe. This is surprising because Stockholm was the first European city to import (in 1919) the early American type of skyscraper (see figure 103).[3] Furthermore, in the 1960s several large Manhattan-like skyscrapers were built in the centre of Stockholm (see figure 104). Today, however, skyscrapers are out of grace. The Swedish architectural critic Hultin says there is a very deep-rooted resistance to high buildings in Sweden. 'In this respect we differ from the USA where no building less than twenty storey is considered to be a high building'.[4]

The Lilla Bommen project of Ralph Erskine may be regarded as an example of Swedish high-rise (see figure 105). The project is part of the revitalisation of the waterfront of Gothenburg, Sweden's second largest town and Scandinavia's largest harbour. With its 23 floors and red and white striped exterior, the building is a remarkable structure. On an international scale, however, it remains rather modest. Nothing in the project approaches the size and scale of waterfront developments such as the London Docklands (see Chapter 3) or the Kop van Zuid project in Rotterdam (see Chapter 7).

102 Workplace layout Ericsson radio systems, Stockholm (Güllstrom & Westerberg, 1994)

103 Early skyscrapers at the Kungsgatan in Stockholm

104 Skyscrapers from the 1960s in the City of Stockholm

105 Lilla Bommen in Gothenburg

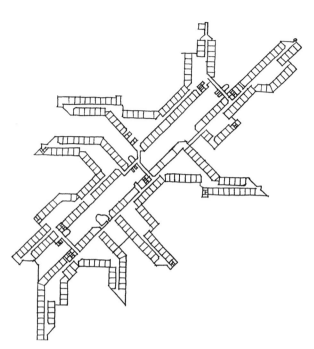

106 Floor plan
SAS Headquarters

107 The SAS
headquarters creates
its own urban setting
with an internal street

So, Sweden has not much of a high-rise tradition. Instead it is better known for its 'groundscrapers'. Such low-rise buildings are most noticeable on the edge of metropolitan areas, where space is not so constrained. SAS's headquarters is probably Sweden's best-known 'groundscraper'. The SAS headquarters, designed by Norwegian architect Niels Torp, is a huge building brought down to a human scale. The building is divided into seven separate building blocks connected by a street covered by a roof of glass (see figures 106 - 107). This glazed street is the 'social heart' of the building, giving access to collective facilities such as a restaurant and a swimming pool. American office experts Becker and Steele remarked that 'Unlike the soaring atria of many modern corporate buildings, which are impressive as a visual statement but devoid of life and activity because they lead nowhere and provide no reason to linger, SAS's street is lined with real shops and cafés'.[5] The street may be regarded as a means of strengthening the company's culture. At the same time, it results in a relatively inefficient ratio of gross to net area because it is basically an over-sized circulation space.

Floor plan

Like most northern European offices, Swedish offices have relatively narrow floor plans. The majority of workplaces are located within a maximum of about 6 m from a window, to provide employees with daylight and an outside view. The limited floor depth has also to do with the natural ventilation of most Swedish office buildings. Instead of air-conditioning, Swedish offices tend to rely on the thermal storage capacity of the building fabric, mechanical ventilation and openable windows for fresh air and cooling of the building. It is typical that an architect who followed the American norm of sealed windows in Stockholm was sharply criticised for a lack of 'functional consideration'.[6]

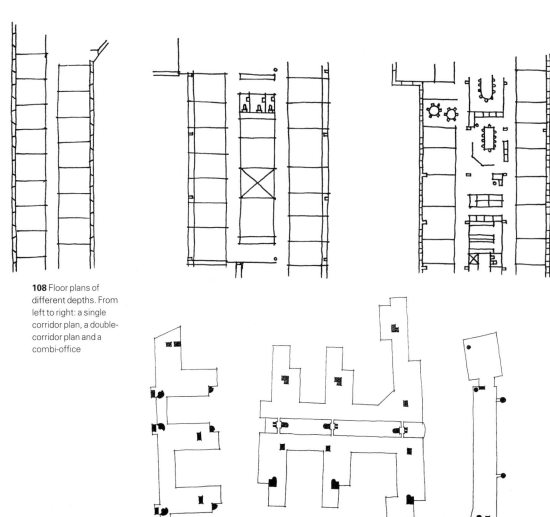

108 Floor plans of different depths. From left to right: a single corridor plan, a double-corridor plan and a combi-office

109 Swedish floor shapes: linear and complex

The narrowest office buildings (or building parts) have a floor depth of 10-11 m. They tend to be single-corridor plans consisting of a central corridor with workplaces along the facade. The deeper floors have a depth of 17-18 m. These are often double-corridor plans which have two corridors with offices along the facade and inner spaces for facilities that do not necessarily need daylight (such as toilets, stairs, elevators and meeting rooms). Combi-offices also tend to have greater depth. In a combi-office, the inner area of the building is left open for informal meeting places and the accommodation of common facilities such as archives, printers and Xerox machines (see figure 108).

The narrow floor plans have a crucial effect on the overall shape of office buildings. Swedish offices tend to have a linear shape rather than a compact one. They may consist of a single office wing, a combination of office wings (forming, for example, an L, an E or

a rectangle) or a set of separated office wings that are connected by a glazed atrium or
street (see figure 109). Deep buildings with central cores are virtually absent.

The disadvantage of such linear floor types is that they are rather inefficient because
you need to build large facades to enclose relatively little office space. This is one of the
reasons why Americans and British tend to choose more compact shapes. Doxtater says
in his book about Swedish offices that some British and Americans may even laugh at
them, as they sense the difficulty of rendering and marketing an external image of these
buildings.[7] British office expert Duffy says 'by the best developer standards these
customised buildings are so inefficient to construct, so profligate in the use of space,
especially circulation, so untouched by conventional norms of efficiency, and thus so
difficult to trade or exchange'.[8]

Workplace
The immediate cause for the linear shapes lies in the workplace layout. It is the result of
giving virtually every employee his or her own private office located next to a window
(*enhetsrum* in Swedish). Regardless of their rank, employees get the same amount of
space, privacy, or offices with an outside view (see figures 110 - 111).

An advantage of these universal plans is that they provide a certain flexibility.[9] In the
case of reorganisation the only things that have to be moved are people and some
furniture components. The time, expense and disruption of moving walls or panels are
eliminated. Yet this flexibility works only as long as you do not want to create teams or
group spaces: Swedish universal plans leave little space for activities other than private
work (at least according to Swedish standards).

A disadvantage of highly cellularised offices may be that people feel socially isolated.
In the literature on office design, cellular offices are often associated with a lack of
interaction.[10] To some extent this disadvantage can be counterbalanced by using glazed
partitions. This at least provides employees with more visual contact. Furthermore,
virtually all Swedish office floors have break areas (*pausrum* in Swedish). These are
separate, specially designed spaces with tables, chairs and a small kitchenette (including
microwave). They are used several times a day for having lunch and drinking coffee with
colleagues.[11]

The Swedish combi-office is a response to the idea that cellular offices are an obstacle
to interaction. Tengbom architects designed the first combi-office in 1977, following the
failure of the office landscape in Sweden (see Chapter 2). Just as in a traditional Swedish
cellular office everybody gets his or her own 'cell'. However, these cells are grouped
around a open space. According to the designers the open space is to function as a sort of
living room, meant for informal meetings and the use of common facilities such as
archives and fax or Xerox machines (see figure 112).

It is clear that the combination of individual offices and common spaces costs more
space than for example an open-plan office. It explains the relatively large amount of
space per employee in Sweden. There are no exact figures on the current situation, but
research has shown that the average use of space in Stockholm in 1993 was 30 m² per
employee (GEA).[12, 13]

This generous use of space is one of the reasons why some Swedish architects and
clients are currently looking for new workplace layouts. Telia – a Swedish telecom

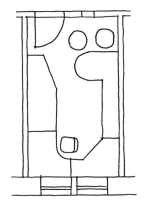

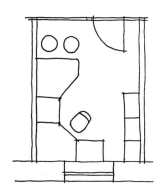

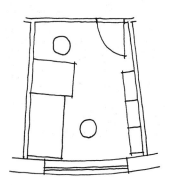

110 Swedish
'enhetsrum'

company – recently decided to use no more than 18 m² per employee. The general criticism is that cellular offices cost too much and hinder communication among employees. The Swedish combi-office is losing its appeal for the same reasons. Even Åke Beijne and Niels Torp, who designed the first combi-offices, advocate more open and economical office solutions.

Some organisations and architects have gone a step further and have replaced individual cells with open-plan solutions. In some cases they have combined them with 'non-territorial' office concepts in which employees no longer have their personal workplace. The reason underlying this is that (just as in other countries) information technology enables employees to work outside the office. When people are teleworking it is no longer necessary to have one's own workplace (from a technical point of view).

Ericsson, the Swedish telecom giant, is one organisation that is experimenting with new office concepts. The architectural firm Gullström and Westerberg has designed a large number of projects for Ericsson in which space was given a more team-oriented and non-territorial character.[14] In these projects we see much more open space than in traditional Swedish offices. Yet, these open spaces still have little in common with the much larger and more dense Anglo-Saxon open plans. The contrast becomes clear when comparing Ericsson offices in Stockholm and those in Guildford, United Kingdom (see figures 113 - 116).[15]

111 Interior individual
room at SAS

112 Workplace layout
Canon headquarters

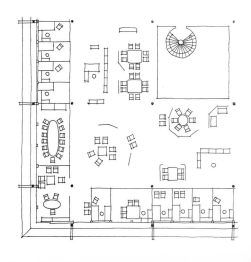

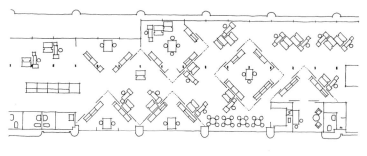

113 Workplace layout
Ericsson Stockholm

114 Flexible furniture
Ericsson Stockholm

115 Mobile phones
Ericsson Stockholm

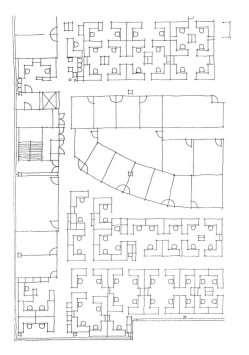

116 Workplace layout
Ericsson Guildford

SWEDISH CONTEXT

Swedish offices tend to be low-rise with narrow, linear floor plans and spacious cellular workplace layouts. Such office design seems to be largely driven by user satisfaction. At the same time, there is a trend to build more open solutions in which employees often share their workplaces. In the following paragraphs we relate these characteristics and developments to the national context.

Urban setting

117 Stockholm's historical urban setting

In Swedish towns, architects and developers work within a historical urban context. They work in cities whose townscape has been shaped by a centuries-old tradition of building with stone. Just like most European cities, they are older and more complex than their American counterparts. Their building stock tends to be smaller and more intricate, possessing a traditionally richer mixture of uses.

Strongly related to the historical nature of Swedish towns are strong emotional reactions against high rises. In the early 1990s in particular, there was a great deal of criticism of skyscrapers. For example *Arkitektur*, Sweden's main architectural magazine, said explicitly 'no to multi-storey buildings'.[16] The magazine 'consistently and strongly maintains that multi-storey buildings do not belong at home in the Swedish urban landscape'. According to Hultin the strongest argument against skyscrapers in Swedish towns and cities is that skyscrapers have nothing to do with European city culture.[17] 'It is quite simply not needed. Instead we should protect and develop the tradition that exists here'. Following the ideas of Leon Krier, Hultin states that buildings should 'reinstate the European city'.[18] He refers to 'the tight-knit low city or town with its systems of streets, blocks, squares and public spaces, where monumental buildings also have a content that corresponds to the outer gesture... These urban qualities are the product of a hundred years of city building. They are wholly superior to the young city culture which gave birth to the skyscraper, a birth which should be seen more as a result of the effects of capitalism's terms and conditions than as an attempt to build a good city'.

The negative attitude towards high-rises has left a clear stamp on Swedish office development, because Swedish planning is very participatory. Since the 1970s, a time when people began to become politically more aware, planning has developed into a process that is no longer confined to experts, making the life of consultants, officials and developers considerably more difficult.[19] Sweden has a democratically oriented type of town planning in which neither the interests of investors nor architectural aesthetics can on their own justify the construction of tall buildings.[20]

The restrictive Swedish urban setting also explains the rarity of very tall buildings in Sweden. The Lilla Bommen project in Gothenburg is of a very modest scale when compared to other projects abroad. Yet even this project has not been devoid of difficulties. The building, with only 23 floors, has been the subject of a 'virtually endless stream' of letters to the press, reflecting a mixed reaction – both positive and negative – to the building among the general public.[21] In response, the local planning authorities asked for 'time out' to adjust their procedures before continuing the waterfront redevelopment.

With the problems surrounding high-rise and inner-city development in mind, it is perhaps not surprising that many large offices in Sweden are suburban groundscraper-like buildings. The tendency to locate outside the city may be strengthened by Sweden's low population density. It is one of the most sparsely populated countries in Europe (see table 5.1).[22] With the availability of so much open space it seems 'natural' that organisations use large sites to build spacious buildings (although we see similar buildings in the Netherlands, which has the highest population density in Europe).

Table 5.1 European population densities (CIA factbook, 1998)

Country	Population density (people/km^2)
Sweden	21.6
Italy	193.1
Germany	234.8
UK	238.9
Netherlands	464.2

Another issue one would expect to be related to the size and population density of the country is teleworking. One would expect that if teleworking took off anywhere, it would be in Sweden because of its remote communities, advanced telecommunications infrastructure, and high level of personal computer ownership.[23] Yet, the proportion of teleworkers in the working population is not as high as one might expect. European research shows that currently 5.4% of the Swedish labour population is teleworking.[24] This is still behind the Netherlands, which has 9.1% teleworkers (see table 5.2).

Table 5.2 Telework in Europe in 1998 (European Commission, 1999)

Country	Percentage of the working population
Netherlands	9.1
UK	7.0
Sweden	5.4
Germany	1.9
Italy	1.2

Market conditions

Sweden may be a relatively 'empty' country but that hasn't stopped it from achieving economic success. For a long time, many other countries have admired Sweden for its mix of social welfare and economic success. 'On the edge of Europe, with one of the highest GDPs per capita in the world (see table 5.3), with a tradition of well ordered city living, the Scandinavians are by definition out of touch with our regressive version of reality'.[25] Today, however, this description is losing some of its validity, as the Swedish economy is no longer as flourishing as it used to be. The social-market economy with its careful blend of market capitalism, strong labour protection and a generous welfare state has served the country well for several decades, but it is now more under pressure than ever before.

Table 5.3 European GDPs per head (The Economist Group, 1997)

Country	GDP per head (US Dollars)
Sweden	25 720
Germany	25 632
Netherlands	23 094
UK	21 848
Italy	19 919

Table 5.4 European rent levels (Richard Ellis, 1999)

City	Prime rent levels (US Dollars per m^2 per annum)
Stockholm	479
Frankfurt	548
Amsterdam	386
London City	1117
Milan	381

Prosperity supported the emergence of very high working standards and funded the relatively high investments in office buildings. Corporations were simply able to spend more money on property than their foreign counterparts. This was strengthened by the relatively low costs of office space in Sweden. Rent levels in Stockholm may be high by Swedish or Continental European standards, but are certainly not so when compared to rents in central London (see table 5.4). This may explain the ample use of space in Swedish offices. It is only logical that organisations put less emphasis on efficiency and flexibility when occupancy costs and rents are relatively low.

Just as important as the ability to invest in office buildings is the willingness to do so. Swedish organisations seem to have few problems with investing in resources such as buildings, that do not have a clear impact on their performance or productivity. Instead of renting commercial offices, they traditionally build their facilities according to their own wishes and company philosophy.[26] They are able to do so because historically capital markets have had little impact on the decisions of Swedish managers.[27] Obviously Swedish managers do take the wishes of shareholders into account, but they also regard their employees as important stakeholders. This puts a premium on providing them with excellent working conditions.

This 'social' attitude of Swedish managers may also have affected the height of buildings. It may explain why Swedish organisations have not expressed their economic success in high-rise showpieces, but in low-rise buildings of a 'human scale'. Such buildings are not efficient or flexible from the point of view of real estate management, but they produce a strong link between the physical layout of the buildings and the organisation's philosophy and activities.[28]

The above may suggest that Swedish organisations are not interested in issues such as the marketability or efficiency of buildings. This is certainly not true. These issues are just as important as in other countries, but within a framework in which user interests also play an important role. The notion that money matters can clearly be seen in experiments that are currently taking place in Swedish office design. Pressure on the

Swedish economy is an important incentive to look for more flexible and economical workplace solutions. It explains why a spacious solution like the combi-office is no longer as popular as it used to be. Organisations are less willing to pay for open spaces that are essentially large circulation areas.

Labour relations

The willingness of Swedish organisations to invest in user-friendly buildings is closely related to the nature of Swedish labour relations. The famous 'Swedish model' is characteristic of harmonious and consensus-oriented relations between employers, unions, employees and government. Today this model is under pressure because of economical problems. Nevertheless, from an international perspective, Swedish labour relations still are the most democratic in Europe.

At an organisational level, this means that power and hierarchy are played down. Almost every employee seems to have the right to contribute to a decision, often resulting in painstaking and time-consuming decision-making processes.[29, 30, 31] Swedish managers are forced to adopt such a participatory style because employees' rights to participate have been formalised in legislation such as the *Co-Determination Act* (1976) and the *Work Environment Act* (1977). According to these acts, the employer is obliged to consult local unions before implementing decisions that involve a major change for employees. Furthermore, unions may appoint employees' representatives to the board of directors of most companies.[32]

The important role of employees in organisational decision-making is reflected in the design process of office buildings. Initially, when the involvement of employees had just been regulated, in the 1970s, their participation took the form of bargaining between employers and union representatives. Mistrust and power struggles characterised the interaction between the two sides.[33] Later on, employers and union representatives became more co-operative. Designers were supposed to achieve better quality designs with the aid of the users' experience.[34] Today, this opinion is still widely shared among architects.[35] 'Visionary architects' or top-down executives who might ignore the needs and desires of the anonymous end-user are rare in Sweden. It is typical that according to some Swedish architects and researchers, today's users are still too passive and should act as experts in the design team.[36, 37]

The key role of employees is probably one of the most important explanations for the user-friendliness of Swedish offices. It explains why user desires for space, privacy and an outside view have been so clearly expressed in Swedish offices. It is also one of the explanations why it took such a long time for teleworking to gain momentum in Sweden and the rest of Scandinavia. Since the first experiments with teleworking in the 1980s, there has been strong criticism from trade unions.[38] Unions objected to the concept on the grounds that telework might prove to be a trap for women, that it would have an adverse effect on work content and that it would increase fragmentation of work duties. Nowadays, however, the focus of telework has shifted from sparsely populated areas to enterprises in the large cities. As a result, telework is no longer associated with women in remote areas but with men in large cities.[39]

The role of unions in the acceptance of teleworking is typical as it shows that employees' representatives rather than employees themselves take most of the decisions concerning the work environment. When reading about participatory design in Scandinavia one might get the impression that all employees gather around the drawing board to design their office building in close co-operation with the architect. This is certainly not the case. Direct participation only takes place at workplace level, where work groups are often able to furnish their own *pausrum*.[40] For the more general issues it is mainly union representatives (sometimes from more than three different unions) or elected users from different departments in the company that are involved in the briefing and functional analysis. Architects translate their information into illustrations and plans, which they feed back to users for their reaction.

Furthermore, it is still the case that in spite of well-developed participation in everyday working decisions, middle managers and higher executives initiate many of the design decisions.[41] In the case of the SAS headquarters, for example, SAS's CEO Jan Carlzon played a crucial role. His ideas about hierarchy and communication were the main driving forces behind the design.

Culture

Swedish labour-relations are closely linked to egalitarian aspects of Swedish culture. There seems to be a general lack of extreme competition for hierarchical advancement and status in Swedish organisations. Swedish organisations tend to strive for equality and uniformity rather than emphasising differences between supervisors and their subordinates. This is expressed in the universal plans of Swedish offices. A Swedish clerk may very well have a similar office to that of his superior. Having one's own office is associated with the equality that is essential in such an egalitarian culture.

Another salient characteristic of the Swedish business culture is its 'socially oriented individualism'.[42] On the one hand Swedes are highly individualistic. They are part of what is termed a neutral culture, meaning that they value privacy and self-control.[43] Trompenaars and Hampden-Turner talk about a relative lack of emotional expression, saying that foreigners may find Swedes 'stiff', 'shy' and 'reserved'.[44] On the other hand, this individualism is counterbalanced by a strong sense of belonging. In day-to-day organisational life, employees are incredibly loyal to their work group.[45] They seek to individualise themselves by what they contribute to their workplace and to their colleagues.

Swedish 'socially oriented individualism' seems to be directly translated into Swedish offices through ample provision of both individual and collective spaces. The individualistic part is reflected in giving everybody a private office. Private offices are an excellent means of controlling your interaction with others. At the same time, however, the office cell carries with it a certain isolation and is a barrier from one's group.[46] To deal with this problem, Swedish offices tend to have relatively large common areas, expressing the social part of the Swedish culture. At workplace level this is manifested in combi-spaces and the provision of *pausrum* (break areas). At the building level, the importance of the group is expressed in spectacular glazed streets and atria. It is typical that the brochure about the SAS building is titled 'Togetherness'.[47]

Regulations

The social element of Swedish culture is also reflected in the large number of institutes that are involved in the development of workplace regulations. Organisations such as the *Arbetslivsinstitutet* (National Institute for Working Life) and the *Arbetarskyddsstyrelsen* (The Occupational Safety and Health Administration) develop regulations, standards and guidelines for the working environment.

Yet Sweden's workplace regulations are not as extensive as one might expect. The current Work Environment Act (*Arbetsmiljölagen*), which took effect in 1977, encompasses a wide area of issues, ranging from work systems, working hours and adaptation of work to human factors. Regulations on the design of offices, however, are fairly limited. The fact that almost everybody has a private office is, for example, not formalised in any regulation or written standards.[48] Also, the size of workplaces and requirements for daylight and an outside view are not specific. Regulations state that a workplace should not be too small or too far from a window, but exact dimensions are not given.

Accompanying recommendations from the Board of Workers' Safety are just as vague.[49] They say that workplaces must give employees 'sufficient freedom to move in relation to the work performed' or that 'workplaces must be arranged so that they receive as much daylight as possible'. It is clear that such recommendations give designers and clients a lot of freedom.

One explanation for the limited number of regulations on office design may be the traditional Swedish focus on blue-collar industries. In spite of the growth of office work, Swedish research and development on workplace design have long focused on industry and neglected working conditions in office environments.[50]

What is interesting is that the lack of regulations concerning workplace design has not resulted in poor working conditions, quite the reverse. One of the underlying reasons is that extensive regulations are not necessary because the employees themselves are significantly involved. As already mentioned, employers are obliged to consult local unions before implementing decisions that involve a major change, either in general or for an individual union member. Furthermore, Swedish law permits that 'safety representatives' to halt work when in their opinion working conditions are dangerous for the health of employees.

SUMMARY AND CONCLUSIONS

This chapter has described Swedish offices by looking at the shape of buildings, their floor plans and the workplace layouts inside.

At the building level, Swedish office buildings tend to be low- or medium-rise. The reasons are that Swedish towns contain historical structures and that there is a rather negative attitude among the general public and architectural critics towards high-rise buildings.

Table 5.5 Summary of results

Offices	Context
Building	*Urban setting*
Low- and medium-rise buildings	Historical urban structure
Groundscrapers	Restrictive planning policies
	Highly participatory planning process
Floor plan	
Narrow floor plans/medium depth double-corridor	*Market conditions*
plans and combi-offices	Strong owner-occupiers
Linear shapes	Low rents
	High GDP
Workplace	
Highly cellular layouts	*Labour relations*
Extra attention to break areas	Strong employee representatives
High use of space per employee	
Trends: pioneer in use of more open, non-territorial	*Culture*
offices and teleworking	Egalitarian
	Social individualism
	Neutral way of interaction
	Regulations
	No specific workplace size given
	Stipulates access to daylight/outside view

Moreover, Swedish corporations show little interest in constructing glamorous high rises to symbolise their success. Instead they seem to prefer to invest in the workplaces of their employees.

At the floor plan level, floor plans tend to be narrow, resulting in linear shaped buildings. Such floor plans are the direct result of giving all employees workplaces with daylight, an outside view and natural ventilation. The fact that these conditions are provided for everybody reflects the egalitarian nature of Swedish culture. It has also to do with the fact that according to Swedish labour legislation, employees (or at least their representatives) have to be involved in decisions concerning their working environment.

At the workplace level, traditionally everbody gets his own, rather spacious private office. Furthermore, employees are provided with common areas such as *pausrum* and combi-spaces for group activities. This combination of both individual and common spaces seems to be a clear reflection of the 'socially oriented individualism' of Swedish culture. The combination of user involvement and the financial means to invest in such workplace layouts obviously plays a crucial role too.

In relation to our research question ('What is the relationship between office design and national context?'), this chapter shows that there are strong parallels between Swedish office buildings and the general Swedish context. The social-democratic nature of Swedish planning processes, labour relations and culture is manifested in a markedly user-oriented approach to office design.

It is interesting to see that a similar image can be seen in Scandinavia as a whole. It is not always correct to perceive the Scandinavian countries as a homogeneous group of nations with common social and economic characteristics. Certainly the Scandinavians themselves would disagree. In office design, however, Scandinavia presents a fairly consistent image. A brief literature study has shown that mainstream offices are fairly similar in Finland, Norway and Denmark. Office experts such as Lapallainen (Finland), Andersen (Denmark) and Blakstad (Norway) all talk about spacious, individual offices with limited floor depths.[51, 52, 53] The main difference lies in the pace of change. Norway and Denmark seem to be rather more conventional in adopting new types of offices, while Finland (e.g. SOL and Nokia) and Sweden (e.g. Ericsson and Digital) seem to be more progressive.

Still, it is hard to judge the progressive image of Swedish office design. It is clear that the situation is not a permanent one. Swedish society and consequently its office buildings are changing. Just like most other European organisations, Swedish organisations are being compelled to become more flexible and cost-efficient. This will also affect the design of their office buildings and it is not clear yet in which direction Swedish office design will evolve. Current experiments, such as those at Ericsson, suggest new Swedish offices will continue to retain their user-friendly character.

Notes

1   Becker, F. (1990), *The total workplace; facilities management and the elastic organization*, Van Nostrand Reinhold, New York
2   Haugen, T.I. and Blakstad, S.H. (1995), *The Scandinavian approach to modern office buildings*, paper presented at the EUROFM/IFMA conference, Frankfurt, Germany
3   Andersson, H.O. and Bedoire, F. (1988), *Stockholm: architecture and townscape*, Prisma, Stockholm
4   Hultin, O. (1985), 'Made in the USA', in: *Arkitektur*, No. 9, pp. 6-7
5   Becker, F. and Steele, F. (1994), *Workplace by design: mapping the high-performance workscape*, Jossey-Bass Publishers, San Francisco
6   Doxtater, D. (1994), *Architecture, Ritual Practice and Co-determination in the Swedish Office*, Ashgate Publishing, Aldershot
7   ibid.
8   Duffy, F. and Crisp, V. (1993), *The Responsible Workplace: the redesign of work & offices*, Butterworth Architecture, Oxford
9   Becker, F. and Steele, F. (1994), *Workplace by design: mapping the high-performance workscape*, Jossey-Bass Publishers, San Francisco
10 Sundstrom, E. (1986), *Workplaces*, Cambridge University Press, New York
11 Doxtater, D. (1994), *Architecture, Ritual Practice and Co-determination in the Swedish Office*, Ashgate Publishing, Aldershot
12 Skolglund, P. (1992), *Lokalyta per anställd I nya kontorslokaler*, USK, Stockholm
13 Gustavsson, B. and Östman, Å. (1993), *Lokalanvändning i kontorverksamhet*, USK, Stockholm
14 Gullström, C. and Westerberg, L. (1996), *Moving Spaces, Knowledge Exchange and Contemporary Work Life*, brochure. Gullström & Westerberg Arkitektkontor AB, Stockholm
15 Caldenby, C. and Waern, R. (1996), 'Looking back it has nevertheless been a good thing on the occasions when we said no', in: *Arkitektur*, No. 5, pp. 4-37
16 Arkitektur (1990), 'No to multi-storey buildings', in: *Arkitektur*, No. 4, p. 2
17 Hultin, O. (1985), 'Made in the USA', in: *Arkitektur*, No. 9, pp. 6-7
18 Krier, L. (1984), 'Houses, Palaces, Cities', *A.D. Profile*, No. 54, *Architectural Design*, London
19 Hultin, O. (1981), 1970-1979: 'Regrets and consideration', in: *Arkitektur*, No. 5, pp. 18-19
20 Polisano, L. (1995), 'Complexity and Contrast; American and European High-Rise Buildings', in: *Architectural Design*, Vol. 65, No. 7/8, pp. 30-35
21 Caldenby, C. (1990), 'Arguments and paradoxes', in: *Arkitektur*, No. 4, pp 3-11
22 European commission (1999), *Status Report on EuropeanTelework 1998*, http://www.eto.org.uk/twork/tw98/index.htm
23 Lake, A. (1996), 'Report on Telework in Sweden', in: *Telework international*, Vol. 4, No. 2, http://www.klr.com/NEWS4206.HTM
24 European commission (1999), *Status Report on European Telework 1998*, http://www.eto.org.uk/twork/tw98/index.htm
25 Duffy, F. (1990), 'Aker Brygge development', in: *Architects' journal*, Vol. 88, No. 8, pp. 56-63
26 Haugen, T.I. and Blakstad, S.H. (1995), *The Scandinavian approach to modern office buildings*, paper presented at the EUROFM/IFMA conference 1995, Frankfurt, Germany
27 Porter, M. (1990), *Competitive Advantage of Nations*, Macmillan, Basingstoke
28 Haugen, T.I. and Blakstad, S.H. (1995), *The Scandinavian approach to modern office buildings*, paper presented at the EUROFM/IFMA conference, Frankfurt, Germany
29 Axelsson, R., Cray, D., Mallory, G.R. and Wilson, D.C. (1991), 'Decision style in British and Swedish organisations: a comparative examination of strategic decision-making', in: *British Journal of Management*, No. 2, pp. 67-79
30 Doxtater, D. (1994), *Architecture, Ritual Practice and Co-determination in the Swedish Office*, Ashgate Publishing, Aldershot
31 Schneider, S.C. and Barsoux, J. (1997), *Managing Across Cultures*, Prentice Hall, Hertfordshire
32 Swedish Institute (1999), http://www.si.se/eng/esverige/esverige.html
33 Granath, J.A., Lindahl, G.A. and Rehal, S. (1996), *From Empowerment to Enablement, An evolution of new dimensions in participatory design*, paper, Chalmers University of Architecture, School of Architecture, Industrial Architecture and Planning
34 Lindahl, G.A. (1996), *Collective Design Processes as a Facilitator for Collaboration and Learning*, paper for the Fourth Conference on Learning and Research in *Working Life*, 1-4-96 to 4-4-97, Steyr, Austria
35 Granath, J.A., Lindahl, G.A. and Rehal, S. (1996), *From Empowerment to Enablement, An evolution of new dimensions in participatory design*, paper, Chalmers University of Architecture, School of Architecture, Industrial Architecture and Planning
36 ibid.

37 Lindahl, G.A. (1996), *Collective Design Processes as a Facilitator for Collaboration and Learning*, paper for the Fourth Conference on Learning and Research in Working Life, 1-4-96 to 4-4-97, Steyr, Austria
38 Regeringskansliet (1998), *The Swedish Government Commission on Telework – Summary*, Stockholm
39 ibid.
40 Doxtater, D. (1994), *Architecture, Ritual Practice and Co-determination in the Swedish Office*, Ashgate Publishing, Aldershot
41 ibid.
42 Hampden-Turner, C. and Trompenaars, A. (1993), *The Seven Cultures of Capitalism*, Doubleday, New York
43 Trompenaars, F. (1993), *Riding the waves of culture*, The Economist Books, London
44 Hampden-Turner, C. and Trompenaars, A. (1993), *The Seven Cultures of Capitalism*, Doubleday, New York
45 Doxtater, D. (1994), *Architecture, Ritual Practice and Co-determination in the Swedish Office*, Ashgate Publishing, Aldershot
46 Etzler, B. (1996), 'University Buildings and Research Parks, A Study of their Origins, Design, and Use', in: *Nordic Journal of Architectural Research*, Vol. 9, No. 4, pp. 97-107
47 Scandinavian Airline Systems, *Togetherness*, SAS Frösundavik
48 Doxtater, D. (1994), *Architecture, Ritual Practice and Co-determination in the Swedish Office*, Ashgate Publishing, Aldershot
49 Board of Workers' Safety (1995), *Arbetarskyddstyrelsens Författningssamling*, Stockholm
50 Etzler, B. (1996), 'University Buildings and Research Parks, A Study of their Origins, Design, and Use', in: *Nordic Journal of Architectural Research*, Vol. 9, No. 4, pp. 97-107
51 Lapalainen, R. (1999), *Presentation at Studio Apertura*, Norway, March 16th
52 Andersen, S.E. (1997), 'Design responses: office buildings in Denmark', in: Worthington, J. (ed.), *Reinventing the Workplace*, Architectural Press, Oxford
53 Blakstad, S.H. (1997), *The Scandinavian Office Building 1900-1980*, Norwegian University of Science and Technology, Department of Architectural History, Trondheim

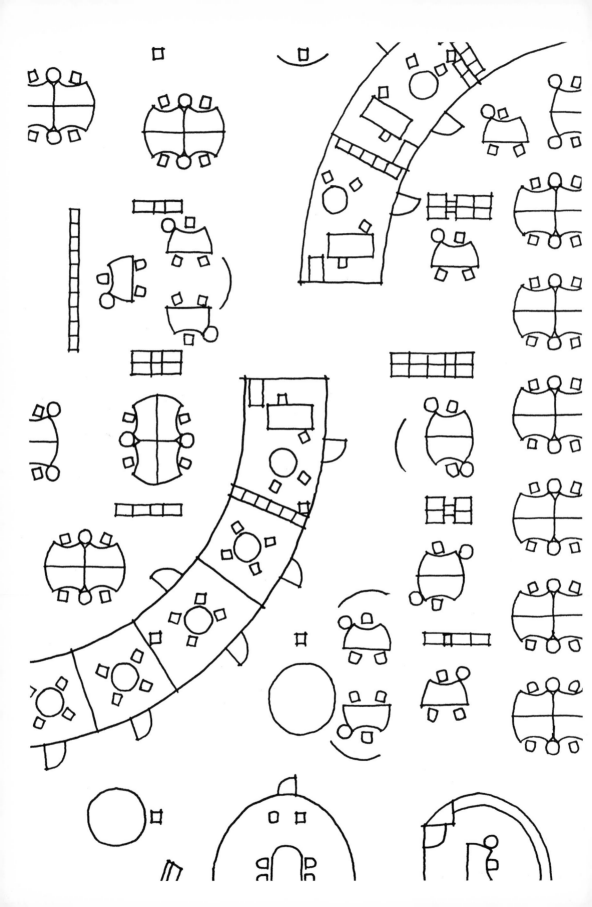

6   Italy

Italy's most famous office building is the 16th century Uffizi in Florence, named after its principal function. The building was designed by Giorgio Vasari for Tuscany's first grand duke, Cosimo de Medici, to accommodate the administration of Florence and its various officials.[1] Although it is currently an art gallery, it is an early example of a complete building that was destined specifically to function as an office.[2, 3]

119 Uffizi in florence: once an office building, now a museum

It is typical that the Uffizi is one of Italy's most famous office buildings. Contemporary Italian examples are virtually absent in the literature on office design. There is plenty of material on Italian office furniture, but Italian office buildings seem to attract little interest. In this chapter we aim to fill that gap. We describe Italian offices and try to explain why they are the way they are. First we will discuss whether there are any typical features of Italian office design. Then we describe Italian office design in terms of the national context. The chapter ends with conclusions.

ITALIAN OFFICES

Building

In the inner cities of Italian towns, large-scale office developments are rare. Not to mention high-rise office buildings. In fact there has been relatively little development at all in the past few years. Most projects have been small-scale, low or medium-rise buildings. As a result there is a shortage of modern inner-city office space in major towns like Milan.[4, 5] This is strengthened by the fact that much of the existing office space is not capable of meeting the requirements of today's occupants. Healey and Baker estimate that 65% of offices in central Milan have no air-conditioning or lifts, despite the warm Italian climate.[6]

To meet demands for new office space, a lot of attention is being paid to renewal and conversion of existing buildings.[7] In particular, historical buildings are much in demand because of their prestigious and impressive appearance. The Palazzo Serbelloni in the historic centre of Milan is a successful example of conversion.[8] This building was constructed in the 18th century as a palace for Duke Gabrio Serbelloni (see figure 120). Now it has been transformed into modern office units, with a total floor space of 12,000 m². The disadvantage of such projects is that there are countless regulations to comply with.[9]

Moreover, the installation of air conditioning, raised floors and suspended ceilings

120 Palazzo Serbelloni
in the centre of Milan

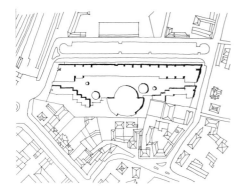

121 Urban setting
Banca Popolare di Lodi

122 Exterior Banca
Popolare di Lodi

is often problematic. Outside the city centre, much attention is being paid to the conversion of industrial areas.[10, 11] This issue is of particular interest in Northern Italy, where Italy's largest industries are located. Milan, for example, has the Bicocca project, the redevelopment of an old Pirelli site. Likewise Turin has the Lingotto project, the redevelopment of a Fiat car factory. A more recent development is the headquarters of the Banca Popolare di Lodi on the site of the former Polengi Lombardo factory in Lodi (see figures 121 - 122). This project is interesting because the architect (the Renzo Piano Workshop) has tried to blend the 90,000 m² building with great care into the existing urban structure around the site.[12] Renzo Piano says that 'the idea of the project was to reconstruct the urban block by creating a homogeneous front, almost a facade, but rendered permeable by clefts, lines of view, and passage ways'.[13]

This concern for the relation between the building and the city seems to be a typical feature of Italian architecture. Famous Italian architects like Rossi, Grassi and Natalini are best known for their use of typologies that refer to the urban and historical context. The Turin-based headquarters of GFT (an apparel manufacturer, the parent company of such labels as Armani and Valentino) is a clear example (see figure 123). Aldo Rossi, the architect of the building, said: 'the building's primary value is the historical element and the understanding of urban values. GFT wants to give Turin a modern, traditional building that is coherent with this city's culture and urban furnishings'.[14]

However, this concern does not apply to all Italian architecture. Especially in the design for the commercial real estate market, it is often absent. On the outskirts of Italian towns you can find the same glass and concrete boxes as anywhere else in the world. The design quality of these buildings varies strongly. Not only in an architectural sense, but also in terms of technical installations and construction. In particular those buildings designed during the speculative construction boom of the 1980s do not match user requirements. According to Richard Ellis overpricing and poor physical specification have resulted in a large supply of buildings remaining vacant for considerable periods of time.[15]

123 GFT headquarters

Floor plan

It is difficult to say something general about floor plans of Italian office buildings. The most important characteristic is the diversity in floor plans. Unlike in other countries, office floors are hardly standardised. There appears to be no clear preference for either deep or shallow buildings, or compact or linear ones (see figure 124).

Depths of office floors in Italy vary from 18-25 m.[16] In that respect Italian offices resemble the deep and compact British and American offices. In American and British offices, however, the full depth of the floors is used for workplaces. In Italy this is rare. Most deep buildings have double-corridor plans. Only the spaces along their perimeter are used for workplaces. The inner areas accommodate secondary areas such as meeting rooms, service rooms and vertical movement cores.[17]

Workplaces are located along the perimeter, to give employees access to daylight and an outside view. Just as in the rest of continental Europe, architects and clients emphasise the importance of 'a maximum penetration of natural light'. Architects Roj and Rivera say 'we no longer need the often excessively deep buildings, where one major difficulty was that the further you moved away from the outer or window edge, the more you tended to lose control of the microclimate, especially in terms of natural light and outdoor views … Being able to look out of a window and open it – even if the air outside is the hopelessly polluted air of some great city – is an old dream that many people have not forgotten'.[19]

Italy's best known example of a double corridor plan is the Quinto Palazzo, designed by Gabetti and Isola (see figures 125 - 126). The client was SNAM, a major Italian developer. The building is known for its expressive shape and design.[20] From the inside it has a typical double-corridor plan, with offices along both exterior facades and a central linear core containing fire stairs, toilet facilities, filing rooms, and so on. SNAM chose this scheme because in their experience the deep double-corridor plan provided a greater compactness and a smaller area for horizontal communication than single corridor plans.[21]

Workplace

Describing workplace layouts in Italian offices is as difficult as describing floor plans. Again, the variety in Italian office design makes it hard to identify a 'typical' Italian workplace layout.

Europroperty says that Italian companies are looking for 'modern open-plan offices

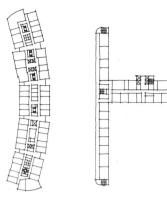

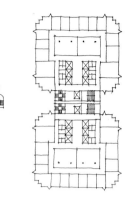

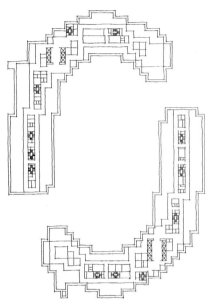

124 Different floor plans: Olivetti in Ivrea, Cerved in Padova, and La Torre degli Affari in Milan

125 Exterior Quinto Palazzo

126 Floor plan Quinto Palazzo

with raised floors'.[22] This gives the impression that they are looking for US-style open plans with vast areas of cubicles. In Italy, however, such large-scale open plans are rare. Casciani says that American open plans are not accepted in Italy because privacy is stripped to a minimum by partitions that afford no concealment whatever.[23] And that 'most unacceptable of all', standard space is cut to 30% less than the normal space allotted in Italy (5 instead of 7 m² per person).

In practice Italian offices tend to be a mix of open and cellular spaces. A good example is the workplace layout of TNT Traco (see figure 127). The floor plan of their new headquarters shows several group spaces for billing and sales functions. On the other side of the corridor are several private offices. The size of room and the number of people working in it differs, depending on the type of work and the hierarchical position of employees.

As in other countries, some architects and consultants regard this type of office as 'outdated' or 'traditional'. Italian magazines such as *Ufficostile*, *Office Layout* and *Habitat Ufficio* write about new offices where people are teleworking, sharing workplaces and moving around in 'activity related settings'. The general argument is that mainstream layouts do not match new ways of working or use the full potential of information technology.

Nevertheless the majority of Italian offices are still rather traditional.[25] Innovative workplace concepts are rare. Research done by the European Commission of 1999 shows, for example, that teleworking is less successful than in the rest of Europe, apart from several trials at Telecom Italia and the Rome City Council (see table 6.1).[26] Also, the combi-office has never attracted the same attention it did in Northern Europe.

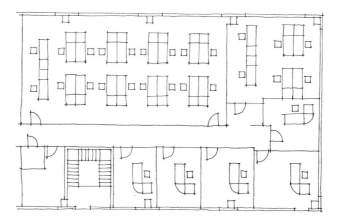

127 Workplace layout
TNT Traco

According to Mangano 'Italy's mental approach is a long way from the European and international dimensions of differentiated working methods and ways of using time and space'.[27] Casciani and Roj say 'unfortunately, any analysis of what is really happening in the property market brings us down with a bump'.[28]

Table 6.1 Telework in Europe in 1998 (European Commission, 1999)

Country	Percentage of the working population
Netherlands	9.1
UK	7.0
Sweden	5.4
Germany	1.9
Italy	1.2

The limited number of projects does not mean that Italian designers are not involved in creating new ideas for the office. Maurzio Morgantini, for example, is involved in a project for the Deutsche Bank on telematics. Likewise, De Lucchi and Sottsass have designed innovative office equipment for Philips and Vitra. Such projects, however, tend to focus on office furniture and equipment rather than office buildings. Furthermore they are very design-oriented and less concerned with new ways of working.

A good example of a design-oriented project is the headquarters of McDonald's Italia designed by Atelier Mendini (see figures 128 - 130). According to *Interni*, an Italian design magazine, it is an icon of a workplace that 'communicates energy and good humour'.[29] It is important to note, however, that the project's main quality lies in its alternative use of colours and materials. The project has little to do with implementing alternative ways of working or using new information technology.

ITALIAN CONTEXT

Large-scale projects and high rises are rare in Italy. Most activity has concerned the re-use and reconstruction of existing buildings and industrial areas. Floor plans and workplace layouts are hardly standardised. Also, experiments with new workplace concepts such as teleworking or combi-offices are rare. In this section we look at why this is so.

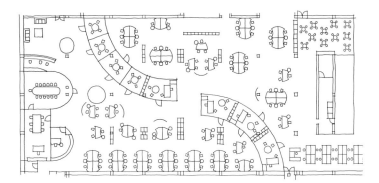

128 Workplace layout
McDonald's Italia

129 Interior
McDonald's Italia

130 Interior
McDonald's Italia

Urban setting

The Italian urban setting is dominated by history. More than in any other European country, towns and cities are shaped by time. Centuries of construction and reconstruction have left their mark on urban structures. Cities have grown organically, with irregular and tight street patterns. Furthermore, there is an 'ever present historical heritage'.[30] Major towns like Milan, Rome and Turin (not to mention Venice or Florence) seem to be full of churches and monumental palazzos and squares.

Italian planning focuses on protecting historical heritage. Town plans and planning permits impose tight constraints within which architects must work. Preservation of urban centres is the rule. Demolition and rebuilding are not allowed.[31] Planning is further complicated by Italian bureaucracy. Although things are changing, the Italian government is still dominated by red tape. The British architectural critic Collinge remarks that 'innumerable political, technical and administrative bodies superintend the planning and construction process'.[32]

The historical urban structure and planning complications partly explain why large-scale developments are rare in Italian cities. In particular, high-rise buildings do not seem to fit into the existing historical fabric of cities. Their size, height and bulk would radically change the character of historical areas. High rises also increase the intensity of activities in the city. This can be a problem in cities like Rome and Milan, which are already congested with traffic.

Planning problems also explain Italy's focus on the redevelopment of disused industrial areas. In most cases these are located in suburban areas where historical context is less present. Just as important is the absence of special zoning constraints.

Offices can be larger, planning is easier and you need fewer permits. This was one of the reasons why, for example, the Banca Popolare di Lodi built its headquarters on a former factory site.[33]

The dominant presence of history also explains Italian expertise in the preservation and renewal of existing buildings. 'In Italy preserving and renewing old architecture is the most rewarding option'.[34] Primarily this is because architects grow up, live and work within this context. As a result Italian architects seem more aware of the urban and historical impact of architecture. Secondly, this is because there is little other work to do in the office market.

Market conditions

In the past few years, there has been relatively little activity on the Italian office market. Years of political scandals and financial debacles have left the market 'battered and bruised'.[35] Property was exposed as a deeply tainted industry during the bribery scandals of the early 1990s.[36] Several major developers were under investigation for accepting kickbacks.[37] It is clear that good design or user satisfaction were not the prime interests of these developers.

These property scandals are a symptom, and perhaps a cause, of the fact that the Italian office market is less well developed than in other countries. Mangano refers to it as an immature market.[38] It is relatively small and few properties are actually being traded.[39] This notion is supported by research done by D'Arcy and Keogh, who characterise the Milan office market (Italy's main office market) as 'emerging', while, for example, the London market is characterised as 'mature' (see table 6.2).[40]

Table 6.2 European market types according to D'Arcy and Keogh (1998)

City	Market type	Real estate service provision	Market information
London	Mature	Very well developed	High
Berlin	Transitional/emerging	Well developed	Moderate
Milan	Emerging	Poorly developed	Poor

These market conditions explain why a great deal of the Italian office stock is of such variable quality. Because of the emerging nature of the market, there is little expertise in office design. The average architectural studio has a very 'romantic' way of working: one day they may be designing a small flat in town, and the next some 3000 m² of office space. This way of working may bring disappointing results for both the client and their architect.[41] It one of the reasons why many large multinational companies find it more convenient to use international specialised design practices. During the last 10 years, however, some new architectural practices have been set up with the idea of specialising in office design.[42] Slowly these practices are changing the Italian office market and introducing more innovative office design concepts.

Another crucial characteristic of the Italian office market is its relatively low rent levels. Both in Milan (Italy's financial centre) and Rome (its administrative centre), rents tend to be lower than in, for example, Frankfurt or London (see table 6.3). This may explain why space-saving concepts such as desk-sharing and non-territorial offices are not that popular, there are fewer financial pressures. It may also explain the absence of high-rise projects, which are often an indication of high rents.

Table 6.3 European rent levels (Richard Ellis, 1999)

City	Prime rent levels
	(US Dollars per m^2 per annum)
Stockholm	479
Frankfurt	548
Amsterdam	386
London City	1117
Milan	381

Rents, however, are not the sole issue. To explain Italian office design, it is also necessary to look at Italy's economy in general. Over the past decades Italy's GDP has been lower than the GDPs of Germany, Sweden or the Netherlands (see table 6.4).[43] At this moment Italy is struggling to put its financial parameters in line with what is needed to qualify for early participation in the European monetary union. These economic conditions may very well explain the hesitance of Italian organisations to invest in large or high-tech office projects.

Table 6.4 European GDPs per head (The Economist Group, 1997)

Country	GDP per head
	(US Dollars)
Sweden	25 720
Germany	25 632
Netherlands	23 094
UK	21 848
Italy	19 919

The problem with such an economic explanation is that Italy's problems vary greatly per region. In particular the North and South of Italy differ strongly. The North of Italy is one of the most prosperous parts of Europe, while the South is relatively poor. This also affects office design. A successful company in the industrialised North is likely to have a different office than a less successful company in the agricultural South. It can also lead to interesting contrasts. For example, DEGW Italia designed one of the most advanced research centres of its kind for Olivetti – a north Italian company (see figures 131 - 132).[44] Surprisingly, the centre is located among olive trees in one of the poorest areas of the country.

Labour relations

Another crucial contextual factor is relations between Italian employers and employees. Just as in other continental European countries, Italian employees are relatively influential. Labour regulations (*Statuti dei Lavoratori*) give employees and union representatives the right to be informed and consulted on matters of organisational decision-making. Despite this basis for employee participation, these rights have never been developed.[45] In that respect, the situation contrasts with the Netherlands, Germany and Sweden, where employees play an important role in workplace decisions.

This difference has to do with Italy's 'low trust culture'.[46] In large professional organisations trust between employers and their employees (or their representatives) tends to be limited. This means that labour relations are characterised by conflict rather than consensus and stability.[47, 48] And within these conflicts, the physical design of the

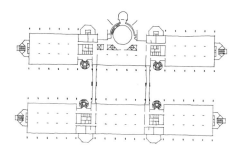 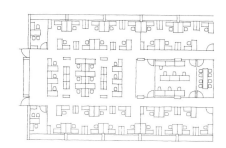

131 Floor plan Olivetti

132 Workplace layout Olivetti

workplace plays only a minor role. Italian unions have never shown as much interest in the design of the physical workplace as their North European counterparts. Problems with wages, labour security and pensions have been much more important in Italy's restless economic development.

Also, there is little interest on the part of architects in employee involvement in design. The architectural debate seems to be dominated by questions about architectural style rather than user satisfaction. This problem is not typically Italian, but more than in other countries the professional culture of designers seems to focus on 'design' rather than 'use'. This idea is in line with the stereotypical idea of Italians as people who 'given the choice between function and beauty, will always choose beauty'.[49] The British critic Hellman said that Italian architects 'unashamedly' see themselves as creative artists.[50] Not without reason, Italian architects have long been known for their 'paper architecture' rather than for the buildings they have actually built.[51]

The limited involvement of employees in design may be one of the reasons why the quality of Italian workplace design can vary so much. It may also explain why Italy has no tradition of office innovation, in which new ideas about work and user needs are translated into design. At the same time, however, office buildings in Italy have little in common with those in the UK or the US, where employees are even less involved. The American open plan for example seems to be 'unacceptable'.[52] Furthermore we do not see Italian employees working in deep spaces as British and American employees do. One explanation for this difference may be that Italian employees' representatives do not become involved in design as long as offices do not deviate too much from the Italian workplace culture.

Culture

The most noticeable characteristic of Italian culture is its lively mode of interaction. According to Trompenaars Italy has an 'affective' culture, meaning that personal relations are important.[53] When people interact they tend to use more emotions, body language and verbal expressions than 'neutral' cultures such as in Germany or the Netherlands.

The affective nature of Italian culture may explain the limited experiments with teleworking. The Italian way of interaction with lots of facial expressions, intonation, touching and gestures is probably less easily replaced by e-mail or video conferencing than more 'neutral' types of interaction.[54] At the same time, however, figures regarding the use of mobile phones in Europe clearly reflect Italy's love affair with this instrument (see table 6.5). Mobile telephones, however, seem to complement rather than replace existing face-to-face interaction.

Table 6.5 Mobile phones per 100 inhabitants in May 1998 (European Commission, 1998)

Sweden	41
Italy	24
United Kingdom	16
Netherlands	13
Germany	12

The liveliness of Italian interaction may also partly explain why large open-plan offices are rare. At first, one might expect that Italians have a preference for open-plan offices, because they are accustomed to a high level of bustle, and are therefore less easily distracted (as the American anthropologist Hall assumes for the French).[55] In practice, however, it seems to be the other way round. Italians seem to have a preference for cellular offices because their affective culture strengthens rather than solves problems of noise and privacy in open plans. Furthermore it is important to take into account that Italians are not only very sociable people, but also rather strong individualists. Ideas of corporate identity and a sense of belonging that come with an American open plan are conceptually remote from Italian offices, where everything is focused on autonomy, individuality and creativity.[56]

The other crucial aspect of Italian culture is hierarchy. According to cross-cultural research, the Italian culture is one of the most hierarchical in Europe.[57] This means that that there is a certain 'power distance' between managers and their employees. Ciferri argues that in Italy subordinates at all levels are heavily dependent on their supervisors; that subordinates expect superiors to act autocratically, and that to most managers the ideal model of a superior is a benevolent autocrat or paternalist.[58]

The importance of hierarchy may have a negative influence on teleworking. When people are working at a distance, the role and status of managers change. Employees have to operate without the direct and visual control of their supervisors. Hierarchy can frustrate this way of working because managers may not believe that employees work at home as hard as they do at the office under their guidance.

Hierarchy may also affect the design of office space. Ciferri says there is a wide expectation that superiors enjoy privileges, laws and rules that are different to those of their subordinates.[59] Status symbols seem to be important in contributing to the authority of the manager. In Italian office buildings one can find several such expressions of hierarchy. In the well-known Pirelli tower, for example (nowadays used by the administration of the Province of Lombardy), the top floor is given over to the President's offices and the Council Chamber.[60] They are literally located 'on top' of the rest of the civil servants. More modest expressions of hierarchy can be seen in the layout of workplaces. The local space planning of Coca-Cola's headquarters in Italy (by the Italian consultants PCMR) shows, for example, that managers get more privacy and more space than the rest of the employees (see figure 133).[61]

Yet the status symbols described are no more remarkable or significant than in other countries. Alone, they do not support the idea that Italian organisations are more hierarchical than their foreign counterparts. The possibility is that in Italy status is not so much expressed in the allocation of space or privacy, as in more subtle things such as office equipment. Gagliardi and Turner say there is a high degree of aesthetic sensibility

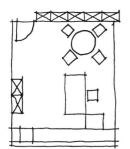 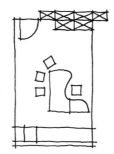 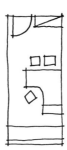 

133 Space standards Coca-Cola Italia. Left: managers' offices. Right: employees' offices

in Italian business culture.[62] Public concern with style in dress and the visual arts is also reflected in managerial life. The freedom to choose your own 'designer' furniture may therefore be more important than the size of your room. This would also explain the extensive activities of Italian designers in this area.

Regulations

As we have already mentioned, Italian bureaucracy and planning regulations tend to be extensive. Not surprisingly there are also many laws and regulations concerning the office workplace. Most important is the '626 law', know officially as *Sicurenzza E Salute Dei Lavoratori Sul Luogo Li Lavoro*, D.LGS.626/94. This is an Italian health and safety law. One of its main features is that, since its adoption in 1994, large companies are obliged to have a department that ensures the quality of the work environment. Employees have a health and safety delegate who checks on the conditions they work under.

Italian legislation scarcely gives specific standards for the design of workplaces. There are various laws and regulations about, for example, ceiling heights of workplaces (not lower than 2.70 m) and corridors (at least 2.40 m). Yet there is no explicit regulation about the size of office workplaces. The regulations say that a workplace has to have sufficient space for carrying out the work, but sizes or dimensions are not given. As a result the effects of these regulations on the layout of workplaces are not very clear.

There are, however, regulations about air-conditioning and ventilation systems, concerning both power consumption and health in working spaces. These limit the maximum number of persons per workspace, but that is as far as they go. For example, the health service requires a minimum of 10 cubic metres per person. But with a minimum ceiling height of 2.70 m this means that workplaces have to be at least 3.7 m². This is hardly a realistic standard for the design of workplaces.

Most importantly, other regulations state that employees must have access to daylight and an outside view, although distances from windows are not specified. This explains why in Italy the majority of workplaces are located next to a window. Consequently, it also explains why most deep buildings tend to have double corridor plans with the inner spaces being used for secondary functions such as toilets and meeting rooms.

SUMMARY AND CONCLUSIONS

Table 6.6 summarises the characteristics of Italian offices and context within which they have developed.

At the building level we have seen that there are few large-scale developments, in particular high rises. There is currently little new activity on the office market, most attention being given to the redevelopment of historical buildings and disused industrial sites. This can be explained by the historical urban setting, extensive bureaucracy and planning regulations.

At the floor plan level there is a large diversity in plan forms. Only the double-corridor plan seems to rank as some sort of typical Italian floor plan. The diversity may be explained by the 'emerging' character of the office market. Office development is fragmented and there are few architects who are specialised in office design. The fact that most deep buildings have double corridor plans has to do with Italian regulations stipulating the provision of daylight and an outside view.

At the workplace level there is no clear preference for open or enclosed layouts. Nevertheless, totally open-plan offices are rare, as are innovative concepts like combi or telework offices. One reason may be that rents are too low or that economic circumstances do not promote investment in office innovations. The other explanation lies in the Italian culture. Its affective, individualistic and hierarchical nature may not match the requirements of new ways of working.

A more general observation is that the quality of Italian offices varies strongly. The causes are several. As we have indicated, developers dominate the office market. Several property scandals have made it clear that quality has not always been their main concern. For clients, economic problems – particularly in the South – may frustrate efforts to invest in good working conditions. Furthermore, employee representatives such as unions have traditionally shown little interest in the workplace. Among architects there is a strong emphasis on fitting buildings in the historical and urban context. Functional issues have attracted less attention, although it is clear that things are changing.

Going back to the research question of this study ('what is the relationship between office design and national context') we conclude that Italian offices, too, are a product of local circumstances. At first, it appeared to be difficult to say something about Italian offices because little has been built in the last few years. Another problem was the large diversity in design. These difficulties, however, are themselves probably the most important characteristics of Italian office design. They reflect an 'emerging' and design-oriented office culture in Italy.

Reflecting on the Italian situation, we consider that other countries can learn a lot from the Italian experts on the conversion and re-use of buildings and sites. This 're-officing' is interesting because the preservation of resources, the environment and cultural heritage is an increasingly important issue. It is clear, however, that it is not the easiest way of creating office space. Design options can be severely restricted in existing buildings. The installation of air-conditioning, raised floors and suspended ceilings is often problematic. But, according to the Italian architect Mario Bellini such restrictions should not be regarded as a problem. Rather it should encourage designers to come up with interesting designs.[63]

Table 6.6 Summary of results

Office	Context
Building Low- and medium-rise buildings Extra attention to urban context and conversion	*Urban setting* Omnipresent historical heritage Restrictive planning policies Strong bureaucracy
Floor plan Narrow floor plans/medium depth double-corridor plans Linear/compact shapes	*Market conditions* Strong developers, but immature market Low rents Low GDP (difference between North and South)
Workplace Mix of cellular and group layouts High use of space per employee Few experiments with new office concepts	*Labour relations* Strong employee representatives, but rights not fully used
	Culture Very hierarchic Individualistic Affective way of interaction
	Regulations No specific workplace size given Stipulates access to daylight/outside view

Another point for reflection is that the Italian situation highlights some of the weaknesses of office innovation. First of all, the Italian situation suggests that to a certain extent workplace innovations are a luxury comodity. New concepts are supposed to make people more productive and reduce the cost of accommodation. Taking these aspects into account, one would think that less successful firms in particular should adopt them. The Italian case, however, shows that they don't. Generally, workplace innovation is just not on the priority list of Italian companies. Given the economic circumstances they tend have other priorities than investing in innovative offices. This is also the reason why the examples in this chapter are either from foreign companies (e.g. Coca-Cola, McDonald's) or from the more prosperous north of Italy (e.g. Olivetti, Banca Popolare di Lodi).

Second, the Italian situation underlines some of the human problems of office innovations. Teleworking for example may not work that well because of the human need for interaction. Likewise, open-plan solutions may not be successful because of the human desire for privacy and status symbols. Such problems can also be seen in other countries, but they are magnified by the affective, individualistic and hierarchical Italian culture.

Notes

1   Goldwaithe, R.A. (1980), *The building of Renaissance Florence*, John Hopkins University Press, Maryland
2   Veldhoen, E. and Piepers, B. (1995), *The demise of the office*, Uitgeverij 010 Publishers, Rotterdam
3   MacCormac, R. (1992), 'The dignity of office', in: *The Architectural Review*, No. 5, pp. 76-82
4   Europroperty (1998), Milan offices, in: *Europroperty*, www.europrop.com/epi_view.asp?art=1587
5   Vastgoedmarkt, Italië, *Vastgoedmarkt*, August 1998, No. 47
6   Healey and Baker (1998), Milan, in: *Europroperty*, www.europrop.com/epi_view.asp?art=1587
7   Lane, D. (1997), 'Italy: keep out', in: *World Architecture*, No. 54, pp. 45-51
8   www.serbelloni.it
9   Roj, M. (1998), 'The project as value added to the production process', in: *Ufficiostile*, No. 1, pp. 72
10 Collinge, J. (1991), 'European outlook Italy and Greece', *Architects' journal*, September 4, pp. 49-53
11 Lane, D. (1997), 'Italy: keep out', in: *World Architecture*, No. 54, pp. 45-51
12 Brandolini, S. (1997), 'Building blocks', in: *World Architecture*, No. 54, pp. 67-71
13 Piano, R. http://www.renzopiano.it/frame_works
14 Rossi, A. (1987), 'Nuovo edificio per uffici <<Casa Aurora>> Torino', in: *Domus*, No. 684, pp. 38-49
15 Lane, D. (1997), 'Italy: keep out', in: *World Architecture*, No. 54, pp. 45-51
16 Evette, T., Bonnet, C., Fencker, M., Michel, P. and Philipon, B. (1992), *L'architecture tertiaire en Europe et aux Etats-Unis*, CSTB, Paris
17 ibid.
18 Matti, L. (1997), 'Come riorganizzare e ottimizarre gli spaziod'ufficio', in: *Office Layout*, No. 74, pp. 86-92
19 Roj, M. and Rivera, A. (1998), 'Involucri ambientali', in: *Habitat Ufficio*, No. 88, pp. 66-69
20 Vitta, M. (1992), 'Quinto: natura e architettura', in *l'Arca*, No. 16, pp. 16-27
21 Gabetti, R. and Isola, A. (1990), 'The Quinto Palazzo Uffici Snam in San Donato Milanese', in: *Zodiac*, No. 3, pp. 100-115
22 Europroperty (1997), 'Milan picks itself up off the bottom', in: *Europroperty*, www.europrop.com/epi_view.asp?art=628
23 Casciani, S.(1997), 'Return to the Planet of the Apes: Jottings from Michigan on office space and differences between Europe and America', in: *Abitare*, http://www.abitare.it/366/366-nautilus.html
24 Fenker, M. (1995), 'The influence of culture on the design and use of office space', in: *InterVIEWS*, No. 1, pp. 2-8
25 Sias, R. (1998), 'Space planning: History and news', in: *Ufficiostile, Special issue*, pp. 14-19
26 European commission (1999), *Status Report on EuropeanTelework 1998*, http://www.eto.org.uk/twork/tw98/index.htm
27 Mangano (1994), 'The new symbols of the office habitat', in: *Habitat Ufficio*, No. 77, pp.65-67
28 Casciani, S. and Roj, M. (1997), 'L'edificio Pensante', in: *Habitat Ufficio*, No. 87, pp. 64-68
29 Caleca, S. (1997), 'Progetto new pop', in: *Interni*, No. 468, pp. 94-99
30 Fenker, M. (1995), 'The influence of culture on the design and use of office space', in: *InterVIEWS*, No. 1, pp. 2-8
31 Lane, D. (1997), 'Italy: keep out', in: *World Architecture*, No. 54, pp. 45-51
32 Collinge, J. (1991), 'European outlook Italy and Greece', in: *Architects' journal*, September 4, pp. 49-53
33 Brandolini, S. (1997), 'Building blocks', in: *World Architecture*, No. 54, pp. 67-71
34 Eciffo (1995), 'Re-officing', in: *Eciffo*, Vol. 27, Autumn Issue, pp. 10-36
35 Europroperty (1998), 'Overseas investors push for market transperency', in: *Europroperty*, www.europrop.com/epi_view.asp?art=1776
36 Leijendekker, M. (1996), *De Italiaanse Revolutie*, Meulenhoff, Amsterdam
37 Europroperty (1998), Italy, in: *Europroperty*, www.europrop.com/epi_view.asp?art=621
38 Mangano, L. (1996), 'Re-inventing the workplace to design the future', in: *Habitat Ufficio*, No. 83, pp. 53-59
39 Collinge, J. (1991), 'European outlook Italy and Greece', in: *Architects' journal*, September 4, pp. 49-53
40 D'Arcy, E. and G. Keogh (1998), 'Territorial Competition and Property Market Process: An Exploratory Analysis', in: *Urban Studies*, Vol. 35, No. 8, pp. 1215-30
41 Cavini, A. (1999), *Italian offices*, Internal report
42 ibid.
43 Penn World Tables (1998), *Italy*, http://datacentre2.chass.utoronto.ca/cgi-bin/pwt/jump?c=120155
44 Vidari, P.P. (1990), 'La citta dell'ufficio', in: *l'Arca*, No. 39, pp. 48-55
45 Brierley, W. (1990), 'The business culture in Italy', in: Randlesome, C. (ed.), *Business cultures in Europe*, Heinemann, Oxford

46 Fukuyama, F. (1995), *Trust: the Social Virtues and Creation of Prosperity*, Hamish Hamilton, London

47 Nacamulli, R. C. D. (1993), 'Italy', in: Rothman, M. (ed.), *Industrial relations around the world: labor relations for multinational companies*, Walter de Gruyter, Berlin

48 Wolleb, E. (1988), 'Belated Industrialisation: The Case of Italy', in: Boyer, R. (ed.), *The Search for Labour Market Flexibility*, Clarendon Press, Oxford

49 Wallace, C. P. (1997), 'Good looks-Italian design carves a niche in the global market and creates an industry that sells as face value', in: *Time International*, April 21, pp. 42-45

50 Hellman, L. (1988), 'Italy: deregulate by definition', in: *Architects' journal*, Vol. 187, No. 20, pp. 46-49

51 Vos, A. (1992), 'Het papier van de plannen en het steen van de stad. Veertig jaar architectonische cultuur', in: Boschloo, A. (ed.), *Italië & Italië*, Meulenhoff, Amsterdam

52 Casciani, S.(1997), 'Return to the Planet of the Apes: Jottings from Michigan on office space and differences between Europe and America', in: *Abitare*, http://www.abitare.it/366/366-nautilus.html

53 Trompenaars, F. (1993), *Riding the waves of culture: understanding cultural diversity in business*, The Economist Books, London

54 Meel, J. J. van, Jonge, H. de and Dewulf, G. P. M. R. (1997), Workplace design: global or tribal?, in: Worthington (ed.), *Reinventing the Workplace*, Architectural Press, Oxford

55 Hall, E.T. and Hall, M.R. (1990), *Understanding cultural differences: keys to success in West Germany, France and the United States*, Intercultural Press Inc., Yarmouth

56 Casciani, S.(1997), 'Return to the Planet of the Apes: Jottings from Michigan on office space and differences between Europe and America', in: *Abitare*, http://www.abitare.it/366/366-nautilus.html

57 Hofstede, G. (1991), *Cultures and organisations: software of the mind*, McGraw-Hill, London

58 Cifferi, M. (1990), *Managerial attitudes, values and perceptions: an Anglo-Italian study*, unpublished research paper

59 ibid.

60 Citterio, http://www.citteriofx.it/italiano/SededellaRegioneLombardia.htm

61 Premoli, D. (1997), 'flessibili e creativi', in: *OFX Office International*, No. 35, p. 44

62 Gagliardi, P. and Turner, B.A. (1993), 'Aspects of Italian Management', in: Hickson, David J. (ed.), *Management in Western Europe: Society, Culture and Organization in Twelve Nations*, Walter de Gruyter & Co., Berlin.

63 Eciffo (1995), 'Re-officing', in: *Eciffo*, Vol. 27, Autumn Issue, pp. 10-36

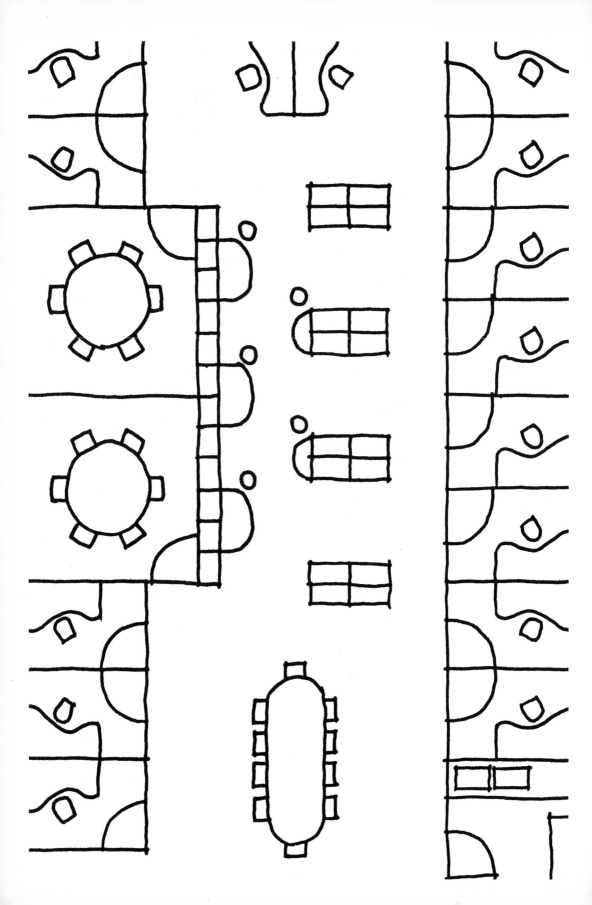

7   The Netherlands

At first sight, Dutch office architecture seems to be highly international. A large number of foreign – mostly British and American – architects are currently working in the Netherlands. Some of them came along with international clients who set up a business there. Others have been commissioned by Dutch organisations that are seeking buildings with an international character. Good examples are the 'World Port Center' in Rotterdam (designed by Norman Foster), the new headquarters of ABN AMRO Bank in Amsterdam (designed by Henry Cobb), and the seat of provincial government in The Hague (designed by Kohn Pedersen Fox).

Despite the large number of foreign architects working in the Netherlands, Dutch office buildings are above all very Dutch. From the outside, these buildings may be similar to those abroad. A closer look, however, reveals that office buildings in the Netherlands are different from offices elsewhere, particularly those in the UK and the US. In this chapter, we discuss Dutch office design and its 'particularities'. Again we look at these offices from the point of view of building, floor plan and workplace level. Then we describe and relate Dutch office design to its national context. Conclusions about the relationship between Dutch office design and its national context are presented in the final section.

DUTCH OFFICES

Building

When looking at Dutch offices, the first thing one notices is that most of them are of low or medium height. Just as in other European countries, the skyline is dominated by churches rather than office towers. New office buildings tend to be of modest scale, relating to the existing urban context. Furthermore, many organisations inhabit converted historic warehouses and residences (see figure 135). These types of buildings are popular particularly among professionals such as lawyers and consultants.

Yet things have been changing during the last ten years. Currently the Netherlands is in the midst of an economic boom. The 'feel good' euphoria seems to be reflected in an end to the moratorium on high-rise buildings.[1] At suburban locations, one can find several tall office buildings. The most prestigious site is the 'Southern Axis', in the south of Amsterdam. It is probably the most expensive piece of land in the Netherlands, because of its excellent connections with motorways, railways and Schiphol Airport.

135 Many of the historic buildings have been transformed into offices: this former archive building in The Hague has been changed into a satellite office for civil servants

The landmark of the Southern Axis is ABN AMRO headquarters, designed by Henry Cobb. This building, which houses over 2500 employees, consists of two slender towers connected by a rectangular base (see figure 136). Typical for the Dutch context is that the bank chose a high-rise structure (105 m) not so much to capitalise on the value of the land, but rather to create a landmark for the company, one corresponding with its corporate identity.[2]

The city of Rotterdam is another exception when it comes to building heights. In the Netherlands, this city is referred to as 'Manhattan on the Maas' (the Maas being the river running through Rotterdam). Over the past few years a number of landmark offices have sprung up in the city centre (see figure 137).

Furthermore, plans have been made for a number of high rises at the 'Kop van Zuid'. Up to the eighties this was a dockland area. With the relocation of dock activities to the edge of the city this area became free for new, high-rise developments like Foster's World Port Center (145 m) and Renzo Piano's KPN Tower (98 m).

By Dutch standards the buildings in Rotterdam are tall, but in a world context the majority of Rotterdam's high buildings would be perceived as mid-rise. In a flat country like the Netherlands a tall building soon becomes a landmark. John Worthington indicates in his report on high rises in Rotterdam that buildings there are dwarfed by their American and Asian counterparts.[3] This becomes clear when we look at the ranking of Dutch high-rises in the list of the world's tallest buildings (see table 7.1).[4] Things may be changing, however. Recently, the city's planning authority has been approached for permission to develop 'super high-rise' (>250 m) buildings. But it is not very likely that these buildings will be developed in the near future.

Table 7.1 Ranking of the world's tallest buildings (based on Gerometta, 1999)

No.	Name	Location	Height (m)
1	Petronas Towers	Kuala Lumpur	452
2	Sears Tower	Chicago	442
3	Jin Mao Building	Shanghai	421
4	One World Trade Centre	New York	417
5	Empire State Building	New York	381
662	Millennium Tower	Rotterdam	157
742	Nationale Nederlanden	Rotterdam	152

Floor plan

Another difference between high rises in the Netherlands and those in America and to a lesser extent the UK, lies in the scale of their floor plans. This difference becomes clear when comparing the One Canada Square Tower in London (which has been developed by Americans, see Chapter 2) and the Rembrandt Tower in Amsterdam. Within their own country, both buildings are regarded as high rises. Furthermore, both buildings have a floor plan that resembles the classic plan of an American skyscraper: a rectangular floor with a central core (see figures 138 - 140). However, when one looks at the scale of the floor plans, there is an enormous difference: the floor depth of the Rembrandt Tower is 9 m, while that of the One Canada Square Tower ranges from approximately 14-22 m.

136 Headquarters ABN AMRO Bank

137 Landmark in the centre of Rotterdam: the Nationale Nederlanden building, designed by Bonnema (152 m)

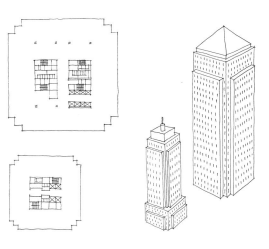

138 Exterior Rembrandt Tower

139 Floor plan One Canada Square Tower and Rembrandt Tower floor plan (same scale)

140 The slender, 135 m high Rembrandt Tower and the 'thicker' 244 m high One Canada Square Tower

The limited floor depth of the Rembrandt Tower is typical of Dutch office buildings. In contrast to British and North-American employees, Dutch employees work in office space with desks in close proximity to windows.[5, 6] In the majority of office buildings nobody is sitting more than 7 m from a window. This difference is crucial because shallow floor plans tend to be less efficient than deep-plan forms: for a similar amount of space you have to build a more expensive facade (approximately one third of the total building costs).[7, 8]

The advantage of shallow floor plans is that they provide employees with an outside view, daylight and the ability to control the indoor climate. About 80% of Dutch office buildings has openable windows and possibilities for individual climate control.[9] In

141 Headquarters ING
Bank

particular the ability to open windows is thought to be of crucial importance for the
well-being of employees.

The Dutch ING bank says of its new headquarters, designed by Meyer and Van
Schooten (see figure 141). 'The building will feature a large number of advantages for the
people who will be working in it, one of which is windows that can be opened'.[10] One
problem, however, was that the building is located next to a busy highway. To deal with
that, the building will have a climate facade made of an outer layer of normal glass and an
inner layer of insulating glass. Between these two layers, air will circulate. This allows
the inhabitants of the building to open the windows of the inner layer of the facade
without being disturbed by the noise and pollution of the highway.

Because of the limited floor depth, buildings may have complex plan forms.
Particularly in inner cities, it is difficult to build a large low-rise building that still
provides employees with seats near a window. A good example of a complex plan form
is the new provincial government building in The Hague, designed by the American
firm Kohn Pedersen Fox (KPF). KPF based its design on a section with a typical depth
of 12.6 m, giving 5.4 m office depth on either side of a 1.8 m corridor. The architects
calculated the length to which the typical section would need to be 'extruded' to produce
a building with the desired amount of office space. Then, using clay models, KPF literally
moulded its elongated office block to wrap around the perimeter of the site. The multiple
curves that emerged from these studies were not only a response to the site's corner
location, but also a means of increasing the overall volume of accommodation while
remaining compatible with the shallow plan (see figures 142 - 143).[11]

According to some designers, Dutch offices are too narrow, providing little option for
innovative layouts. For this reason, there is a trend to design buildings with larger
depths. A good example is the new KLM office, designed by the architectural firm Van
den Broek & Bakema. The office floors in this building have a depth of 14.4 m (see figure
144). Workplaces are still located along the facade. The inner areas are used for meeting
spaces. Glazed partitions allow maximum penetration of daylight.

Other buildings even have depths over 20 m. These buildings, however, have atria to

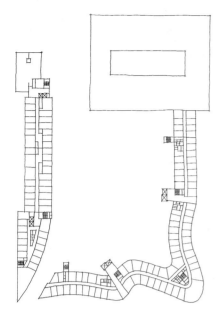

142 Floor plan, seat of provincial government in The Hague

143 Exterior seat of provincial government in The Hague

ensure that work areas are still located next to an (internal) window. The Dynamic office in Haarlem, for example, is a pioneer in Dutch office innovation. The Dynamic office (Rudy Uytenhaak, 1998) is an experimental building belonging to the Dutch central government. One of its most striking features is its unusual floor depth of 25 m. This is compensated for by a series of 7 m x 7 m patios that convey daylight into the interior of the building (see figures 145 - 146).[12]

Even more radical is Villa VPRO, the office of a progressive Dutch broadcasting company (see figures 147 - 148). With a 50 m x 50 m square floor plan, it is one of the deepest office building in the Netherlands. A large number of atria and light wells bring daylight into the building. MVRDV, the building's architects, say: 'a precision bombardment of snake-like holes makes it possible to combine light and air with a view of the surroundings'.[13]

The VPRO building deviates in many other ways from mainstream Dutch office designs. The building has sloping floors and a totally open layout. This is highly unusual in the Netherlands.

Workplace

In the Netherlands open-plan offices are rare. The narrow floor plans of Dutch office buildings mostly have a cellular layout. After a strong rejection of the office landscape in the mid-1970s (see Chapter 2), Dutch organisations chose to accommodate their employees in rooms rather than open plans.[14] Veldhoen, a Dutch workplace consultant, describes the average Dutch office as a building block with long dark corridors with closed and deserted rooms running along both sides.[15] This image may be too negative, but research done in 1998 indeed shows that the majority of Dutch offices are highly cellularised (see table 7.2).[16] Whether you actually have a room to yourself depends on your

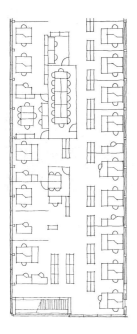

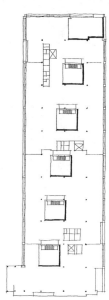

144 Workplace
layout KLM Office

145 Patio in the
Dynamic office with
patio in background

146 Floor plan
Dynamic office

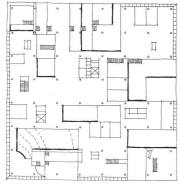

147 Floor plan Villa
VPRO

148 Interior Villa VPRO

149, 150, 151: Dutch office interiors: long corridors, cellular offices and spacious managers' offices

function and your position in the organisational hierarchy. Managers will have a room of their own while the lower echelons may be accommodated in rooms containing up to 8 people.

Table 7.2 Dutch workplace layouts (based upon research by Inbo among 764 Dutch organisations[17])

Dominant type of layout	Percentage of organisations (%)
Cellular office (1-2 persons)	40%
Group office (3-8 persons)	23%
Combination of cellular and group offices	21%
Open plan	11%
Others	5%

Typical of the Dutch situation, cellular layouts are highly standardised. The modules and grids being used are very similar in both public and commercial buildings. British architects have observed that there is no discussion or debate on what sort of grid should be used.[18] Currently both commercial and public buildings currently tend to be based on an office module of 1.8 m x 5.4 m.[19, 20, 21, 22] Employees can get an office of one module (1.8 m x 5.4 m), two modules (3.6 m x 5.4 m), three modules (5.4 m x 5.4 m) etc. Research has shown that this type of module is not that efficient from a space planning point of view.[23] But, apparently, both clients and architects regard these sizes as appropriate. Another crucial factor is that the construction industry uses these sizes for the production of products such as prefabricated floor slabs, ceilings and HVAC units.

One of the side effects of cellular layouts and the module sizes chosen is a relatively great use of space per employee. Available data put typical London densities at 14-16 m² lettable space per person, while in Amsterdam the average employee has an ample 24 m².[24]

According to some Dutch designers and consultants, the situation described above will soon become outdated. The spacious cellular office is thought to be inefficient and frustrating to employee communication. In response to organisational developments such as working in project teams, there is a trend towards more open layouts.

Several Dutch organisations, mainly those in the IT business, are adopting American-style open plans with cubicles. Yet, most of the inspiration for the new layouts comes from Scandinavia. In particular, the Swedish combi-office (see Chapter 5) is strongly associated with office innovation. This concept was introduced in the Netherlands in

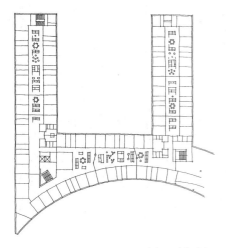

152 Fragment floor plan combi-office of Schiphol Airport

153 Interior of the Schiphol office

articles with titles such as 'The combi-office: office of the future?' and 'The combi-office; Scandinavian fiction or irreversible development?'.[25, 26] The general message of these articles was that the combi-office is a perfect solution (despite losing its appeal in Sweden itself; (see Chapter 5), combining the advantages of both cellular and open plan-offices.

A good example of a Dutch combi-office is the headquarters of Amsterdam Airport Schiphol, designed by Wim Quist (see figures 152 - 153). The organisation chose this type of layout because it wanted to be 'faster, more open and more market-oriented'.[27] Before Schiphol decided to choose a combi-office, the executive board went to visit the SAS building in Stockholm.

In many cases the adoption of new layouts goes hand in hand with new ways of using office space. Just as in other countries, Dutch consultants are promoting such concepts as teleworking, desk-sharing and non-territorial offices. Some present the adoption of such concepts as something inevitable rather than futuristic.[28] In line with a tradition of innovative buildings such as the Centraal Beheer Building and the NMB Headquarters, many Dutch organisations seem indeed to be starting to implement innovative solutions on a large scale.

This idea seems to be supported by the relatively large number of Dutch organisations currently experimenting with other-than-traditional Dutch office solutions. Teleworking has been around for some years now, and it has become a widely accepted option. When compared to other European countries, the Netherlands is first in teleworking, with 9.1% of the workforce actively employed in this manner (see table 7.3). Research by INBO shows that a similar proportion of organisations are working with new office concepts, such as desk-sharing (see table 7.4).[29]

Table 7.3 Telework in Europe in 1998 (European Commission, 1999)

Country	Percentage of the working population
Netherlands	9.1
UK	7.0
Sweden	5.4
Germany	1.9
Italy	1.2

154 Interior
Interpolis

Table 7.4 Emergence of new office concepts (based upon research by Inbo among 764 Dutch organisations[30])

Stage of transition	Percentage of organisation (%)
Working with new concepts	9%
Experimenting with new concepts	4%
Studying new concepts	3%
Thinking about new concepts	15%
Not thinking about new concepts	69%

The Interpolis building in Tilburg is an instance of an insurance organisation that has adopted office innovation on a large scale. Basically, the building has a standard floor plan with a depth of 12 m based on a module of 1.80 m (see figures 154-156). What makes this building different from other Dutch offices is its workplace layout and the way in which the building is being used (developed by Veldhoen and Partners, 1998). There are small, closed-off 'cockpits' where employees can work in peace and quiet. In addition there are open spaces in the centre of the office floors for more interactive work. Employees are free to choose in which type of space they want to work. Every employee has his entire department at his disposal. The general idea is that 'your workplace is where you are'.[31]

DUTCH CONTEXT

With exception of Rotterdam and the South of Amsterdam, Dutch cities have a relatively low skyline. Offices tend to have relatively narrow floor plans with spacious and cellular workplace layouts. Furthermore, there are many organisations experimenting with new workplace concepts such as combi-offices, desk-sharing and teleworking. In this section we relate these characteristics to the context in which Dutch offices are being designed, produced and used.

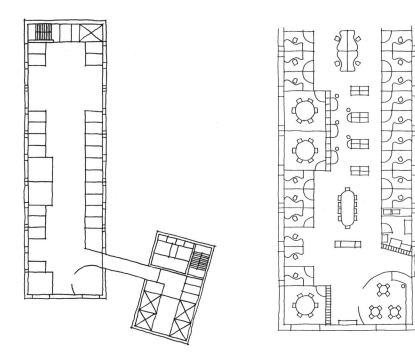

Urban setting

The Dutch urban setting is an important explanation for the absence of a high-rise tradition in the Netherlands. Most Dutch cities have historical cores. They were settled and achieved their identities centuries before the modern office was invented.[32] In Amsterdam's city centre, for example, most buildings are historical, and there are now plans to turn its historical centre into a conservation area.[33] Because of their willingness to preserve this heritage, the public tends to disapprove of commercial structures that overshadow religious and public buildings.

The sustained limit on the height of buildings in most city centres (in combination with traffic congestion) has encouraged the development of offices on the outskirts of cities. There one can also find taller buildings, such as the ABN AMRO Bank building on the Southern Axis of Amsterdam. The major exception is Rotterdam. The historical city of Rotterdam was destroyed by bombing in 1940. After the war the city rapidly rebuilt itself following the modern town planning principles of CIAM. Because of the modern zoning, with broad boulevards, there are less obstacles to high-rise development.

Another complication in high-rise development is Dutch urban planning. Dutch planning is concerned with preserving of the existing historical content of cities. Planning regulations follow a relatively 'loose' advisory system, which allows evaluation of projects case by case.[34] This way of working provides the necessary flexibility for local officials to accommodate the occasional skyscraper, while at the same time avoiding the impression that high-rises are as a general rule acceptable.[35]

Furthermore, the Netherlands generally speaking has a long tradition of participatory planning, including face-to-face contact between interested parties during development negotiations.[36] A good example of the democratic nature of Dutch planning is the Larmag Tower. In 1991, the Amsterdam municipality broke its low-rise tradition by granting planning permission to a skyscraper, designed by Skidmore, Owings and Merrill (SOM) and the Dutch architect Liag. The building was to be the tallest building in the Netherlands, with a height of 210 m. However with planning well ahead of schedule, the project was stopped. One reason was strong local opposition: there were complaints that the building would be visible from as far as 40 km from Amsterdam, not to mention the shadow it would cast on its surroundings.[37]

Market conditions

Just as important as the urban setting in explaining Dutch office design is the Dutch office market. In the Netherlands, owner-occupiers have traditionally played an important role in the office market. At this moment about 50% of all office users are owner-occupiers.[38] Not unexpectedly, most of the total floor area is being used by them.[39]

The dominance of the office market by owner-occupiers partly explains why Dutch office buildings are relatively inefficient from an investment point of view. When users themselves are the client in a project, they can exercise a direct influence on the design. Consequently, they are able to create buildings that have more to do with corporate identity than with marketability. They put less emphasis on construction efficiency, gross-to-net ratios and the marketability of a building than investors do. It also gives organisations more opportunities to experiment with new building types. Famous Dutch office buildings such as the Centraal Beheer building and, lately, Villa VPRO are the best examples of this tendency.

The dominance of users does not, however, imply that developers and investors play a minor role in Dutch office design. Also in the Netherlands there is a large commercial office market in which offices are being built without the user being identified beforehand. In fact, the number of organisations that prefer to rent office space instead of owning it is increasing.[40] Yet this has not resulted in differences in the typology of Dutch offices. It is clear that developers are part of the same national culture as the users of their buildings. To develop a commercially successful building developers have to anticipate the expected acceptability of their buildings by users.

The main impact of commercial office development on Dutch design is that floor plans and workplace layouts have become heavily standardised. Dutch developers have standardised the narrow and cellular floor plan into a 1.80 m corridor with 5.40 m deep office spaces on both sides.

Another crucial feature of the Dutch office market is that prices are relatively low (see table 7.5). This may be surprising for such a small and densely populated country (the highest population density in Europe) (see table 7.6). One would expect that in the Netherlands, space is scarce and, therefore, expensive. However this is not the case because office development is greatly dispersed throughout the country. It has no top location, in the way that, say, the UK has London and France has Paris, where services, government and organisational headquarters are concentrated around a single point on the map. In the Netherlands these functions are spread over Amsterdam, Rotterdam, Utrecht, The Hague and many small towns in between – the agglomeration known as *Randstad*. As a result, land is relatively cheap and, consequently, so is office space.[41]

Table 7.5 European rent levels (Richard Ellis, 1999)

City	Prime rent levels (US Dollars per m² per annum)
Stockholm	479
Frankfurt	548
Amsterdam	386
London City	1117
Milan	381

Table 7.6 European population densities (CIA factbook, 1998)

Country	Population density (people/km²)
Sweden	21.6
Italy	193.1
Germany	234.8
UK	238.9
Netherlands	464.2

Table 7.7 European GDPs per head (The Economist Group, 1997)

Country	GDP per head (US Dollars)
Sweden	25 720
Germany	25 632
Netherlands	23 094
UK	21 848
Italy	19 919

The combination of a relatively prosperous economy (one the highest GDPs in Europe, see table 7.7) and low rents explains why Dutch organisations can afford to build spacious buildings with narrow floor plans. It also explains the hesitation to build tall buildings, as rent levels necessary to justify such developments scarcely exist.

The fact that office space is relatively cheap also affects office innovation. Research shows that at current Dutch rent levels, office innovation hardly saves any costs.[42] Not surprisingly, Dutch consultants propagate that office innovation should not be seen merely as a means to save costs.[43] Instead, they promote it as a tool to increase productivity or to change the culture of an organisation. This way of thinking may explain why relatively expensive concepts such as the combi-office are currently popular in the Netherlands.

Labour relations

The focus on organisational issues in innovations may also be connected with the nature of Dutch labour relations. Dutch office design is a reflection of the Dutch 'consultation model' which stands for consensus, bargaining and compromise. Labour relations are characterised by an inclination to reconcile opposing interests and to create balances between them.[44] Whereas in Anglo-Saxon countries companies traditionally have one overriding goal – to maximise returns to shareholders – Dutch organisations often accept broader obligations. They tend to balance the interests of shareholders against those of other 'stakeholders', notably employees.

Harmonious labour relations within organisations are reflected in an on-going process of consultation between employers and employees at different levels.[45] Most companies are obliged to have a works council, an independent body within the company that is made up of employees' representatives. Its main task is to advise management on important decisions regarding the company. Management is legally obliged to ask for the council's advice when, for example, it wants to sell off part of the company, but also when it wants to implement important changes in the working environment. The actual decision-making, however, is done exclusively by management.

157 Ministry of Housing, Spatial Planning and the Environment, designed by Jan Hoogstad. The image shows the large atria of the building, which have to ensure that employees are able to open windows without being bothered by noise and polluted air from outside.

In the design of office buildings, works councils play a crucial role. Depending on the size of the project, management must seek its advice and even its consent. This leaves its mark on the design of office buildings. It explains why Dutch office buildings are so much focused on the satisfaction of individual employees rather than on cost-benefits or flexibility for the organisation as a whole.

A recurrent theme in the involvement of works councils is the extent to which employees have the possibility to control environmental conditions (e.g. light level, temperature, and flow of fresh air). Piet Vroon, a Dutch psychologist, has stated that individual control is crucial for the well-being of employees. Open spaces with air conditioning, artificial lighting, little outside view and no possibilities of opening a window are regarded as harmful. Works councils have picked up this issue and made it one of their main criteria in judging office design.

In particular, in government the influence of employee representatives is clear. Herman Hertzberger said of the civil servants at the Ministry of Social Affairs: 'They want a lot of room. They want a view. They want windows that will open. They don't want air conditioning because of headaches. They want good lighting. ... The employees' committee has significant rights as far as the working environment is concerned. They can say, "No we don't want it". And if so, we [architects] can't do it, whatever it is'.[47]

Also in the case of the Ministry of Housing, Spatial Planning and the Environment's building in The Hague, designed by Jan Hoogstad, the users wanted openable windows with a view and daylight (see figure 157).[48] There was also a long-standing bone of contention between the heads of the ministry and staff representatives about whether the minimum area of office workplaces should be 8 or 9 m².[49]

But the involvement of user representatives in office design is not just something for government projects. The design of the new ABN AMRO bank headquarters by the American Henry Cobb was also influenced by employees' representatives. The design was presented to the works council by a member of the board of directors and discussed thoroughly with them.[50] One of the main points of discussion was the windows in the high-rise towers. Initially, these could not be opened. The works council, however, demanded openable windows because they regarded it as important for the well-being of employees. As a result the building is equipped with small 'psychological' windows.

Culture

Because of the crucial role of employees in office design, offices are a fairly clear reflection of Dutch organisational culture. The Dutch tend to have an individualistic culture, which explains their preference for cellular offices, which are an excellent means to achieving a certain degree of autonomy and privacy.[51] The walls and doors prevent conversations, meetings and telephone calls from being overheard; they prevent you from being disturbed by the sounds of others, and they block out the view and prevent social control by your colleagues (partitions are seldom glazed in Dutch offices). These characteristics match results of cultural studies that indicate that the Dutch, like most other North Europeans, are members of a neutral culture.[52] This means that they share a tendency towards social independence. Interaction has to be functional and 'to the point' while self-regulation, autonomy and privacy are highly valued. Trompenaars and Hampden-Turner, two authorities on organisational culture, say that this might have to do with the high density of population in the Netherlands: with so many people on a small piece of land, privacy is a scarce item.[53]

The importance of privacy to Dutch employees is clearly illustrated in the building of the Ministry of Social Affairs, which was designed by Herman Hertzberger (who refers to the building as the 'friendly castle'). The basic plan module of the building is an octagon. Originally, Hertzberger divided its octagons into open and spacious workplaces, somehow similar to those of the Centraal Beheer building (see Chapter 2). These plans, however, were rejected by employees, who demanded a cellular solution. Hertzberger said that the employees 'locked' themselves up in cells.[54] The result is a rather complex workplace layout with many awkward corners, which contrasts with the open structure of the rest of the building (see figures 158 - 159). Hertzberger: 'It was a fight that has been won in the common areas, but lost in the rooms. It is disappointing that there no larger rooms, but the building does have a structure that can be broken up by the next generation'.[55] A Dutch critic wrote that the civil servants didn't 'deserve' such a building and that they should have been accommodated in an 'anonymous-corridors-with-rooms' building.[56]

The case of the Ministry of Social Affairs may not be representative of the Dutch situation as a whole. Privacy is an important issue in the Netherlands, but it is not like in Sweden where, traditionally, every employee gets his or her own private office. Besides, there are several cases in which organisations have (again) chosen landscape-like solutions, as in the case of Villa VPRO. Yet in this case, too, privacy was an issue. 'Dissident' employees stated that it is impossible to concentrate and work in an open building where people are constantly moving around, making calls and conferring.[57, 58, 59] To the Dutch this criticism may seem understandable. Yet it is important to note that Villa VPRO is still very spacious and quiet when compared to, for example, the offices of Channel 4 in the UK, which are 'crowded, with lots of equipment, monitors and filing cabinets'.[60]

Another aspect of Dutch culture that seems to be reflected in office design is egalitarianism. Research has shown that Dutch managers are more egalitarian and less hierarchical than those in other countries.[61] Authority is not so much connected with position as with personal credibility.[62] This idea is closely linked to the tendency of the Dutch to distrust anyone showing off or drawing attention to themselves.[63]

The urge for equality is reflected in the layout and use of office buildings. In Dutch offices, outside view and privacy have a less symbolic meaning than in the Anglo-Saxon offices. These features have always been more or less equally distributed among employees. Also in the case of workplace innovation, it is stressed that management should be involved and should set an example.[64] A brochure on the Interpolis project (see p. 137) says: 'Your place of work is wherever you are... And that goes for everyone, management staff and departmental heads included'.[65]

Yet Dutch offices are not completely free of status. In general, managers still have certain privileges such as a room on the upper floor of a tall building or a private parking

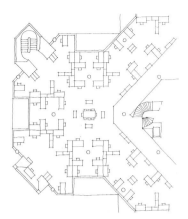 

158, 159 Workplace layouts for the Ministry of Social Affairs. Left: one of the more open layouts as proposed by Hertzberger. Right: the final cellular layout.

space. In the ABN AMRO building, for example, the rooms of members of the board of directors are located on the upper floors of the building. Generally the working space allocated to a person depends on their position in the hierarchy: an executive receives 27 m², a manager 19 m², an employee 18 m², the section head 18 m², and the administrative staff are allocated 15 m².[66] To outsiders, though, Dutch offices may still seem very egalitarian. When a group of Germans visited the famous Centraal Beheer building of Hertzberger they found it anarchic: 'Now you can no longer see who the boss is', they exclaimed.[67]

Regulations

The last crucial factor in explaining Dutch office design is legislation. The Netherlands has extensive health and safety regulations for the design of office workplaces. Most important are *Arbeidsomstandigheden* (*Arbo*) regulations. These determine various aspects of the physical working environment. The most important of these are regulations stipulating the dimensions of workplaces and those governing access to daylight.

Arbo regulations prescribe that a workplace should comprise at least 7 m². This concerns the basic space needed for a desk and a chair. For other features such as the entrance to the workplace, a filing cabinet and a conference table more space is required (see table 7.8). Furthermore, Dutch law prescribes that an enclosed office space should be at least 8 m². In new office buildings this minimum is 10 m².

Table 7.8 Minimum workspace size according to Dutch Health and Safety Regulations

Minimal workspace	7 m²
Entrance to workspace	+ 1 m²
Filing cabinet	+ 1 m²
Conference table with max. 4 persons	+ 1 m² per person
Conference table for 5 persons or more	+ 1.5 m² per person

These space requirements may partly explain the great amount of space used in the Netherlands. If you add extra spaces for toilets, corridors, and reception and storage areas a gross external area of 25 to 30 m² per employee can easily be reached. Yet it is questionable to what extent regulations are actually a 'shaping force'. Regulations are based on existing standards for space within organisations, and not the other way round.[68] The same seems to be true for the minimum width of a workplace. This is 1.80 m, which corresponds exactly with the most common window module in Dutch offices (see table 7.9).[69]

Table 7.9 Office space dimensions according to Dutch Health and Safety Regulations

Office space dimensions	Existing office building	New office building
Width (window module)	1.8 m	1.8 m
Total surface	8.0 m² *	10.0 m² *
Height	2.1 m	2.4 m

*These m² can be spread over several spaces

Concerning daylight, Dutch regulations stipulate that workplaces that are being used for more than two hours per day have to have access to daylight. The accompanying guidelines comment that a lack of daylight and lack of an outside view can result in dissatisfied employees.[70] This may very well be one explanation for the limited floor depth of Dutch offices. Yet, regulations do not specify the distance from the workplace to the window; they do state that the total window surface should be at least 1/20th of the total floor area of the office space. However, this hardly puts any constraint on the depth of office floors.

SUMMARY AND CONCLUSIONS

Dutch office design and the influence of its context are summarised in table 7.10.

On the building level, Dutch cities have a low skyline, punctuated by the occasional high-rise office. This can be explained by the centuries-old structure of Dutch cities, and planning policies aimed at preserving this image. The only exception is Rotterdam, which had been bombed during World War II. Another explanatory factor is the low level of rents.

In terms of floor plans, Dutch offices tend to have limited floor depths. This is due to the Dutch practice of providing all employees with daylight, an outside view and openable windows, which has also been formalised in regulations. It reflects the important role employee representatives play in organisational decision-making. Low rents also probably influence this since such plans are relatively inefficient in their use of space.

On the workplace level we have seen that Dutch offices tend to have spacious, cellular workplace layouts. These layouts reflect the individualist and egalitarian nature of Dutch culture. The link between culture and office design can be explained by the involvement of employees in the design and the fact that Dutch organisations also have the financial means to invest in such buildings.

Table 7.10 Summary of results

Offices	Context
Building	*Urban setting*
Low- and medium-rise buildings	Historical urban structure
Major exception: Rotterdam and outskirts of	Major exception: Rotterdam
Amsterdam	Restrictive planning policies
	Highly participatory planning process
Floor plan	
Narrow floor plans	*Market conditions*
Linear shapes	Strong owner-occupiers
Strong emphasis on daylight, openable windows	Low rents
and an outside view	High GDP
Workplace	*Labour relations*
Cellular layouts	Strong employee representatives
High use of space per employee	
Trends: combination of open and cellular layouts,	*Culture*
non-territorial offices and teleworking	Egalitarian
	Individualistic
	Neutral way of interaction
	Regulations
	Minimum workplace size: 7 m^2
	Stipulates access to daylight/outside view

This situation is in flux. A relatively large proportion of Dutch organisations are working with workplace innovations such as combi-offices, desk-sharing and teleworking. Because of the low cost of space and the important role of employees, these innovations seem to focus on organisational issues rather than cost-savings.

In terms of the research question of this study ('What is the relation between office design and national context'), there appears to be a clear relation between Dutch offices and the Dutch context. The urban setting, market conditions, labour relations, culture and to a lesser extent regulations all affect Dutch office design. Above all, Dutch offices are a reflection of the Dutch consultation model in which various stakeholders are involved in decisions about the size, shape and layout of a building.

The role of architects in Dutch office design is interesting. There are many international architects working in the Netherlands, yet their influence on the height of buildings, their floor plans and workplace layouts is limited. Buildings such as the seat of provincial government in The Hague (designed by KPF) and the ABN AMRO headquarters in Amsterdam (designed by Henry Cobb) are all very Dutch. The concept of these buildings was already captured in the brief, in regulations and in urban plans, before an architect was even involved in the project. This says something about the role of architects. Their main activity seems, indeed, to be to materialise and shape a predetermined concept. Developing a vision of how the inhabiting organisation and its people work no longer seems to be part of that job. That role appears to have been taken over by consultants.

Notes

1   Vaughan Bowden, V. (1998), 'Country Focus - The Netherlands', in: *World Architecture*,
    No. 69, September, pp. 61-69
2   Meel, J. J. van (1998), *Case ABN AMRO Bank*, internal report, Delft University of
    Technology, Department of real estate and project management, Delft
3   DEGW (1998), *High Rise Rotterdam: A Strategy for Intensification and Innovation*, DEGW,
    London
4   Gerometta, M. (1999), *Marshall Gerometta's Hot 500*,
    http://www.worldstallest.com/hot500.html
5   Blyth, A. (1993), 'Working in the Netherlands', in: *Architects' journal*, September 1,
    pp. 26-27
6   Wislocki, P. (1998), 'New buildings in The Netherlands: Power and ambition', in: *World
    Architecture*, No. 69, September, pp. 72-77
7   Gerritse, C. (1998), 'Inpandigheid', in: *Bouwadviseur*, January/February, pp. 16-19
8   Leaman, A. and Bordass, B. (1997), *Productivity in buildings: the 'killer' variables*, paper
    presented to the Workplace Comfort Forum, London, 19-30 October
9   Dewulf, G. P. M. R. and De Jonge, H. (1994), *Toekomst van de kantorenmarkt 1994-2015*,
    Delft University of Technology, 1994
10 ING Bank (1999), press release
11 Wislocki, P. (1998), 'New buildings in The Netherlands: Power and ambition', in: *World
    Architecture*, No. 69, September, pp. 72-77
12 Rijksgebouwendienst (1997), *Dynamischkantoor Haarlem*, 010 Publishers, Rotterdam
13 MVRDV (1999), http://www.archined.nl/mvrdv/vpro/index.html
14 Van Wagenberg, A. (1998), 'interview', in: *Quintessence*, Vol. 6, No. 5, p. 14-17
15 Veldhoen, E. and Piepers, B. (1995), *The demise of the office*, 010 Publishers, Rotterdam
16 Antwerpen, J. van, and Hermans, W. (1998), *Huisvestingsvoorkeuren van kantoren: over
    wens en werkelijkheid*, INBO, Woudenberg
17 ibid.
18 Blyth, A. (1993), 'Working in the Netherlands', in: *Architects' journal*, September 1,
    pp. 26-27
19 ibid.
20 Wislocki, P. (1998), 'New buildings in The Netherlands: Power and ambition', in: *World
    Architecture*, No. 69, September, pp. 72-77
21 Van Wagenberg, A. (1998), 'Interview', in: *Quintessence*, Vol. 6, No. 5, pp. 14-17
22 Dewulf, G. P. M. R. and De Jonge, H. (1994), *Toekomst van de kantorenmarkt 1994-2015*,
    Delft University of Technology, 1994
23 Gerritse, C. (1998), 'Programma en stramienkeuze', in: *Bouwadviseur*, April, pp. 14-16
24 Hakfoort, J. and Lie, R. (1996), 'Office Space per Work: Evidence from Four European
    Markets', in: *The Journal of Real Estate Research*, Vol. 11, No. 2, pp. 183-196
25 Kamphuis, H. (1992), 'Het cocon-kantoor, kantoorvorm van de toekomst?', in: *Facility
    Management Magazine*, Vol. 5, Oct. pp. 24-26
26 Veldhoen, E. (1995), 'Beproefde kantoorconcepten bestaan niet meer: het coconkantoor;
    een Scandinavische fictie of een onomkeerbare ontwikkeling', in: *Facility Management
    Magazine*, Vol. 8, No. 46, pp. 27-29
27 Visser-de Boer, M. (1996), 'Goede communicatie en efficiëntie in combikantoor', in:
    Facility Management Magazine, Vol. 9, No. 47, pp. 8-13
28 Regterschot, J. (1995), 'It is finally going to happen', in: *New European Offices*, Twijnstra
    Gudde, Amersfoort
29 Antwerpen, J. van, and Hermans, W. (1998), *Huisvestingsvoorkeuren van kantoren: over
    wens en werkelijkheid*, INBO, Woudenberg
30 ibid.
31 Interpolis, (1997), 'Je werkplek is waar je bent', *Interpolis Facilitair Bedrijf*, Tilburg
32 Duffy, F. (1997), *The New Office*, Conran Octopus, London
33 Vaughan Bowden, V. (1998), 'Country Focus - The Netherlands', in: *World Architecture*,
    No. 69, September, pp. 61-69
34 DEGW, (1998), *High Rise Rotterdam: A Strategy for Intensification and Innovation*,
    DEGW London
35 Polisano, L. (1995), 'Complexity and Contrast; American and European High-Rise
    Buildings', in: *Architectural Design*, Vol. 65, No. 7/8, pp. 30-35
36 DEGW (1998), *High Rise Rotterdam: A Strategy for Intensification and Innovation*, DEGW,
    London
37 Architects' journal (1991), 'Getting High', in: *Architects' journal*, Vol. 194, No. 17, p. 10
38 Twijnstra Gudde (1999), *Het nationale kantorenmarktonderzoek 1999 - het periodieke
    onderzoek naar de huisvestingssituatie van kantoorgebruikers in Nederland*, Twijnstra
    Gudde, Amersfoort
39 Israel, F.J. (1992), *Kantoren in gebruik*, Stichting voor Beleggings- en Vastgoedkunde,
    Amsterdam
40 Twijnstra Gudde (1999), *Het nationale kantorenmarktonderzoek 1999 - het periodieke
    onderzoek naar de huisvestingssituatie van kantoorgebruikers in Nederland*, Twijnstra
    Gudde, Amersfoort

41 Vries, A.M.E. de, and P.P. Kohnstamm (1991), *Kansen en knelpunten voor de ontwikkeling van commercieel onroerend goed in dertien stedelijke knooppunten*, Stichting voor Beleggings- en Vastgoedkunde, Amsterdam

42 Troost, K. (1998), *(Werkplek)Kosten van kantoorinnovatie*, Stichting voor Beleggings- en Vastgoedkunde, Amsterdam

43 Vollebregt, J. (1998), 'Huisvesting als kapstok voor integraal verandermanagement', in: *Facility Management Magazine*, Vol. 11, No. 61, pp. 26-29

44 Dijk, N. van and Punch, M. (1993), 'Open Borders, Closed Circles: Management and Organization in The Netherlands', in: Hickson, D. J. (ed.), *Management in Western Europe: society, culture and organisation in twelve nations*, Walter de Gruyter, New York

45 Empel, F. van (1997), *The Dutch Model: the power of consultation*, http://www.ser.nl/engels/adviezen/dutchmo.html

46 Vroon, P. (1995), 'Building', in: *NRC Handelsblad*, October 7, 1995

47 Hertzberger, H. (1988), 'Interview', in: *Architects' journal*, January 13, 1988

48 Rossum, V. van, (1990), 'Milestone in office architecture', in: Rutten, J. (ed.), *VROM Ministry*, 010 Publishers, Rotterdam

49 Rutten, J. (1990), 'A single face for a single organisation', in: Rutten, J. (ed.), *VROM Ministry*, 010 Publishers, Rotterdam

50 Meel, J. J. van (1998), *Case study ABN AMRO Bank*, internal report, Delft University of Technology

51 Hofstede, G. (1991), *Cultures and Organisations, Software of the Mind*, McGraw-Hill, London

52 Trompenaars, F. (1983), *Zakendoen over de grens: leren omgaan met andere culturen*, Uitgeverij Contact, Amsterdam

53 Hampden-Turner, C. and Trompenaars, F. (1994), *The Seven Cultures of Capitalism*, Piatkus, London

54 Maas, T. (1991), 'Ministerie SZW: Meesterlijke spanning tussen delen en geheel', in: *Architectuur/Bouwen*, 1991-I, pp. 26-28

55 ibid.

56 ibid.

57 Gijssel, R. van (1997), 'De open werkplek', in: *Intermediair*, http://www.intermediair.nl/Loopba…s/modern_werken/openwerkplek.html

58 Zwaap, R. (1997), 'Villa Hommeles', in: *De Groene Amsterdammer*, http://www.groene.nl/1997/36/rz_vpro.html

59 Amsberg, K.; Gaag, P van der; Koolhaas, M.; Leenders, G.;Nauta, A.;Slager, K. (1998), 'Foute gebouwen 2', in: *NRC Handelsblad*, September 15

60 Duffy, F. (1997), *The New Office*, Conran Octopus, London

61 Hampden-Turner, C. and Trompenaars, F. (1994), *The Seven Cultures of Capitalism*, Piatkus, London

62 Dijk, N. van and Punch, M. (1993), 'Open Borders, Closed Circles: Management and Organization in The Netherlands', in: Hickson, D. J. (ed.), *Management in Western Europe: society, culture and organisation in twelve nations*, Walter de Gruyter, New York

63 Hampden-Turner, C. and Trompenaars, F. (1994), *The Seven Cultures of Capitalism*, Piatkus, London

64 Dewulf, G. P. M. R. and Vos, P. G. J. C. (1998), 'De (on)mogelijkheden van kantoorinnovatie', in: *Management en Organisatie*, Vol. 52, No. 1, pp. 7-28

65 Interpolis (1997), Je werkplek is waar je bent, *Interpolis Facilitair Bedrijf*, Tilburg

66 NRC Handelsblad (1997), 'Profiel Kantoren', in: *NRC Handelsblad*, 24 April, pp. 33

67 Staal, G. (1987), *Between Dictate and Design: The Architecture of Office Buildings*, 010 Publishers, Rotterdam

68 Ministery of Social Affairs and Labour (1998), *Arbo-Informatieblad* 'Kantoren', Sdu Publishers, Den Haag

69 Boer, J.R.; Diehl, P.J. and Koenders, H. (1996) *Arbo-normenboek*, Samsom Bedrijfsinformatie, Alphen a/d Rijn

70 Ministery of Social Affairs and Labour (1998), *Arbo-Informatieblad 'Kantoren'*, Sdu Publishers, Den Haag

REVOLUTION!

8   Conclusions and reflections

This research started with the observation that there are international differences in office design. This observation triggered the desire to acquire a better understanding of office buildings. Why do international differences in office design exist? What are the forces that shape office design?

To answer these questions we first studied the historical development of European office design (see Chapter 2). We then looked in more detail at office design in the UK, Germany, Sweden, Italy and the Netherlands. For each country, office design was described by looking at offices from the building, floor plan and workplace level. Subsequently, the urban setting, market conditions, labour relations, culture and regulations were analysed.

This final chapter integrates the results of the previous chapters. Subsequently we return to the research question and try to answer it. After that we discuss the implications of the research findings for office design in practice. The chapter ends with recommendations for further research and final reflections on the future of office design.

RESEARCH FINDINGS

The research findings have been summarised in table 8.1. Below we discuss the results by explaining the differences observed in office design at building, floor plan and workplace level.

Building

When looking at the mass and shape of buildings, the main observation is that none of the European countries studied has a high-rise tradition. Europe is known for its 'groundscrapers' rather than for its skyscrapers. This can largely be explained by the historical European urban setting and restrictive planning policies. Relatively low rent levels also play a role, but their influence is not decisive.

The historic description in Chapter 2 shows that at the start of the 20th century high rises were virtually unknown in Europe. It was only in the 1950 that Europeans started to build high rises, copying American glazed towers. The European buildings, however, were of a smaller scale than their American prototypes. The same holds for high rises built in the 1980s and today.

The absence of a European high-rise tradition is strongly related to the fact that the

Offices

Building level	Floor plan level	Workplace level	Urban setting
United Kingdom			
Low- and medium-rise buildings Major exception: Canary Wharf, with occasional high-rises in the City	Deep floor plans Compact shapes with central cores or atria Air-conditioning and raised floors	Open plans with cellular offices for management Low use of space per employee Trends: more open, non-territorial offices and teleworking	Historical urban structure Restrictive planning policies Struggle between conservationists and business
Germany			
Low- and medium-rise buildings Major exception: Frankfurt	Narrow floor plans Linear shapes Natural ventilation/mixed mode systems, attention to ecological issues	Cellular layouts High use of space per employee Trends: combination of open and cellular offices, relatively few experiments with non-territorial offices and teleworking	Historical urban structure/bombed cities Major exception: Frankfurt Restrictive planning policies
Sweden			
Low- and medium-rise buildings Groundscrapers	Narrow floor plans/medium depth double-corridor-plans and combi-offices Linear shapes	Highly cellular layouts Extra attention to break areas High use of space per employee Trends: pioneer in use of more open, non-territorial offices and teleworking	Historical urban structure Restrictive planning policies Highly participatory planning process
Italy			
Low- and medium-rise buildings Extra attention to urban context and conversion	Narrow floor plans/medium depth double-corridor-plans Linear/compact shapes	Mix of cellular and group layouts High use of space per employee Few experiments with new office concepts	Omnipresent historical heritage Restrictive planning policies Strong bureaucracy
Netherlands			
Low- and medium-rise buildings Major exception: Rotterdam and outskirts of Amsterdam	Narrow floor plans Linear shapes Strong emphasis on daylight, openable windows and outside view	Cellular layouts High use of space per employee Trends: combination of open and cellular layouts, non-territorial offices and teleworking	Historical urban structure Major exception: Rotterdam Restrictive planning policies Highly participatory planning process

National context

Market conditions	Labour relations	Culture	Regulations
Strong developers High rents Relatively low GDP	Strong shareholders	Hierarchic Strongly individualistic Neutral way of interaction	No specific workplace size given No requirements for daylight/outside view
Strong owner-occupiers Low rents High GDP	Strong employees' representatives	Hierarchic/formal Strong emphasis on privacy and personal space Neutral way of interaction	Minimum workplace size: 8 m^2 Stipulates access to daylight/outside view
Strong owner-occupiers Low rents High GDP	Strong employees' representatives	Egalitarian Social individualism Neutral way of interaction	No specific workplace size given Stipulates access to daylight/outside view
Strong developers, but immature market Low rents Low GDP (difference between North and South)	Strong employees' representatives, but rights not fully used	Very hierarchic Individualistic Affective way of interaction	No specific workplace size given Stipulates access to daylight/outside view
Strong owner-occupiers Low rents High GDP	Strong employees' representatives	Egalitarian Individualistic Neutral way of interaction Regulations	Minimum workplace size: 7 m^2 Stipulates access to daylight/outside view

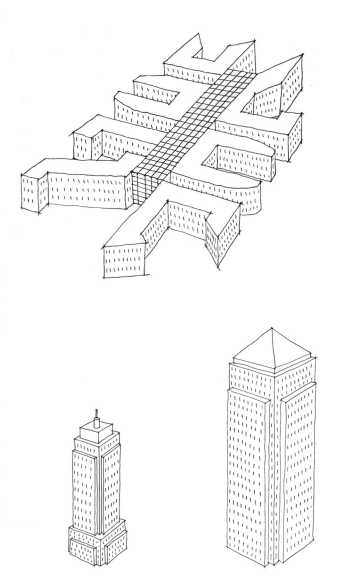

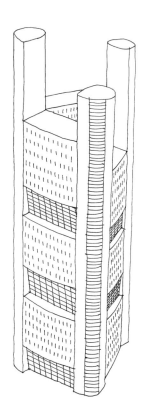

161 Low-rise European 'groundscraper'

162 Small-scale European skyscraper

163 Imported American skyscraper

164 New ecological type of skyscraper

majority of European cities are old, with complex and intricate city structures. This limits the possibilities for high-rise office development.

First of all, there are practical difficulties. Fragmented ownership structures form an obstacle to the acquisition of large plots; tight street patterns cannot cope with the activities or the traffic volumes that accompany high rises – a major issue because most European cities are already congested.

Second, there are planning difficulties. European planners tend to be conscious of retaining their historical urban design. Building height is restricted because tall buildings do not 'fit' in the historical character of cities or because they obstruct the view of monuments. This is, for example, particularly important in Italian cities with their 'ever present historical heritage'.

A third problem is the fact that European planning processes can be complex and lengthy. A typically Northern European problem is the democratic nature of planning processes. Large-scale projects can meet resistance from all kinds of pressure groups. A typically Italian problem is bureaucracy. Large-scale projects are frustrated by a large number of political, technical and administrative bodies that superintend the planning process.

The impact of the historical urban setting on office design in Europe is underlined by three exceptions: Frankfurt, London and Rotterdam. Each of these cities has a skyline dominated by high-rise buildings. This is not surprising because in each of these cities, the historical structure was destroyed by bombing during World War II. In particular Frankfurt and Rotterdam were badly damaged. Post-war reconstruction plans were specifically designed to encourage every opportunity for development. To a lesser extent the same holds for London, where the 'blitz' created empty sites in the city structure.

The case of London is interesting because it highlights the impact of another crucial factor, namely market conditions. Because of London's role as a global city, market pressures and rent levels are higher than anywhere else in Europe. Given the large demand for modern office space and the scarcity of land in the City, skyscrapers would be a natural solution. Yet there are relatively few high rises there. London's largest office blocks can be found in Canary Wharf, outside the City. Apparently, the historical and restrictive urban setting has a larger impact than market pressure.

Just as high rent levels do not automatically result in high buildings, low rents do not necessarily result in low-rise buildings. In most European cities, low rents indeed discourage the development of tall buildings. In Frankfurt, however, rent levels are just as low as in the rest of Europe. Yet Frankfurt is the only European city with high rises that match world standards. The underlying reason is Frankfurt's desire to show its increasingly important position as a financial centre. The tall buildings have to signify prosperity, modernity and power. A relatively new – typically German – feature is that tall buildings like the Commerzbank Tower also have to express a certain ecological awareness.

Floor plan

When looking at floor plans of European office buildings, there is a crucial difference in the depth of floors between the UK and Continental Europe. British offices tend to have deep, compact floor plans. Workplaces can be located as far as 14-16 m from a window. In contrast, Continental European buildings tend to have narrow, more linear floor plans. Workplaces tend to be located next to windows. This difference can be explained by differences in power relations within organisations and on the office market. Legislation also plays a role, but it does not have a decisive influence.

This difference began in the 1960s. At that time, European organisations started – for the first time – to use air-conditioning to realise deep buildings. By the end of the 1970s, however, Continental European organisations rejected deep solutions. The main criticism was, and still is, that deep buildings provide too little possibilities for outside view, daylight and natural ventilation. In the UK, these issues were regarded as less of a problem. Influenced by of American practice, British organisations adopted deep air-conditioned plans (although air-conditioning is no necessity in the British climate as it is in Houston or New York).

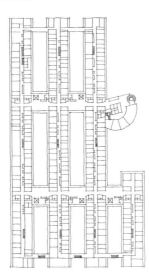

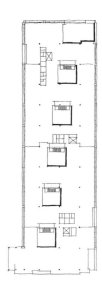

165 British deep plan

166 Continental European narrow plan

167 Continental European deep plan with atria to ensure entrance of daylight

The divergence between the UK and the other European countries can largely be explained by differences in labour relations. In the 1970s, the power of Continental European employees increased strongly. Extensive labour regulations gave employees the right to be involved in organisational decision-making. Using their newly acquired rights, employee representatives took a firm stand against deep air-conditioned buildings. In the UK this did not happen. Unlike their European counterparts, British employees had, and still have, no formal right to be involved in organisational decision-making. Just as in the US, the interests of shareholders are regarded as more important than those of employees.

Office buildings mirror this difference in labour relations. The efficiency of the deep British floors reflects the interests of the corporation and its shareholders. The narrow Continental European floors express the interests of employees: they are the product of the employees' desire for daylight, an outside view and openable windows.

A related explanation has to do with health and safety regulations. Due to the strong role of employee representatives, Continental European countries have adopted regulations that stress the importance of daylight and an outside view. Only in the UK are such regulations absent. The impact of regulations, however, should not be overestimated. In none of the European countries studied, do regulations specify the distance from workplaces to windows.

More important than regulations are market conditions. In Continental Europe, employees have been able to put their stamp on office design, because there organisations traditionally build their own buildings. As owner-occupiers they have to be less concerned about issues such as standardisation, efficiency or marketability than office developers. In Sweden, Germany and the Netherlands this is further strengthened by prosperity. Having both the means and the willingness to invest in office buildings, Northern European organisations have been able to build innovative buildings such as the Centraal Beheer Building in the 1970s, the SAS Building in the 1980s and the Commerzbank Tower in the 1990s.

In the UK the situation is the opposite. The British office market is dominated by developers and investors, who are often strongly influenced by American practice. By nature, these parties are more interested in the efficiency and flexibility of buildings than in end-user desires. Particularly in London, developers have for a long time been able to ignore user interests because of all-time high market pressures.

Workplace

At the workplace level there is a crucial difference in the layout of workplaces between – again – the UK and the rest of Europe. In the UK, office buildings tend to have open and dense workplace layouts. Employees work in cubicles while their managers are accommodated in glass-partitioned cells. In contrast, Continental European offices have more cellular and spacious workplaces. Layouts vary from totally individual ones in Sweden to a mix of cellular and group layouts in Italy. A crucial side effect is that use of space per employee differs strongly. It varies from as little as 14.5 m² lettable space per employee in London to over 27 m² in Amsterdam and Frankfurt.

These differences can be explained by differences in labour relations and market conditions. Culture also plays a crucial role. The way in which culture is expressed, however, depends strongly on market conditions and the extent to which users are actually involved in workplace design.

The origins of these differences can again be placed in the 1960s. At that time, the German Quickborner Team launched the office landscape. The office landscape was a completely open layout with an apparently random arrangement of workplaces. In Continental Europe, the office landscape quickly became a hit. Ten years later, however, it was rejected with the same force as it had been welcomed. As said before, employees had become increasingly powerful. Their major complaints were that the landscape provided them with too little privacy and too little personal control. Therefore organisations started to build cellular office solutions.

In the UK, the office landscape was never adopted on a large scale. Influenced by America, British organisations transformed the ideological concept of the office landscape into an updated version of the Tayloristic open plan. The 'organic' arrangement of workplaces was replaced by an efficient orthogonal grid. The opinion of employees hardly influenced this transformation. During the 1980s and 1990s this flexible solution became increasingly popular as businesses became more dynamic.

Partly, these differences can be explained by market conditions. Because office space has always been relatively cheap in Continental Europe, organisations can afford to use ample space. In Germany, Sweden and the Netherlands, the high workplace standards furthermore fit the general image of high living standards and excellent secondary labour conditions.

British organisations have to be more economical in their use of space. London's high rents have always put great pressure on accommodation budgets. But because of the general focus on cost savings, buildings outside London follow the same pattern even though rents are much lower.

Regulations also seem to be an important explanation. In the UK, regulations for the size of workplaces are minimal. In contrast, German and Dutch regulations explicitly set minimum workplace sizes (7 and 8 m², respectively). In Sweden and Italy, however, the use of space is also relatively high, while regulations are just as minimal as in the UK.

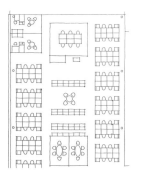
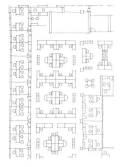
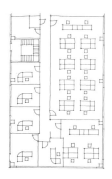
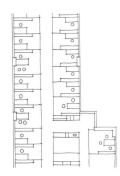

168 Totally open plan (UK)

169 Classic open plan with cells for management (UK)

170 Mix of cellular and group spaces (Italy)

171 Totally individual layout (Sweden)

More important than regulations is the culture factor culture. There are three aspects of culture that have an impact on workplace design: hierarchy, individualism and the way people interact.

The first aspect of a country's culture to influence workplace design is hierarchy. In Sweden's egalitarian culture, every employee gets his own private room. In the more hierarchic British culture, such offices are privileges meant for the higher echelons. In Germany, the Netherlands and Italy, hierarchy is expressed in the size of rooms and the number of people per room.

A second aspect of culture that has an impact on workplace design is individualism. In Germany, cellular layouts can be explained by the individualistic culture in which privacy and personal space are very important. Likewise, Swedish offices reflect Sweden's 'social individualism'. The individual aspect is reflected in offices being private. The social aspect is reflected in the ample provision of communal spaces such as *pausrum* (break areas). It is also no surprise that the combi-office is a Swedish invention – providing employees with both private and common spaces. Nowadays, however, the combi-office is past its prime in Sweden. Changing economic circumstances have taken their toll on this rather spacious solution.

Only in the UK is the relation between individualism and office design unclear. According to the literature, British culture is highly individualistic. The British are supposed to put a premium on privacy and self-control. Yet they are accommodated in open plans. As explained earlier, this has partly to do with costs and hierarchy. Just as importantly, British employees are hardly involved in the design of and briefing for the buildings they work in. Therefore they have not been able to leave their cultural stamp on workplace layouts in the way their Continental counterparts have.

A third aspect of culture that seems to affect workplace design is the way people interact. We have seen that all countries except for Italy have what are called 'neutral' cultures. This means that the Dutch, Swedes and British tend to be more 'restrained' in their communication than Italians. The exact impact of this difference on office design is hard to prove. It may explain, however, why in Italy workplace innovations such as teleworking are less popular than in the rest of Europe. The Italian expressive way of interaction may be less easily replaced by e-mail or video conferencing than more 'neutral' types of interaction.

UNDERSTANDING EUROPEAN DIFFERENCES

Based on our research findings we conclude that there is a clear relation between office design and national context. International differences in the height, depth and workplace layout of buildings correspond with differences in urban setting, market conditions, labour relations, culture and regulations. This supports the idea that office buildings are not just a translation of functional needs or technological possibilities, but also a reflection of the national context in which they are produced.

The impact of national context is most clear in the adoption of office concepts. In each country there is a diversity of office concepts, but some office types are more popular than others. In the UK, for example, one can find both open-plan and combi-offices. Still, open offices predominate while combi-offices are rare (in fact, we have found only one combi-office, built by a Swedish contractor for a Swedish corporation). Likewise, both Italian and Dutch organisations have implemented teleworking concepts. In the Netherlands, however, the percentage of teleworkers is much higher than in Italy.

Furthermore, national context affects perception of office concepts. Similar concepts can have a different meaning in different countries because architects and clients have another frame of reference. For example, the term 'high rise' has a different meaning in the Netherlands than it has in the UK. In the Netherlands buildings with a height of 150 m are perceived as skyscrapers, while in the UK they would be regarded as medium rises. Likewise, an open-plan office in Sweden is not the same as an open plan in the UK. In both cases ceiling-high partitions are absent, but the density and the arrangement of workplaces differ.

The question still remains of how it is possible that national context can leave such a strong mark on a country's office design. In the introduction we said that function is generally regarded as the primary shaping factor in office design. After all, office buildings are a factor of production. Therefore their design should be based on the 'production' process. In other words: form should follow function. Yet, similar organisations are accommodated in strongly varying buildings in different countries.

Roughly, there are three reasons why national context can 'overrule' the impact of functional requirements: differences in the interpretation of functional requirements, the relative importance of these requirements and their translation into design solutions.

First of all, functional requirements are not as clear-cut or universal as they seem. This study shows that functional requirements are open to interpretation. Efficiency, for example, has a different meaning in London than in Amsterdam, where rents are twice as low. The same goes for the term flexibility. In the UK it refers to open office spaces in which workplaces can be easily rearranged. In the Netherlands, it refers to cellular offices with moveable partitions.

Secondly, the relative importance of functional requirements can differ per country. There is always a multiple set of requirements buildings have to comply with. The importance of the various requirements depends on the powers and interests of the parties involved (developers, owners, real estate managers, shareholders, employees). In a developer-led market like the UK, flexibility is more important than user comfort. In Continental Europe it is the other way round.

Thirdly, and most fundamentally, the impact of national context can be explained by the notion that the relationship between the design of a building and the function that it has to fulfil is not as strong as is often thought. Handbooks on office design lead designers into believing that each activity or function requires its own type of space. Yet international differences clearly illustrate that similar functions can take place in markedly different buildings, and vice versa. Rapoport uses the term 'low criticality', meaning that there is a wide range of solutions available in any design situation.[1] Which solution is actually chosen depends largely on the national context.

Over time, a country's social, cultural and economic forces create design solutions that become generally accepted. These solutions are institutionalised in corporate standards, design guidelines, handbooks or even regulations. Furthermore, they are part of what can be called 'tacit' design knowledge. Every designer has a head full of design principles picked up during his education and practice. Clients also have certain design concepts in their minds, based on what they see around them and what they are used to. Together they develop a common repertoire of solutions, influenced by the context in which they work and live. In the Netherlands, for examples when an office building has to be 'marketable', both designers and clients automatically think of a grid of 1.80 m. In doing so they rely heavily on 'tacit' knowledge transferred by precedents. This knowledge is not necessarily right, but part of the local design culture, which is hard to change.

IMPLICATIONS FOR PRACTICE

We have concluded that office design is not just a translation of functional requirements, but also a reflection of the social, cultural and economic context in which they are produced. In what follows we discuss the implications of this conclusion for practice.

Real estate managers

Real estate management is becoming an increasingly international and therefore complex discipline. One way to deal with the increasing complexity is to use a single, infinitely replicable, office concept all over the world. This is the same strategy as international hotels, retail stores and fast food chains successfully use. Such a 'McOffice' approach seems very convenient and well-ordered. It gives the corporation a single, consistent image all over the world and contributes to the establishment of a common corporate culture.

The differences discussed in this study make clear that such a universalist approach does not work, at least not within Europe. In some cases it may simply not be possible because of legal considerations. For example, a British open-plan workplace of 6 m² is not allowed in the Netherlands, where a workplace has to be at least 7 m². The German *Sicherheitsregeln* even prescribe that an open-plan workplace should be 12 -15 m². Similar problems occur when you want to build US-style deep offices, because of European regulations on daylight in the workplace.

More fundamental problems lie in the employees' perception of the working environment. Their expectations are being influenced by what they are used to and see around them. This is probably not a problem when transferring an office concept from

172, 173 Continental
European office
design versus British
office design

Sweden to the UK. British employees – used to American-style cubicles – may welcome the extra space and increased privacy. The other way round, however, is more difficult. Many Continental European employees regard their high accommodation standards as 'acquired rights'. They are not likely to give them up easily.

In particular American corporations are confronted with this difference. An American bank, for example, is currently implementing an American workplace concept on an international scale. In their new headquarters in London the implementation did not cause major problems because the concept provided employees with more space than they were used to (American standards tend to be higher than those in London). In Germany, however, implementation was more difficult. For German employees, the concept meant a decline in space and privacy. This can be a major problem because in Germany employees play a crucial role in organisational decision-making processes.

One way to deal with these differences is to work with performance specifications rather than design specifications.[2] Instead of prescribing a solution, real estate managers can focus on the performance of real estate. Examples of performance specifications are costs per workplace, rate of churn and employee satisfaction (although there are few organisations that structurally evaluate the satisfaction of their employees). The advantage of such an approach is that it leaves the actual solution to the local businesses. The idea of a single corporate image can still be expressed in the materialisation of office concepts, using similar colours, materials and logos.

Eventually, the success of international workplace management depends on the real estate managers' ability to sensitively respond to cultural differences, regulatory constraints, different power-relations and local market conditions. The more real estate managers understand the local context, the more likely they are to respond intelligently by providing local businesses with satisfactory buildings.

It is clear, however, that a single, central real estate department cannot do this alone. Peter Krumm states in his dissertation about corporate real estate management that 'it is hard – if not impossible – for a corporation to maintain up-to-date knowledge on all the different real estate markets in numerous countries and regions all over the world'.[3] Therefore international real estate managers must identify and tap multiple sources of information to gain the local competitive intelligence they require.

Architects

One of the major findings of this study is that the nationality of the architect hardly matters in office design. We have seen, for example, that in the Netherlands there is a trend to invite foreign architects to design office projects. Yet Dutch office buildings are above all very Dutch when it comes to the height of buildings, floor plans, and workplace design. The reason is that these features are determined long before the architect is actually involved in a project. They are incorporated in planning policies, regulations and corporate standards. For architects they are just a part of the brief or the masterplan that they have to materialise.

This situation supports the widespread idea that the architects' role is becoming increasingly limited to designing the proverbial ten-centimetre-deep facade of an office building. In Continental Europe, architects are in some cases still responsible for the design of the office building as a whole. In most British cases, however, the role of architects is much smaller. The architect's role in office design is only one small component among those of many other professionals such as space planners, interior designers and workplace consultants. A good example is a building by Aldo Rossi in Canary Wharf. Basically Aldo Rossi just designed the outside of the building; the developer provided the floor plans and users used their own interior designers for the fitting-out.

It is clear that in such a case as the Canary Wharf project an architect does not require detailed knowledge of the local social-economic context to design a building. Knowledge of national context is crucial, however, when your work goes beyond facade architecture and includes a design for the working environment. When designing workplaces, architects need to be fully aware of what is going on in the building. Yet, we have already stated that just a functional analysis is not enough. To develop a successful working environment, architects need to be aware of how floor plans and workplace layouts affect cultural issues like privacy, status and interaction. Furthermore they need to know what the expectations of their clients are and how employees will respond to new solutions.

This does not mean that designers should uncritically accept or copy local conventions in office design. Questioning the brief and local standards may give clients food for thought and may encourage them to analyse their own organisation.[4] In doing so, architects can play a role that is far more important than just dealing with the aesthetic aspects of building design.

The European Union

The countries investigated in this study are all part of the European Union. The study makes clear that the creation of a European Union (EU) does not imply that member states are becoming more alike. Government, economic policy and even currency may become more European, but the underlying power structures, beliefs, cultures and working conditions remain different.

The European Union is striving for the harmonisation of rules about office workplaces. It enforces executive regulations, which serve as a basis for more particular regulations that are then determined by the member states. The question is which standards should be used. Enforcing the extensive Dutch or German standards would mean costly renovations and refurbishment of British offices. At the same time it is clear that the excellent working conditions of these states cannot just be degraded in the name of integration.

The question is whether we really need extensive European workplace regulations. Extensive regulations may limit the flexibility and potential for innovation in office design. When labour relations are very extensive, as in the Netherlands, workplace changes require a lot of time and energy. On the other hand, they may also result in healthier and safer working conditions. This last issue is, however, very hard to prove. One should not forget that office design is just one of the many factors that affect the performance of employees. When we look, for example, at figures on absenteeism, we see that German and Dutch employees with their excellent working conditions are absent more often than other European employees (see table 8.2).[5]

Table 8.2 Absenteeism in Europe: percentage of the workers who were more than five days absent due to health problems caused by their job (European Foundation for the Improvement of Living and Working Conditions, 1996)

Country	Percentage of workers (%)
(West) Germany	28%
Netherlands	19%
Italy	12%
United Kingdom	9%
Sweden	9%

FURTHER RESEARCH

This study has been exploratory in its nature. Further validation of the outcomes of this study should, therefore, use 'harder', quantitative methods. Four research instruments could be used: post-occupancy evaluations, in-depth case studies, surveys and experiments. Another option would be to test the outcomes of this study in America and Asia. All five options are discussed below.

Post-occupancy evaluations

We have described and explained a wide variety of office types. One obvious question is: which type is better? Which type of office is most productive? For example, are German employees working in their spacious offices more productive than their British counterparts, who are crammed into open plans? Or are human beings very flexible and quickly able to adapt to their environment, however it may look?

To answer such questions it would be interesting to do to post-occupancy evaluations (POEs) in different countries. There is already a large tradition of POEs that dates from the 1970s. International comparisons, however, are absent. Preferably, such research should concern similar organisations, doing the same type of work, in different countries. Using existing questionnaires, we could compare employee satisfaction, absenteeism, interaction patterns and productivity across different countries.[6]

Case studies

Case studies can be used to describe international differences on a project level. To get a better understanding of how offices become the way they are, it would be very interesting to chart decision-making in the briefing and design stages of projects. We have seen, for example, that in Sweden employee representatives play a crucial role in office design. Case studies could describe their role in more detail: the stages of the project in which they are involved; their formal and informal status in the project, and their main interests. Such questions could be investigated by interviewing all participants in a project. Preferably the researcher should also follow the project all the way through, attending design meetings and observing the way different stakeholders co-operate. By comparing cases in different countries we could perhaps get a better understanding of how power relations affect office design.

Surveys

Surveys can be used to get a more quantitative view of international differences in occupants' needs and desires. They could be based on existing methods for the assessment of buildings, such as the REN (Real Estate Norm) and Serviceability Tools. Both are means to identify occupant requirements. They present occupants with a list of options on a wide diversity of design issues, ranging from the type of facade to the type of footprint. It is the client's task to rate the different options. In the REN, for example, the client is presented with five different workplace layouts, which he has to rate on a scale from one to five. Such questions can be used to get a more exact idea of how clients interpret building requirements such as flexibility, user comfort, efficiency and quality.

Experiments

Experiments can be used to support our observations of international differences. We could give architects a hypothetical commission for a hypothetical site. Their task would be to develop a broad concept for the building in a relatively short period of time. After that we could compare the designs and discuss the differences with the participants. The goal would be to better understand how architects make decisions on the planning and layout of a building. Experiments could give us a better understanding of how architects perceive and translate briefs and commissions into design. A similar experiment could be done with clients. Using a standardised method,[7] we can ask clients to develop a brief for their organisation. Comparing and discussing differences among these briefs would give us the opportunity to study the client's perception of office design as well.

America and Asia

The most interesting option for further research is to extend our research area to America and Asia. The United States is interesting because it is the cradle of modern office design. In this study we have referred many times to Manhattan-like skyscrapers and American-style open plans but we have not studied the background of these concepts in depth.

Asia is interesting because there has been an enormous boom in office construction during the last ten years. The list of the world's tall buildings is currently dominated by buildings in countries such the Philippines, China and Singapore. Even more interesting, however, is that Asia's cultural conventions are completely different from those of the Western world. In Japan, for example, finding yourself with a window seat does not augur well. *Mado-giwa* means 'those by the window' and indicates that you have been moved out of the mainstream, or sidelined.[8] Another radical difference can be seen in the meaning of privacy. The Japanese work very closely together, but isolate themselves by avoiding eye contact.[9] This is in total contrast from what we have seen in Europe.

FINAL REFLECTIONS: THE OFFICE OF THE FUTURE

Now that we have reached a better understanding of office design, we should be able to expand our views to its future development. Unfortunately, one of the main lessons of this research turns out to be that predictions are hazardous. The historical analysis in Chapter 2 has shown that the course of office architecture is driven by new office concepts: the Tayloristic open-plan office, the office landscape, the combi-office, and lately the virtual office. In each case proponents of new concepts wish to set themselves apart from the past to highlight the novelty of their ideas. They glorify the benefits of their solutions and invariably present them as more productive, cost-efficient and more flexible than 'conventional' or 'traditional' concepts.

In reality, predictions about new concepts are very often wrong. Office concepts have a life cycle of their own: they emerge, they become popular, and then they are replaced by other ideas – a pattern similar to that of management theory. The most radical example of the coming and going of concepts is the office landscape. In the 1960s, this concept was hailed as the perfect solution. Ten years later the initial euphoria had completely vanished, which came rather as a surprise since the concept seemed to have proved its merits in extensive tests and investigations. In retrospect, however, what had been regarded as visionary ideas ultimately said more about their own time than about what was really going to happen.

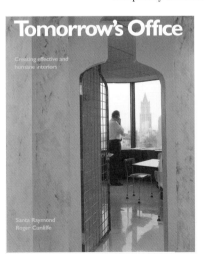

174 TBWA Chiat/Day presented as tomorrow's office

A more recent example is the virtual office of the American advertisement company TBWA Chiat/Day. Until recently, the TBWA Chiat/Day office had been widely regarded as an unquestioned exemplar of how the office of the future would look like. The project has been discussed in almost every book on office design (see figure 174).[10],[11],[12],[13] The project was virtual, non-territorial and open. Its design resembled a three-dimensional pop art painting with vibrant colours, expressive shapes and unconventional materials. This famous case, however, proved to be a failure. Employees couldn't find each other, they couldn't find workspace and their productivity plummeted.[14],[15]

The failure of a concept such as the office landscape or a single project such as TBWA Chiat/Day is interesting because it shows how willing we are to accept new concepts as much for their novelty, aesthetics (glamorous packaging) and prestige (the glitter of the designer or organisation involved) as for the real reasons (does it actually do the job?). Designers and consultants flirt with fashionable concepts, while users are dissatisfied. As Steward Brand puts it: 'fashion is fun for (certain) architects, but it's deadly for users'.[16]

Still, criticising ambitious innovations that have failed in hindsight might all be a bit too easy. Radical and visionary ideas are necessary to rethink and question implicit assumptions that underlie often tedious mainstream office design. Moreover, it is evident that society is changing. New technologies are emerging, economic circumstances are changing and so are cultures. In line with our conclusion that office buildings reflect the context in which they are designed, these changes will have a large effect on office design. We should, however, remember not to take changes simply for granted. Contemporary office design should always take the 'human factor' into account. In the past it may have been possible to ignore user needs, but today the working population in the Western world is shrinking. Therefore, firms will have to work harder to attract young talented people into the labour market. This may require better payment and career opportunities, but also a more humane office environment. With this notion in mind we will reflect on the main trends in office design detected in this study.

Building

At the building level the main trend seems to be to keep on building higher and higher office towers. Driven by economic success, the moratorium on high-rise buildings seems to have come to an end in Europe. In Frankfurt there are plans for an extra fifteen high rises; in London plans have been presented for a 460 m high 'Eco Tower' and in Rotterdam developers have come up with a plan for a 350 m high tower.

This research has shown that it is uncertain whether these plans will actually be realised. The problem is the absence of a 'natural fit' between such buildings and the European context. Existing high-rise cities like Manhattan and Hong Kong were not created out of well-meaning attempts to compose an overall effect. Instead, they have been created by real and powerful market forces. In Europe such strong forces are either absent or have been overruled by the impact of the urban setting.

Yet one should also realise that building tall structures is an inherently human activity. People have always had the desire to show that they are different, more powerful or more prosperous than others. This desire may not be 'politically correct', but it is certainly persistent. Constructing great and impressive – though often deficient – buildings seems to be a need of all times and all people. Therefore, European buildings will grow taller and taller too, though not to the same extent as in the US or Asia.

A typically European feature of tall buildings might be their increasing 'greenness'. Foster's Commerzbank tower certainly set an example in building ecological skyscrapers. Double facades, with their climate-buffering interstitial layer of air, are slowly becoming commonplace in Northern Europe. And so are skygardens, green roofs and the use of recycled materials. It is typical, however, that most green buildings are owner-occupied. It is doubtful whether commercial office development will follow the same line – especially when economic circumstances are becoming less favourable.

Floor plan

Looking at the design of floor plans, the most striking trend today is to design medium-depth buildings (14-15 m). In Continental Europe, there is an increasing awareness of the relative inefficiency of narrow floor plans. Deep old warehouses have proved to accommodate new office concepts more easily than today's narrow buildings.[17] Therefore both users and developers are looking for new, medium-depth solutions.

In the UK too there is a growing trend to build medium-depth offices. In previous decades, depths of over 20 m were still regarded as normal. Artificial lighting and air-conditioning were believed to create a perfect climate. It has become clear, however, that human beings want to be in control of their own environment; they want to be able to open a window; they want an outside view; they prefer daylight to artificial light. The importance of having an office with a window is actually stressed in the traditional layout of deep-plan offices. Here top managers inhabit the perimeter offices which lend them part of their status within the company.

Workplace

At the workplace level we have seen three trends. The first is to build more open and transparent layouts. In the UK, completely open plans are increasingly popular among clients. In Continental Europe, new offices are combinations of open and enclosed spaces with many glazed partitions. Again, the success of these solutions depends largely on cultural and psychological factors.[18] We have seen that in the Netherlands, open solutions may present problems since the Dutch tend to think highly of their personal space. In Italy open plans may not work either because the Italian expressive manner of interaction may turn it into chaos. On the other hand, in the UK these layouts have been used for several years now and people have grown quite accustomed to them. At all events, there remains some sort of desire for privacy and personal territory. Workplaces should not only be efficient and flexible, they also have to fulfil a basic human need for identity and security. This has to be taken into account in any country.

The second trend is the emergence of the non-territorial office. Here an increasing number of employees share their workplaces because they spend little time behind their own desks. Intranets, mobile technology and electronic archives have made it possible to work at different locations in the office. The success of such a concept depends on the actual need for it: how much time do employees spend in the office and what is the financial gain of sharing offices? This gain will differ internationally. In Frankfurt, for example, the financial advantages of desk-sharing are considerably lower than in London because space is cheaper. But here too cultural issues play a crucial role. In Germany the firm awareness of the distinction between 'personal space' and 'communal space' can be a major obstacle when it comes to sharing. To some extent similar issues will arise in other countries as well because, just like many other animals, humans tend to mark and defend their spatial territory.

The third trend is the most radical; workplaces are becoming increasingly virtual. Teleworking is no longer a novelty, it has become a widespread phenomenon. Improvements in information technology enable employees to work anywhere and anytime they want (at least from a technical point of view). This development contrasts strongly with the tendency to build taller and thus larger office buildings. When more

175 Mobile phone of the near future

people switch to teleworking, offices can become smaller, functioning merely as meeting places for 'nomadic' employees. Judging from this perspective, the end of the corporate superblock seems imminent.

As with all modern office innovations, the apparent merits of teleworking should not be overestimated. Our research findings suggest that the acceptance of workplace innovations such as teleworking depends largely on psychological factors. This is particularly clear in the case of the Italians, as it magnifies the human problems office innovation inevitably brings. In a fairly hierarchical culture like the Italian one, managers are likely to feel rather powerless and lacking control when their employees are teleworking. Employees in their turn will develop feelings of social isolation because their normal social interaction cannot easily be replaced by e-mail or video conferencing.

In the future things may be change as today's 'Nintendo generation' will be more at ease with electronic interaction than their parents are now. Yet, people remain social animals. Just like monkeys, we are used to living in tight groups. Face-to-face interaction with others is part of our daily routine, and we need it. Therefore, the idea of the isolated teleworker, free from all pressures of the world, is a romantic but rather unrealistic one. Still, this does not mean that uniform and impersonal office blocks are our only alternative.

The general message of these final reflections is that apart from international differences there are also a number of common human needs, such as the need for daylight, an outside view, interaction, privacy and territory. At first sight these factors may appear 'soft' in the sense that they are intangible or even irrational. But the impact of these soft factors is hard. Human nature can throw a spanner into the best-laid office designs. To avoid that, designers and consultants should take these issues into account. To create an office concept that will last, they should not focus one-sidedly on changes and trends, but also on those human needs that remain constant.

Technology and organisational theories may change, but human nature will not.

Notes

1 Rapoport, A. (1969), *House Form and Culture*, Prentice-Hall, London
2 Ang, K.I. and D.P. Wyatt (1998), *The role of performance specifications in the design agenda*, Paper for CIB W96 Design Agenda Conference, 18-19 September, Brighton
3 Krumm, P.J.M.M. (1999), *Corporate Real Estate Management in Multinational Corporations*, Arko, Nieuwegein
4 Hoogdalem, H. van (1984), 'Organization and buildings – some contributions from architectural psychology', in: Drenth, P.J.D., Thierry, H., Willems, P.J. and Wolff, C.J. (eds.), *Handbook of Work and Organizational Psychology*, John Wiley & Sons, New York
5 European Foundation for the Improvement of Living and Working Conditions (1996) *Second European Survey on Working Conditions,* Dublin
6 Vos, P. and Dewulf, G.P.M.R. (1999), *Searching for data: a method to evaluate the effects of working in an innovative office*, Delft University of Technology, Department of Real Estate and Project Management, Delft
7 Wijk, M. and Spekkink, D. (1998), *Bouwstenen voor het PvE*, Stichting Bouwresearch, Rotterdam
8 Schneider, S.C. and Barsoux, J. (1997), *Managing Across Cultures*, Prentice Hall, Hertfordshire
9 Raymond, S. and Cunliffe, R. (1997) *Tomorrow's Office: Creating effective and humane interiors*, E & FN Spon, London
10 Vos, P. G. J. C., Meel, J. J. van and Dijcks, A. (1999), *The Office, the whole office and nothing but the office version 1.2*, Delft University of Technology, Department of Real Estate and Project Management, Delft
11 Raymond, S. and Cunliffe, R. (1997) *Tomorrow's Office: Creating effective and humane interiors*, E & FN Spon, London
12 Becker, F. and Steele, F. (1994), *Workplace by design: mapping the high-performance workscape*, Jossey-Bass Publishers, San Francisco
13 Duffy, F. (1997), *The New Office*, Conran Octopus, London
14 Berger, W. (1999), 'Lost in Space', in: *Wired*, No. 7.02, http://www.wired.com/wired/archive/7.02/
15 Meel, J. J. van (1999), 'You probably know the slides off by heart!', *Usable Buildings*, http://www.usablebuildings.co.uk/Opinion.html
16 Brand, S. (1994), *How buildings learn: what happens after they're built*, Phoenix Illustrated, London
17 De Jonge, H. (1999), *Real Estate in the Corporate Setting*, Course in Successful Corporate Real Estate Strategies, April 20-24, Delft University of Technology, Delft
18 ibid.

BIBLIOGRAPHY

AiT (1998), 'Nonterritoriale Bürowelt',
http://www.quickborner-
team.de/english/newspresse/index.htm

AiT (1999), 'Auf sendung', http://www.quickborner-
team.de/english/newspresse/index.htm

Altman, I. and Chemers, M. (1980), *Culture and
environment*, Brooks/Cole, Monterey

Amsberg, K., Gaag, P. van der, Koolhaas, M., Leenders,
G., Nauta, A. and Slager, K. (1998), 'Foute gebouwen 2',
in: NRC *Handelsblad*, September 15

Andersen, S.E. (1997), 'Design responses: office buildings
in Denmark', in: Worthington, J. (ed.), *Reinventing the
Workplace*, Architectural Press, Oxford

Andersson, H.O. and Bedoire, F. (1988), *Stockholm:
architecture and townscape*, Prisma, Stockholm

Ang, K.I. and D.P. Wyatt (1998), *The role of performance
specifications in the design agenda*, Paper for CIB W96
Design Agenda Conference, September 18-19, Brighton

Antwerpen, J. van, and Hermans, W. (1998),
*Huisvestingsvoorkeuren van kantoren: over wens en
werkelijkheid*, INBO, Woudenberg

Apgar IV, M. (1998), 'The Alternative Workplace:
Changing Where and How People Work', in: *Harvard
Business Review*, May-June, pp. 121-136.

Arch+ (1997), Your Office is Where You Are, *Arch +*,
No. 136

Architects's journal (1991), 'Getting High', in: *Architects'
journal*, Vol. 194, No. 17, p. 10

Arkitektur (1990), 'No to multi-storey buildings', in:
Arkitektur, No. 4, p. 2

Atkinson, T. (1994), 'Mercedes immerses executives in
"Bama drawl" ', in: *International Herald Tribute*,
No.1, p. 4

Axelsson, R., Cray, D., Mallory, G.R. and Wilson, D.C.
(1991), 'Decision style in British and Swedish
organisations: a comparative examination of strategic
decision-making', in: *British Journal of Management*,
No. 2, pp. 67-79

Bailey, S. (1990), *Offices: a briefing and design guide*,
Butterworth Architecture, Oxford

Bak, L. (1980), *Kantoorprofiel; struktuur en ontwikkeling van
de kantorensektor*, Van Loghum Slaterus, Deventer

Baldry, C. (1997), 'The social construction of office space',
in: *International Labour Review*, Vol. 136, No. 3,
pp. 365-378

Balfour, A. (1995), *World Cities Berlin*, Academy Editions,
London

Banham, R. (1969), *The Architecture of the Well-Tempered
Environment*, Architectural Press, London

Bar-hillel, M. (1999), 'City anger at bid to protect London
sights', in: *This is London*, May 10,
http://www.thisislondon.com

Barlow, J. (1995), *Public Participation in Urban
Development: The European Experience*, Brookings
Institute, Washington D.C.

Becker, F. (1990), *The total workplace; facilities management
and the elastic organization*, Van Nostrand Reinhold,
New York

Becker, F. and Steele, F. (1994), *Workplace by design:
mapping the high-performance workscape*, Jossey-Bass
Publishers, San Francisco

Bedford, M. and Tong, D. (1997), 'Planning for diversity:
new structures that reflect the past', in: Worthington, J.
(ed.), *Re-inventing the Workplace*, Architectural Press,
Oxford

Bedoire, F. (1979), 'Open plan offices, landscape offices and
celltype office', in: *Arkitektur*, No. 1, pp. 16-26

Bennett, P.H. (1958), 'Offices for rent', in: *Architectural
Design*, Vol. 28, No. 7, pp. 256-258

Bennetts, R.(1995), 'Building study: The choice of a new
generation: Architect's account', in: *Architects' journal*,
March 2, pp. 44-48

Berger, W. (1999), 'Lost in Space', in: *Wired*, No. 7.02,
http://www.wired.com/wired/archive/7.02/

Blakstad, S.H. (1997), *The Scandinavian Office Building
1900-1980*, Norwegian University of Science and
Technology, Department of Architectural History,
Trondheim

Blenner, H. and Mannervik, S.C. (1967), 'How information
was organized', in: *Arkitektur*, No. 12, pp. 696-699

Blyth, A. (1993), 'Working in the Netherlands', in:
Architects' journal, September 1, pp. 26-27

Board of Workers' Safety (1995), *Arbetarskyddstyrelsens
Författningssamling*, Stockholm

Boer, J.R.; Diehl, P.J. and Koenders, H. (1996) *Arbo-
normenboek*, Samsom Bedrijfsinformatie, Alphen a/d Rijn

Bor, W. (1995), 'A meeting of minds', in: *Architects' journal*,
March 2, pp. 60-61

Brand, S. (1994), *How buildings learn: what happens after
they're built*, Phoenix illustrated, London

Brandolini, S. (1997), 'Building blocks', in: *World
Architecture*, No. 54, pp. 67-71

Branzi, A. (1984), *The Hot House; Italian New Wave
Design*, MIT Press, Cambridge

Brierley, W. (1990), 'The business culture in Italy', in:
Randlesome, C. (ed.), *Business cultures in Europe*,
Heinemann, Oxford

British Council for Offices (1997), *Best Practice in the
Specification of Offices*, British Council for Offices

Burland, J. (1997), 'Building study: Stockley Park updated:
Architect's account', in: *Architects' journal*, March 20,
pp. 30-31.

Bussel, A. (1992), '(In)visible Giant', in: *Progressive
Architecture*, No. 3, pp. 96-100

Cairns, S. (1996), *The North American Influence on the
London Docklands*,
http://www.macalstr.edu/~geograph/world-
urbanization/scairns/noam.html

Caldenby, C. (1990), 'Arguments and paradoxes', in: *Arkitektur*, No. 4, pp 3-11

Caldenby, C. and Waern, R. (1996), 'Looking back it has nevertheless been a good thing on the occasions when we said no', in: *Arkitektur*, No. 5, pp. 4-37

Caleca, S. (1997), 'Progetto new pop', in: *Interni*, No. 468, pp 94-99

Carp (1999), 'Carp International: Marc Straat, business development manager bij ICO Global Communication in London', in: *Carp*, No. 12, pp. 7

Casciani, S. and Roj, M. (1997), 'L'edificio Pensante', in: *Habitat Ufficio*, No. 87, pp. 64-68

Casciani, S.(1997), 'Return to the Planet of the Apes: Jottings from Michigan on office space and differences between Europe and America', in: *Abitare*, http://www.abitare.it/366/366-nautilus.html

Castells, M. (1994) 'European Cities, the information society, and the global economy', in: *New Left Review*, No. 204, pp. 18-32

Cavini, A. (1999), *Italian offices*, Internal report

CB Richard Ellis (1999), *Global Market Rents*, http://www.cbcommercial.com/corp/markets.htm

Çelik, Z. (1998), 'Cultural intersections: re-visioning architecture and the city in the twentieth century', in: Koshalek, R., Smith, E.A.T. and Ferguson, R. (eds.), *At the end of the century: one hundred years of architecture*, Abrams, New York

Center for Building Performance & Diagnostics (1995), *Flexible grid –flexible density – flexible closure officing: the intelligent workplace*, Carnegie Mellon University, Pittsburg

Charkham, J.P. (1995), *Keeping good company; a study of corporate governance in five countries*, Clarendon, Oxford

Charles, Prince of Wales (1989), *A vision of Britain; a personal view of architecture*, Doubleday, London

Checkland, P. (1981), *Systems thinking, Systems Practice*, Wiley, Chichester

Cifferi, M. (1990), *Managerial attitudes, values and perceptions: an Anglo-Italian study*, unpublished research paper

Citterio, http://www.citteriofx.it/italiano/SededellaRegioneLombardia.htm

Coleman, C. (1997), 'Going Global', in: *Perspective*, Winter, http://www.iida.com/communications/publications/perspective/winter97/GoingGlobal/index.htm

Collinge, J. (1991), 'European outlook Italy and Greece', in: *Architects' journal*, September 4, pp. 49-53

Congena (1994), *Zukunftsstrategie Kombi-Büro*, Callway/FBO, Munich

Cowan, P. (1969), *The office: a facet of urban growth*, Heineman, London

Crouzier, M. (1965), *The world of the office worker*, The University of Chicago Press, Chicago

D'Arcy, E. and Keogh, G. (1998), 'Territorial Competition and Property Market Process: An Exploratory Analysis', in: *Urban Studies*, Vol. 35, No. 8, pp. 1215-30

Daft, R.L. (1983), 'Learning the Craft of Organisational Research', in: *Academy of Management Review*, Vol. 8, No. 4, pp. 539-546

Davey, P. (1999), 'Critique: Could Piano's Debis Tower in Berlin have been built in the US? The answer reveals the flaws affecting American architecture', in: *The Architectural Record*, No. 4, pp. 35-36

Davies, C. (1992), 'Critique: On the Waterfront', in: *Progressive Architecture*, No. 4, pp.122-124

Davies, C. and Lambot, I. (1997), *Commerzbank Frankfurt, Prototype for an Ecological High-Rise*, Watermark/Birkhäuser, Surrey

Davies, N. (1996), *Europe: a history*, Oxford University Press, London

Dawson, L. (1991), 'Hamburg Headquarters', in: *Architects' journal*, June, pp.34-39

Dawson, L. (1997), 'Architecture for the people', in: *World Architecture*, No. 60, pp. 85

De Wit, O. and Ende, J. van den (1998), 'Het gemechaniseerde kantoor 1914-1940', in: Lintsen, H.W., Rip, A., Schot, J.W. and Albert de la Bruhèze, A.A. (eds.), *Techniek in Nederland in de twintigste eeuw*, Walburg Pers, Zutphen

DEGW (1998), High Rise Rotterdam: *A Strategy for Intensification and Innovation*, DEGW, London

Dewulf, G.P.M.R. and De Jonge, H. (1994), *Toekomst van de kantorenmarkt 1994-2015*, Delft University of Technology, Delft

Dewulf, G.P.M.R. and Vos, P.G.J.C. (1998), 'De (on)mogelijkheden van kantoorinnovatie', in: *Management en Organisatie*, Vol. 52, No. 1, pp. 7-28

Dichmann, D. W. (1984), *Ein freundliche Welt für jedes Büro, Handbuch Moderne Burogestaltung*, Verlag Moderne Bürogestaltung, Detmold

Dijk, N. van and Punch, M. (1993), 'Open Borders, Closed Circles: Management and Organization in The Netherlands', in: Hickson, D.J. (ed.), *Management in Western Europe: society, culture and organisation in twelve nations*, Walter de Gruyter, New York

Doxtater, D. (1994), *Architecture, Ritual Practice and Co-determination in the Swedish Office*, Ashgate Publishing, Aldershot

Driemeyer, T. (1998), *Working in the USA: Experiences of a European*, http://www.bitrot.de/workinusa.html

Drucker, P.F. (1991), 'The New Productivity Challenge', in: *Harvard Business Review*, Vol. 69, No. 6, pp. 109-118

Drucker, P.F. (1992), 'The new society of organizations', in: *Harvard Business Review*, September/October, pp. 95-104

DTZ Zadelhoff (1995), Flächen pro Arbeitsplatz, *internal report DTZ Zadelhoff*, Frankfurt

DTZ Zadelhoff (1996), *European Commercial Property Markets Overview 1996*, DTZ Zadelhoff

Duffy, F. (1980), 'Office buildings and organisational change', in: King, A.D. (ed.), *Buildings and Society*, Routledge, London

Duffy, F. (1983), 'Taming the beast from the wild', in: *Computer Weekly*, January 19, pp. 18-20

Duffy, F. (1990), 'Aker Brygge development', in: *Architects' journal*, Vol. 88, No. 8, pp. 56-63

Duffy, F. (1992) *The Changing Workplace*, Phaidon Press, London

Duffy, F. (1997), *The New Office*, Conran Octopus, London

Duffy, F. and Cave, C. (1976), 'Bürolandschaft: an appraisal', in: Duffy, F., Cave, C. and Worthington, J. (eds.), *Planning office space*, The Architectural Press, London

Duffy, F., Laign, A. and Crisp, V. (1993), *The Responsible Workplace: the redesign of work & offices*, Butterworth Architecture, Oxford

Eciffo (1995), 'Re-officing', in: *Eciffo*, Vol. 27, Autumn Issue, pp. 10-36

Econy (1998), 'Büros in bewegung', in: *Econy*, January, http://www.quickborner-team.de/english/newspresse/index.htm

Eisenhardt, K.M. (1989), 'Building Theories from Case Study Research', in: *Academy of Management Review*, No 14, pp. 532-550

Eley, J. and Marmot, A. (1995), *Understanding offices*, Penguin, London

Ellen, R.F. (1984), *A Guide to the general conduct of ethnographic research*, Academic Press, London

Empel, F. van (1997), *The Dutch Model: the power of consultation*, http://www.ser.nl/engels/adviezen/dutchmo.html

Etzler, B. (1996), 'University Buildings and Research Parks, A Study of their Origins, Design, and Use', in: *Nordic Journal of Architectural Research*, Vol. 9, No. 4, pp. 97-107

European commission (1999), *Status Report on European Telework 1998*, http://www.eto.org.uk/twork/tw98/index.htm

European Foundation for the improvement of Living and Working Conditions (1996), *Second European Survey on Working Conditions*, Dublin

Europroperty (1998), 'Overseas investors push for market transparency', in: *Europroperty*, www.europrop.com/epi_view.asp?art=1776

Europroperty (1995), Cross-Border Business, *Europroperty*, special issue

Europroperty (1997), 'Milan picks itself up off the bottom', in: *Europroperty*, www.europrop.com/epi_view.asp?art=628

Europroperty (1998), Italy, in: *Europroperty*, www.europrop.com/epi_view.asp?art=621

Europroperty (1998), Milan offices, in: *Europroperty*, www.europrop.com/epi_view.asp?art=1587

Evette, T., Bonnet, C., Fencker, M., Michel, P. and Philipon, B. (1992), *L'architecture tertiaire en Europe et aux Etats-Unis*, CSTB, Paris

Farrell, T. (1991), 'Response Farrell', in: *Architects' journal*, Vol. 193, May 22, pp. 38-39

Fenker, M. (1995), 'The influence of culture on the design and use of office space', in: *InterVIEWS*, No. 1, pp. 2-8

Ferner, A. and Hyman, R. (1999), *Changing Industrial Relations in Europe*, Blackwell, London

Foster, P. (1993), Towers of Depth: *Rise and Fall of the Reichmanns*, Hodder & Stoughton, London

Fukuyama, F. (1995), *Trust: the Social Virtues and Creation of Prosperity*, Hamish Hamilton, London

Gabetti, R. and Isola, A. (1990), 'The Quinto Palazzo Uffici Snam in San Donato Milanese', in: *Zodiac*, No. 3, pp. 100-115

Gagliardi, P. and Turner, B.A. (1993), 'Aspects of Italian Management', in: Hickson, David J. (ed.), *Management in Western Europe: Society, Culture and Organization in Twelve Nations*, Walter de Gruyter & Co., Berlin.

Gascoine, C. (1996), 'The office lines are open at Stockley Park', in: *Architects' journal*, April 11, p. 38

Geertz, C. (1973), *The Interpretation of Cultures*, Basic Books, New York

Gelernter, M. (1995), *Sources of architectural form: a critical history of Western design theory*, Manchester University Press, Manchester

Gerometta, M. (1999), *Marshall Gerometta's Hot 500*, http://www.worldstallest.com/hot500.html

Gerritse, C. (1998), 'Inpandigheid', in: *Bouwadviseur*, January/February, pp. 16-19

Gerritse, C. (1998), 'Programma en stramienkeuze', in: *Bouwadviseur*, April, pp 14-16

Gier, H.G. de (1991), *Arbeidsomstandigheden in Europees perspectief, implementatie van EG-richtlijnen op het vlak van arbeidsomstandigheden en produktveiligheid*, Kluwer Deventer

Gijssel, R. van (1997), 'De open werkplek', in: *Intermediair*, http://www.intermediair.nl/Loopba...s/modern_werken/openwerkplek.html

Goldwaithe, R.A. (1980), *The building of Renaissance Florence*, John Hopkins University Press, Maryland

Gottschalk (1994), *Verwaltungsbauten, Flexibel, Kommunikatief, Nutzorientiert*, Bauverlag, Wiesbaden

Gottschalk, O. (1984), 'Zur Entwicklug des Verwaltungshaus', in: *Bauwelt*, No. 43, pp. 1836-1850

Gottschalk, O. (1992), *Use and appropriation in office buildings*, Proceedings of the international symposium Corporate space and Architecture, Lille, Lyon, Nantes, Paris, June 30 - July 3

Granath, J.A., Lindahl, G.A., and Rehal, S. (1996), *From Empowerment to Enablement, An evolution of new dimensions in participatory design*, paper, Chalmers University of Architecture, School of Architecture, Industrial Architecture and Planning

Grimston, J. (1999), 'City builds itself up to be second Manhattan', in: *Sunday Times of London*, April 18, http://www.sunday-times.co.uk

Gruner + Jahr (1994), *The Gruner + Jahr Media Building*, Gruner + Jahr, Hamburg

Gullström, C. and Westerberg, L. (1996), *Moving Spaces, Knowledge Exchange and Contemporary Work Life*, Gullström & Westerberg Arkitektkontor AB, Stockholm

Gustavsson, B. and Östman, Å. (1993), *Lokalanvändning i kontorverksamhet*, USK, Stockholm

Hakfoort, J. and Lie, R. (1996), 'Office Space per Work: Evidence from Four European Markets', in: *The Journal of Real Estate Research*, Vol. 11, No. 2, pp. 183-196

Hall, E.T. and Hall, M.R. (1990), *Understanding cultural differences: keys to success in West Germany, France and the United States*, Intercultural Press Inc., Yarmouth

Hampden-Turner C. and Trompenaars, F. (1993), *The seven cultures of capitalism*, Doubleday, New York

Hanscomb (1998), 'USA/Europe comparisons', in: *World Architecture*, No. 64, p. 82

Haugen, T.I. and Blakstad, S.H. (1995), *The Scandinavian approach to modern office buildings*, paper presented at the EUROFM/IFMA conference, Frankfurt, Germany

Healey and Baker (1998), Milan, in: *Europroperty*, www.europrop.com/epi_view.asp?art=1587

Health & Safety Executive (1992), *Approved Code of Practice and Guidance. Workplace health, safety and welfare*, London.

Hellman, L. (1988), 'Italy: deregulate by definition', *Architects' journal*, Vol. 187, No. 20, pp. 46-49

Henn, W. (1962), 'Large-size Office and the Architect', in: *Baumeister*, July, pp. 655-660

Hertzberger, H. (1988), 'Interview', in: *Architects' journal*, January 13, pp. 36-39

Hillier, B. (1996), *Space is the machine: a configurational theory of architecture*, University Press, New York

Hofstede, G. (1991), *Cultures and Organisations*, Software of the mind, McGraw-Hill, London

Hohl, R. (1968), *International Office Buildings*, Verlag Gerd Hatje, Stuttgart

Hoogdalem, H. van (1984), 'Organization and buildings- some contributions from architectural psychology', in: Drenth, P.J.D., Thierry, H., Willems, P.J. and Wolff, C.J. (eds.), *Handbook of Work and Organizational Psychology*, John Wiley & Sons, New York

Hopf, H.A. (1931), 'Physical factors', in: Donald, W.J. (ed.), *Handbook of Business Administration*, McGraw-Hill, New York

http://www.boomtown-frankfurt.com/wolkenkratzer/reportagen/skyline/bericht-03/e_index.shtml

http://www.commerzbank.com/navigate/zent_frm

http://www.fosterandpartners.com/projects/1991/80

http://www.serbelloni.it

Hultin, O. (1981), 1970-1979: 'Regrets and consideration', in: *Arkitektur*, No. 5, pp. 18-19

Hultin, O. (1985), 'Made in the USA', in: *Arkitektur*, No. 9, pp. 6-7

ING Bank (1999), press release

Interpolis (1997), *Je werkplek is waar je bent*, Interpolis Facilitair Bedrijf, Tilburg

Israel, F.J. (1992), *Kantoren in gebruik*, Stichting voor Beleggings- en Vastgoedkunde, Amsterdam

Jenkin, D. (1997), 'Emerging building forms', in: Worthington, J. (ed.), *Re-inventing the Workplace*, Architectural Press, Oxford

Jick, T. (1979), 'Mixing qualitative and quantitative methods: Triangulation in action', in: *Administrative Science Quarterly*, Vol. 24, December, pp. 602-611

Jockusch, P.R.A. (1992), *Recent German experience with changes of existing administrative organizations in the public sector*, Proceedings of the international symposium Corporate space and Architecture, Lille, Lyon, Nantes, Paris, June 30 - July 3, 1992

Jong, H.W. de (1996), 'Rijnlandse ondernemingen presteren beter', in: *Economisch Statistische Berichten*, Vol. 81, Nr. 4049, pp. 228-232

Jonge, H. de (1999), *Real Estate in the Corporate Setting*, Course Successful Corporate Real Estate Strategies, April 20-24, Delft University of Technology, Delft

Joroff, M.L., Louargand, M., Lambert, S. and Becker, F. (1993), *Strategic Management of the Fifth Resource: Corporate Real Estate*, Industrial Development Research Foundation, Atlanta

Kammerer, H. (1985), 'From Open Plan to Individual Offices', in: *Baumeister*, Vol. 82, No. 10, pp. 17-27

Kamphuis, H. (1992), 'Het cocon-kantoor, kantoorvorm van de toekomst?', in: *Facility Management Magazine*, Vol. 5, October, pp. 24-26

Kannenberg, S. (1997), 'The Alexander-platz of the future', in: *Berliner Morgenpost*, http://www.berliner-morgenpost.de/bm/international/

Krall, H. (1972), 'Offices: the issues related', in: *Built Environment*, Vol. 1, No. 7, pp. 468-469

Krier, L. (1984), 'Houses, Palaces, Cities', A.D. *Profile*, No. 54

Krinsky, C.H. (1988), *Gordon Bunshaft of Skidmore, Owings & Merill*, Architectural History Foundation, New York

Krumm, P.J.M.M. (1999), *Corporate Real Estate Management in Multinational Corporations*, Arko, Nieuwegein

Lake, A. (1996), 'Report on Telework in Sweden', in: *Telework international*, Vol. 4, No. 2, http://www.klr.com/NEWS4206.HTM

Lane, D. (1997), 'Italy: keep out', in: *World Architecture*, No. 54, pp. 45-51

Lapalainen, R. (1999), *Presentation at Studio Apertura*, Norway, March 16

Leaman, A. (1994), *Complexity and manageability: pointers from a decade of research on building occupancy*, paper, National Conference of the Facility Management Association of Australia, Sidney, 30 November - 2 December

Leaman, A. and Bordass, B. (1996), *Buildings in the Age of Paradox*, paper, Institute of Advanced Architectural Studies, University of York

Leaman, A. and Bordass, B. (1997), *Productivity in Buildings: the "killer" variables*, paper presented to the Workplace Comfort Forum, Central Hall, Westminster, London 29-30 October

Lee, A.S. (1991), 'Integrating positivist and interpretative approaches to organizational research', in: *Organizational Science*, Vol. 2, No. 4, pp. 342-365

Leffingwell, W.H. (1925), *Office Management: Principals and Practice*, A.W. Shaw, Chicago

Leijendekker, M. (1996), *De Italiaanse Revolutie*, Meulenhoff, Amsterdam

Lewin, K. (1936), *Principles of Topological Psychology*, McGraw-Hill, New York

Lindahl, G.A. (1996), *Collective Design Processes as a Facilitator for Collaboration and Learning*, paper for the Fourth Conference on Learning and Research in Working Life, April 1-4, Steyr, Austria

Lockwood, D. (1958), *The Blackcoated Worker*, Allen and Unwin, London

London County Council (1956), *High Buildings in London*, 28 Town Planning Report, No. 2

London Planning Advisory Committee (1998), *High Buildings and Strategic Views: A Guide to Draft Strategic Planning Advice*, http://lpac.gov.uk/hbguide

Maas, T. (1991), 'Ministerie SZW: Meesterlijke spanning tussen delen en geheel', in: *Architectuur/ Bouwen*, 1991-1, pp. 26-28

MacCormac, R. (1992), 'The dignity of office', in: *The Architectural Review*, No. 5, pp. 76-82

MacInnes, K. (1998), 'The challenge of globalisation', in: *World Architecture*, No. 62, pp. 92-93

Mangano (1994), 'The new symbols of the office habitat', in: *Habitat Ufficio*, No. 77, pp.65-67

Mangano, L. (1996), 'Re-inventing the workplace to design the future', in: *Habitat Ufficio*, No. 83, pp. 53-59

Matti, L. (1997), 'Come riorganizzare e ottimizzarre gli spaziod'ufficio', in: *Office Layout*, No. 74, pp. 86-92

Max Planck Institute for the study of societies (1998), *The development of co-determination as an institution*, http://www.mpi-fg-koeln.mpg.de/bericht/endbericht/

Mayo, E. (1933), *The Human Problems of an Industrial Civilization*, MacMillan, New York

McGregor, D. (1960), *The Human Side of the Enterprise*, McGraw-Hill, New York

Meel, J.J. (1998), *Case study of a Dutch Bank*, Internal report, Delft University of Technology, Department of Real Estate and Project Management, Delft

Meel, J.J. (1998), *Businesses globalise, buildings don't*, Internal report, Delft University of Technology, Department of Real Estate and Project Management, Delft

Meel, J.J. van (1999), 'You probably know the slides off by heart!', *Usable Buildings*, http://www.usablebuildings.co.uk/Opinion.html

Meel, J.J. van, Jonge, H. de, and Dewulf, G.P.M.R. (1997), Workplace design: global or tribal?, in: Worthington (ed.), *Reinventing the Workplace*, Architectural Press, Oxford

Meel, J.J. van (1998), *Case study Lloyd's TSB Bank Bristol*, Internal report, Delft University of Technology, Department of Real Estate and Project Management, Delft

Meel, J.J. van, Blakstad, S., Dewulf, G. and Duffy, F. (1997), *Power-relations in office design*, Internal report, Delft University of Technology, Department of Real Estate and Project Management, Delft

Meel, J.W. van (1994), *The Dynamics of Business Engineering: Reflections on two case studies within the Amsterdam Municipal Police Force*, Van Meel, Dordrecht

Melvin, J. (1996), "I want one like that", in: *World Architecture*, No. 52, pp. 62-67

Miles, M. (1979), 'Qualitative data as an attractive nuisance: The problem of analysis', in: *Administrative Science Quarterly*, Vol. 24, December, pp. 590-601

Miles, M.B. and Huberman, A.M. (1994), *Qualitative data analysis*, Sage publications, London

Mills, C.W. (1958), *White Collar; the American middle classes*, Oxford University Press, New York

Ministry of Social Affairs and Labour (1998), *Arbo-Informatieblad 'Kantoren'*, Sdu Publishers, The Hague

Mintzberg, H. (1979), 'An emerging strategy of 'direct' research', in: *Administrative Science Quarterly*, Vol. 24, December, pp. 582-589

Moore, R. (1996), 'Record-breaking tower "would lift City" ', in: *Electronic Telegraph*, September 10, http://www.telegraph.co.uk

Moore, R. (1998), 'High and low really can line together', in: *This is London*, April 7, http://www.thisislondon.com

Moore, R. (1998), 'The future office has landed', in: *This is London*, July 21, http://www.thisislondon.com

Moran, R.T. (1992), *Cultural Guide to Doing Business in Europe*, Butterworth-Heinemann, Oxford

MVRDV (1999), http://www.archined.nl/mvrdv/vpro/index.html

Nacamulli, R.C.D. (1993), 'Italy', in: Rothman, M. (ed.), *Industrial relations around the world: labor relations for multinational companies*, Walter de Gruyter, Berlin

Naisbett, J. (1984), *Megatrends*, Warner, New York

Nathanson, N. and Andersen, A. (1993), *Real Estate Financing in Europe*, Arthur Andersen

Newman, P. and Thornley, A. (1996), *Urban planning in Europe: International Competition, National Systems and Planning Projects*, Routledge, London

North, R. (1999), 'Flights of future fancy?', in: *Electronic Telegraph*, October 22, http://www.telegraph.co.uk

NRC Handelsblad (1997), 'Profiel Kantoren', in: NRC *Handelsblad*, 24 April, p. 33

Piano, R. (1998), http://www.renzopiano.it/frame_works

Pile, J. (1978), *Open office planning*, The Architectural Press, London

Pile, J.F. (1976), *Interiors 3rd book of offices*, Whitney Library of Design, New York

Polisano, L. (1995), 'Complexity and Contrast; American and European High-Rise Buildings', in: *Architectural Design*, Vol. 65, No. 7/8, pp. 30-35

Pollard, I. (1993), 'Academy international forum: learning from London', in: Powell, K. (ed.), *World Cities: London*, Academy Editions, London

Porter, M. (1990), *Competitive Advantage of Nations*, Macmillan, Basingstoke

Powell, K. (1993), *World Cities: London*, Academy Editions, London

Premoli, D. (1997), 'Flessibili e creativi', in: OFX *Office International*, No. 35, p. 44

Quinan, J. (1987), *Frank Lloyd Wright's Larkin building; myth and fact*, MIT Press, Cambridge

Rapoport, A. (1969), *House Form and Culture*, Prentice-Hall, London

Rapoport, A. (1980), 'Vernacular architecture and the cultural determinants of form', in: King, A.D. (ed.) (1980), *Architecture and society*, Routledge & Kegan Paul Ltd, London

Raymond, S. and Cunliffe, R. (1997), *Tomorrow's Office: Creating effective and humane interiors*, E & FN Spon, London

Regeringskansliet (1998), *The Swedish Government Commission on Telework – Summary*, Stockholm

Regterschot, J. (1995), 'It is finally going to happen', in: *New European Offices*, Twijnstra Gudde

Richard Ellis St Quintin (1998), News, http://www.richardellis.co.uk/news

Rijksgebouwendienst (1997), *Dynamischkantoor Haarlem*, 010 Publishers, Rotterdam

Roberts, B.C. (1985), *Industrial Relations in Europe: The Imperatives of Change*, Croom Helm, London

Rodermond, J. (1996), 'Globalisering initieert ook pluraliteit', in: *De Architect*, No. 9, pp. 44-45

Roj, M. (1998), 'The project as value added to the production process', in: *Ufficiostile*, No. 1, p. 72

Roj, M. and Rivera, A. (1998), 'Involucri ambientali', in: *Habitat Ufficio*, No. 88, pp. 66-69

Ronen, S. and Shenkar, O. (1985), 'Clustering Countries on Attitudinal Dimensions: A review and Synthesis', in: *Academy of Management Review*, Vol. 10, No. 3, pp. 435-454

Rossi, A. (1987), 'Nuovo edificio per uffici <<Casa Aurora>> Torino', in: *Domus*, No. 684, pp. 38-49

Rossum, V. van, (1990), 'Milestone in office architecture', in: Rutten, J. (ed.), VROM *Ministry*, 010 Publishers, Rotterdam

Rutten, J. (1990), 'A single face for a single organisation', in: Rutten, J. (ed.), VROM *Ministry*, 010 Publishers, Rotterdam

Sassen, S. (1991), *The Global City: New York, London, Tokyo*, Princeton University Press, New York

Saxon, R. (1994), *The atrium comes of age*, Longman, Harlow

Scandinavian Airline Systems, *Togetherness*, SAS Frösundavik

Schneider S.C. and Barsoux, J. (1997), *Managing Across Cultures*, Prentice Hall, Hertfordshire.

Schnelle, E. (1963), Preface, in: Gottschalk (1963), *Flexibele Verwaltungsbauten: Entwürfe, Ausbau, Einrichtung, Kosten, Beispiele*, Verlag Schnelle, Quickborn

Searing, J.E. and Goldstein, J.C. (1992), '10 Myths and realities American real estate managers need to know', in: *National Real Estate Investor*, Vol. 34, No. 2, pp. 17-21

Segelken, S. (1994), 'Vorschriften für den Bürobetrieb', in: Gottschalk, O. (ed.) *Verwaltungsbauten, Flexibel, Kommunikatief, Nutzorientiert*, Bauverlag, Wiesbaden

Sias, R. (1998), 'Space planning: History and news', in: *Ufficiostile*, Special issue, pp. 14-19

Siegel, C. (1962), 'What does a large-size office cost?', in: *Baumeister*, July, pp. 667-672

Simon, R. D. (1996), 'Skyscrapers and the new London Skyline: 1945-1991', in: *Architronic*, Vol. 5, No. 2, http://www.saed.kent.edu/Architronic/v5n2.06html

Sims, W., Joroff, M. and Becker, F. (1996), *Managing the Re-invented Workplace*, International Development Research Foundation, Atlanta

Singmaster, D.(1996), 'Peopling the Ark', in: *Architects' journal*, Vol. 204, October 31, pp. 47-51

Skolglund, P. (1992), *Lokalyta per anställd nya kontorslokaler*, USK, Stockholm

Slavid, R. (1998), 'Opel HQ in Russelheim, Germany, by BDP', in: *Architects' journal*, August 13, No. 6, pp. 32-28

Sommar, I. (1995), 'The Lean Office', in: *Arkitektur*, No. 1, pp 28-35

Staal, G. (1987), *Between Dictate and Design: the architecture of office buildings*, 010 Publishers, Rotterdam

Steward, T.A. (1998), *Intellectual Capital*, Nicholas Brealey Publishing, London

Stimpel, R. (1997), 'Country Focus: Germany', in: *World Architecture*, No. 60, pp. 53-58

Sullivan, L. (1896), 'The Tall Building Artistically Considered', in: *Lippincott's*, March, pp. 403-409

Sundstrom, E. (1986), *Workplaces*, Cambridge University Press, New York

Swedish Institute (1999), http://www.si.se/eng/esverige/esverige.html

Tayeb, M. (1993), 'English Culture and Business Organizations', in: Hickson, D.J. (ed.), *Management in Western Europe: Society, Culture and Organization in Twelve Nations*, Walter de Gruyter, New York

Taylor, F. (1975), *Scientific Management*, Greenwood Press, Westport, Conn. (originally published by Harper Row, New York, 1911)

The Economist (1996), 'Divided still, A survey of Germany', in: *The Economist*, November 9, http://www.economist.co.uk

The Economist (1996), 'Unhappy families', in: *The Economist*, February 10, http://www.economist.co.uk

The Economist (1999), 'The sick man of the euro', in: *The Economist*, June 5, http://www.economist.co.uk

Toffler, A. (1981), *The Third Wave*, Pan Books, London

Trompenaars, F. (1983), *Zakendoen over de grens: leren omgaan met andere culturen*, Uitgeverij Contact, Amsterdam

Trompenaars, F. (1993), *Riding the Waves of Culture*, London, Nicholas Brealey Publishing Limited, 1993

Troost, K. (1998), *(Werkplek)Kosten van kantoorinnovatie*, Stichting voor Beleggings- en Vastgoedkunde, Amsterdam

Twijnstra Gudde (1999), *Het nationale kantorenmarkt-onderzoek 1999- het periodieke onderzoek naar de huisvestingssituatie van kantoorgebruikers in Nederland*, Twijnstra Gudde, Amesfoort

Vastgoedmarkt, Italië, *Vastgoedmarkt*, Augustus 1998, No. 47

Vaughan Bowden, V. (1998), 'Country Focus - The Netherlands', in: *World Architecture*, No. 69, pp. 61-69

Veldhoen, E. (1995), 'Beproefde kantoorconcepten bestaan niet meer: het coconkantoor; een Scandinavische fictie of een onomkeerbare ontwikkeling', in: *Facility Management Magazine*, Vol. 8, No. 46, pp. 27-29

Veldhoen, E. and Piepers, B. (1995), *The demise of the office*, Uitgeverij 010 Publishers, Rotterdam

Vidari, P.P. (1990), 'La citta dell'ufficio', in: *l'Arca*, No. 39, pp. 48-55

Visser-de Boer, M. (1996), 'Goede communicatie en efficiëntie in combikantoor', in: *Facility Management Magazine*, Vol. 9, No. 47, pp. 8-13

Vitta, M. (1992), 'Quinto: natura e architettura', in *l'Arca*, No. 16, pp. 16-27

Vollebregt, J. (1998), 'Huisvesting als kapstok voor integraal verandermanagement', in: *Facility Management Magazine*, Vol. 11, No. 61, pp. 26-29

Vos, A. (1992), 'Het papier van de plannen en het steen van de stad. Veertig jaar architectonische cultuur', in: Boschloo, A. (ed.), *Italië & Italië*, Meulenhoff, Amsterdam

Vos, P. and Dewulf, G.P.M.R. (1999), *Searching for data: a method to evaluate the effects of working in an innovative office*, Delft University of Technology, Department of Real Estate and Project Management. Delft

Vos, P.G.J.C.; Meel, J.J. van and Dijcks, A. (1999), *The Office, the whole office and nothing but the office version 1.2*, Delft University of Technology, Department of Real Estate and Project Management, Delft

Vries, A.M.E. de, en P.P. Kohnstamm (1991), *Kansen en knelpunten voor de ontwikkeling van commicieel onroerend goed in dertien stedelijke knooppunten*, Stichting voor Beleggings- en Vastgoedkunde, Amsterdam

Vroon, P. (1995), 'Gebouw', in: NRC *Handelsblad*, October 7, 1995

Wagener, W. (1997) 'Officing: The Office in the Age of Information', in: *Arch+*, No. 136, pp. 90-92

Wagenberg, A. van (1998), 'Interview', in: *Quintessence*, Vol. 6, No. 5, pp. 14-17

Wallace, C.P. (1997), 'Good looks Italian design carves a niche in the global market and creates an industry that sells as face value', *Time International*, April 21, pp. 42-45

Warner, M. and Campbell, A. (1993), 'German management', in: Hickson, D. (ed.), *Management in Western Europe, Society, Culture, and Organization in Twelve Nations*, De Gruyter, New York

Wijk, M. and Spekkink, D. (1998), *Bouwstenen voor het PvE*, Stichting Bouwresearch, Rotterdam

Willis, C. (1995), *Form follows finance*, Princeton Architectural Press, New York

Wineman, J.D. (1982), 'Office Design and Evaluation: An Overview', in: *Environment and Behavior*, Vol. 14, No. 3, pp. 271-299

Wislocki, P. (1998), 'New buildings in The Netherlands: Power and ambition', in: *World Architecture*, No. 69, pp. 72-77

Wislocki, P. (1998), 'Old-fashioned boy', in: *World Architecture*, No. 64, pp. 86-87

Wolleb, E. (1988), 'Belated Industrialisation: The Case of Italy', in: Boyer, R. (ed.), *The Search for Labour Market Flexibility*, Clarendon Press, Oxford

World Architecture (1995), 'Country Report Germany', in: *World Architecture*, No. 54, pp. 89-111

World Architecture (1995), 'KPF International', in: *World Architecture*, No. 34, pp. 26-65

World Architecture (1999), 'Jahn tower offends, Bonn residents' wishes ignored', in: *World Architecture*, No. 75, p. 22

Worsley, G. (1998), 'A perfect place for work?', in: *Electronic Telegraph*, August 15, http://www.telegraph.co.uk

Yin, R.K. (1989), *Case study research: design and methods*, Sage publications, London

ZH 1/168 *Sicherheitsregeln für Bildschirmarbeitsplätze im Bürobereich* 10.80

Zwaap, R. (1997), 'Villa Hommeles', in: *De Groene Amsterdammer*, http://www.groene.nl/1997/36/rz_vpro.html

United Kingdom

M. Bott	Citibank Realty Services
J. Burland	Arup Associates
F. Duffy	DEGW
P.J. Leadbeatter	Foster and Partners
A. Leaman	Building Use Studies
Prof. T.A. Markus	University of Strathclyde
H.D.C. Stebbing	Lloyds TSB Group

Germany

Prof. O. Gottschalk	Hochschule der Künste Berlin
R. Horn	University of Westminster
H. K. Kuhn	DTZ Zadelhoff GmbH
C. Kohlert	Henn Arkitekten Ingenieure
A. Schlote	Quickborner Team

Sweden

G. Årberg	Catella
Prof. F. Bedoire	Kungliga Konsthögskolan
T. Gromer	Catella
R. Granström	Johnson Controls
C. Gullström-Hughes	Gullström & Westerberg Arkitektkontor
S. Holgersson	National Premises Authority
B. Jonsson	National Premises Authority
S. af Klinteberg	DTZ Swede Property
M. Låtth	Catella
A. Öhrn	Canon Svenska
Prof. E. Persson	Catella
I. Sand	STM Consumer Electronics
P.V. Verboog	Skanska Sverige

Italy

A. Andrean	TNT Traco
C. Caruso	PCMR
C. T. Castelli	Castelli Design Milano
A. Cavini	Casanova R&S
Prof. P. Gagliardi	ISTUD
S. Gelonese	FAAR Institute
L.V. Mangano	DEGW Italia
M. Morganitini	ICS Design/FAAR Institute
G. Origlia	Studio Ideo
A. Vallenzasca	Acropoli

Netherlands

K.I. Ang	Dutch Government Buildings Agency
G.P.M.R. Dewulf	Delft University of Technology
Prof. H. de Jonge	Delft University of Technology
A. Rietveld	ABN AMRO Bank
A.A. van de Velde	ABN AMRO Bank
H.J. Verbij	Architectenbureau Van den Broek en Bakema
P.G.J.C. Vos	Adviesgroep voor Kantoorinnovatie

INDEX

SUMMARY IN DUTCH

Introductie

Kantoorgebouwen zijn iconen van de huidige postindustriële maatschappij. Het stadsbeeld wordt niet langer overheerst door kerken en paleizen, maar door glimmende kantoortorens. Meer dan de helft van de beroepsbevolking in de westerse wereld brengt haar arbeidstijd door achter een bureau in een kantoorgebouw.

Ondanks de belangrijke rol van kantoren in de economie en architectuur, is de kennis van kantoren nog relatief beperkt. De bestaande literatuur schrijft voor hoe kantoorgebouwen ontworpen moeten worden of hoe het kantoor van morgen eruit moet zien. Er is echter weinig bekend over de kantoren van vandaag en waarom die gebouwen zijn zoals ze zijn. Dit onderzoek moet daarin verandering brengen. Het moet inzicht geven in de vormende krachten bij het ontwerp van kantoorgebouwen.

Over het algemeen wordt aangenomen dat de functie van gebouwen de belangrijkste vormende factor is bij het ontwerp van kantoorgebouwen. De achterliggende gedachte is dat huisvesting dient ter ondersteuning van het primaire proces. Vanuit die optiek weerspiegelen kantoren de activiteiten van de gehuisveste organisaties. Met andere woorden: vorm volgt functie.

De logica van de relatie tussen vorm en functie is duidelijk. Goede gebouwen worden gevormd door de functies die ze moeten vervullen. Toch lijkt functie niet zo belangrijk te zijn als vaak wordt aangenomen. Als functie zo belangrijk is, zouden soortgelijke organisaties gehuisvest zijn in soortgelijke kantoren. Dit is echter niet altijd het geval. Dit blijkt duidelijk wanneer er wordt gekeken naar kantoren in verschillende landen.

Op het eerste gezicht lijken kantoorgebouwen in verschillende landen wellicht sterk op elkaar. Op heel de wereld staan ogenschijnlijk identieke anonieme kantoortorens. De massa van deze gebouwen, hun plattegronden en hun werkpleklayouts verschillen echter sterk. Deze verschillen doen zich zelfs voor tussen vestigingen van internationale organisaties, waar in principe overal soortgelijk werk wordt verricht. Klaarblijkelijk zijn locale factoren van grotere invloed op het ontwerp dan organisatorische factoren.

Het doel van dit onderzoek is om te kijken hoe nationale context van invloed is op het ontwerp van kantoorgebouwen. Daarbij moet het een antwoord geven op de vraag waarom kantoren zijn zoals ze zijn. Verder moet dit onderzoek van praktische waarde zijn voor architecten en opdrachtgevers die internationaal opereren. Kennis van buitenlandse ontwerpculturen en hun achtergrond is cruciaal voor het slagen van internationale projecten.

Aanpak

Om de relatie tussen kantoren en nationale context te kunnen bestuderen, richt het onderzoek zich op Groot-Brittannië, Duitsland, Zweden, Italië en Nederland. Deze landen verschillen sterk in hun sociaal-economische context en hun kantoortypologie.

Het startpunt van het onderzoek was een historische analyse van het kantoorgebouw en een korte literatuurstudie van internationale verschillen in Europa. Op basis daarvan is een onderzoeksraamwerk ontwikkeld. Dit raamwerk is als leidraad gebruikt voor het bestuderen van de afzonderlijke landen.

Het onderzoeksraamwerk bestaat uit twee delen (zie tabel). Het eerste deel van het raamwerk betreft de analyse van kantoorgebouwen. Gaande van groot naar klein, wordt onderscheid gemaakt in gebouw-, plattegrond- en werkplekniveau. Het tweede deel betreft de nationale context waarin kantoorgebouwen ontworpen worden. Daarbij wordt specifiek gekeken naar de stedenbouwkundige context, de condities op de kantorenmarkt, arbeidsverhoudingen, cultuur en regelgeving.

Bij het invullen van het raamwerk voor de afzonderlijke landen is gebruik gemaakt van een grote verscheidenheid aan bronnen en onderzoeksinstrumenten: interviews met locale experts, casestudies en literatuuronderzoek. Door het constant vergelijken van de verschillende uitkomsten is getracht van elk land een goed beeld te schetsen.

Bevindingen

De bevindingen van dit onderzoek worden samengevat aan de hand van de drie analyseniveaus: gebouw-, plattegrond- en werkplekniveau.

Tabel Onderzoeksraamwerk

Kantoor

Gebouw
De massa van gebouwen

Plattegrond
De vorm en diepte van plattegronden

Werkplek
De grootte en omslotenheid van werkplekken

Context

Stedenbouwkundige context
De stedelijke structuur en de daaraan gerelateerde stedenbouwkundige planning

Marktcondities
De verhoudingen en huurniveaus op de kantorenmarkt

Arbeidsverhoudingen
De rol van werknemersvertegenwoordigers in organisatorische besluitvorming

Cultuur
Normen en waarden over hiërarchie, privacy, persoonlijke ruimte en interactie

Regelgeving
Wetgeving met betrekking tot arbeidsomstandigheden in kantoren

Gebouw

Op gebouwniveau is de belangrijkste observatie dat geen van de landen in dit onderzoek een hoogbouwtraditie heeft. Dit kan grotendeels verklaard worden door de Europese stedenbouwkundige structuur en de daaraan gerelateerde stedenbouwkundige planning. Relatief lage huurniveaus zijn ook van invloed, maar hun invloed is niet doorslaggevend.

De historische analyse laat zien dat hoogbouw aan het begin van de 20ste eeuw praktisch niet voorkwam in Europa. Pas in de jaren '50 beginnen Europeanen de Amerikaanse kantoortorens te kopiëren. De Europese gebouwen waren echter van een kleinere schaal dan de Amerikaanse prototypen. Vandaag bestaat dit verschil nog steeds.

De afwezigheid van een Europese hoogbouwtraditie kan grotendeels worden toegeschreven aan de stedenbouwkundige context. De meeste Europese steden zijn oud en hebben complexe structuren. In de eerste plaats levert dit praktische problemen op. Gefragmenteerde eigendomsverhoudingen en smalle stratenpatronen zijn een obstakel voor grootschalige ontwikkelingen. Bovendien zijn Europese planners sterk gericht op het behoud van het historische karakter van hun steden.

De invloed van de stedenbouwkundige context wordt benadrukt door drie uitzonderingen: Rotterdam, Frankfurt en Londen. Deze steden hebben relatief veel hoogbouw. In Frankfurt en Rotterdam is dat te verklaren door het feit dat een groot deel van hun oorspronkelijke stedelijke structuur is verwoest tijdens de tweede wereldoorlog. In mindere mate geldt hetzelfde voor Londen.

Londen is bovendien interessant omdat het duidelijk de invloed van een andere factor naar voren brengt, namelijk die van marktcondities. Vanwege Londens rol als wereldstad zijn de marktdruk en huren veel hoger dan in de rest van Europa. Het is dan ook de enige Europese stad waar hoogbouw echt verklaard kan worden door economische noodzaak. Toch is de hoeveelheid hoogbouw gering wanneer er ook wordt gekeken naar steden buiten Europa zoals New York en Hong Kong, waar een soortgelijke marktdruk is. Blijkbaar is in Europa de stedenbouwkundige context belangrijker dan de hoogte van de huren.

Net zo als hoge huren niet automatisch resulteren in hoge gebouwen, resulteren lage huren niet automatisch in lagere gebouwen. In de meeste Europese steden remmen lage huren de ontwikkeling van hoogbouw. In Frankfurt zijn huren echter net zo laag als in de rest van Europa. Dat Frankfurt toch veel hoge gebouwen heeft, heeft te maken met Franfurts wens zich te profileren als een financieel centrum op wereldniveau.

Plattegrond

Op het niveau van plattegronden blijkt een cruciaal verschil te bestaan tussen Groot-Brittannië en Continentaal Europa (Duitsland, Zweden, Italië en Nederland). Britse kantoren hebben over het algemeen diepe en compacte plattegronden. Continentaal Europese kantoren daarentegen hebben doorgaans ondiepe lineaire plattegronden. In Groot-Brittannië kunnen werkplekken 14-16 m van de gevel liggen. In Continentaal Europa liggen de meeste werkplekken direct aan de gevel.

Deze verschillen zijn het gevolg van verschillen in machtsverhoudingen binnen organisaties en op de kantorenmarkt. Wetgeving speelt eveneens een rol, maar heeft geen beslissende invloed.

Het verschil in plattegronddiepte heeft zijn oorsprong in de jaren '60. In die periode beginnen Europese organisaties voor het eerst airconditioning te gebruiken voor het bouwen van diepe kantoren. Eind jaren '70 ligt dit type kantoren echter hevig onder vuur in Continentaal Europa. De kritiek is dat ze te weinig mogelijkheden bieden voor uitzicht, daglicht en natuurlijke ventilatie. In Groot-Brittannië zien opdrachtgevers dit niet zozeer als een probleem. In plaats van terug te keren naar ondiepe plattegronden, geven ze de voorkeur aan de Amerikaanse diepe plattegronden met airconditioning en verhoogde vloeren.

Deze scheiding van wegen kan grotendeels worden verklaard aan de hand van verschillen in arbeidsverhoudingen tussen Groot-Brittannië en de andere landen. In de jaren '70 nam in Continentaal Europa de macht van werknemers sterk toe. Britse werknemers daarentegen hadden, en hebben nog steeds, nauwelijks invloed op de besluitvorming binnen organisaties.

Kantoorgebouwen weerspiegelen dit verschil. De efficiënte en flexibele Britse plattegronden reflecteren de belangen van organisaties en hun aandeelhouders. Omgekeerd, weerspiegelen de Continentaal Europese kantoren de belangen van werknemers. Ze zijn het product van hun behoefte aan daglicht, uitzicht en te openen ramen.

Een hieraan gerelateerde verklaring ligt in de arbeidsomstandighedenwetgeving. Door de sterke positie van werknemers hebben Continentaal Europese landen wetten aangenomen die het belang van daglicht en uitzicht benadrukken. Alleen in Groot-Brittannië is dergelijke wetgeving afwezig. Toch is de invloed van wetgeving op dit gebied beperkt. In geen van de landen wordt de afstand van de werkplek tot de gevel gespecificeerd.

Van grotere invloed zijn de marktcondities waaronder kantoren geproduceerd worden. In Continentaal Europa bouwen organisaties traditioneel hun eigen kantoren. Als eigenaar-gebruikers hoeven zij zich minder te druk te maken om zaken als standaardisatie, efficiëntie of marktconformiteit dan projectontwikkelaars. In Zweden, Duitsland en Nederland wordt deze situatie versterkt door de grotere welvaart. Organisaties kunnen het zich veroorloven toe te geven aan de wensen en behoeften van hun werknemers.

In Groot-Brittannië bestaat een tegenovergestelde situatie. De Britse markt wordt gedomineerd door projectontwikkelaars en beleggers. Van nature zijn deze partijen meer geïnteresseerd in de efficiëntie en flexibiliteit van gebouwen dan in de wensen en behoeften van eindgebruikers. Ook Italië kent een dergelijke situatie. De invloed van de markt is daar echter minder sterk dan in Groot-Brittannië, doordat de Italiaanse markt sterk gefragmenteerd en minder ontwikkeld is.

Werkplek

Op werkplekniveau bestaat een groot verschil in de layout van werkplekken tussen (weer) Groot-Brittannië en de andere landen. Britse kantoren hebben over het algemeen open layouts met grote dichtheden aan werkplekken. Werknemers werken in zogenaamde cubicles, terwijl hun managers gehuisvest zijn in cellen met glazen wanden. In tegenstelling tot de Britse kantoren hebben Continentaal Europese kantoren meer cellulaire en ruimere werkplekken. Een cruciaal effect van dit verschil is de variëteit in het vierkante-metergebruik van werknemers in Europa. Dit verschil varieert van 14,5 m² per werknemer in Londen tot meer dan 27 m² in Amsterdam en Frankfurt.

Deze verschillen hebben sterk te maken met de cultuur van organisaties. Werkplekken weerspiegelen normen en waarden over status, privacy en interactie. De wijze waarop en de mate waarin cultuur terugkomt in het ontwerp is echter sterk afhankelijk van de marktomstandigheden en de inbreng van werknemers in het ontwerpproces.

De oorsprong van de verschillen in werkpleklayout ligt in de jaren '60. Toen ontwikkelde het Duitse Quickbornerteam het 'kantoorlandschap'. Het kantoorlandschap was een compleet open kantoor met daarin een ogenschijnlijk willekeurige plaatsing van werkplekken. In Continentaal Europa werd dit nieuwe type kantoor als snel populair. Tien jaar later werd het concept echter even snel verworpen als het was verwelkomd. De oorzaak ligt in het feit dat in die periode, zoals eerder gezegd, werknemers meer te vertellen kregen binnen organisaties. Hun voornaamste klachten betroffen de beperkte privacy en persoonlijke controle over de werkomgeving.

In Groot-Brittannië is het kantoorlandschap nooit zo populair geweest als in Continentaal Europa. Onder invloed van Amerika transformeerden Britse organisaties het idealistische concept in een geavanceerde versie van het Tayloristische open kantoor uit de jaren '20. De 'organische' ordening van werkplekken werd vervangen door een efficiënte orthogonale opstelling. De mening van werknemers speelde nauwelijks een rol in deze verandering.

Gedeeltelijk kunnen deze verschillen verklaard worden door marktcondities. Door de lage kosten van kantoorruimte kunnen Continentaal Europese organisaties relatief kwistig met hun ruimte omgaan. In Duitsland, Zweden en Nederland past het hoge vierkante meter gebruik bovendien in het totaalbeeld van een hoge levensstandaard en uitstekende secondaire arbeidsvoorwaarden. Britse organisaties moeten meer economisch zijn in het gebruik van kantoorruimte. In Londen drukken de hoge huren op het huisvestingsbudget.

Wetgeving lijkt hierbij eveneens een rol te spelen. In Groot-Brittannië is de wetgeving voor de oppervlakte van werkplekken minimaal. In Nederland en Duitsland daarentegen geeft de wetgeving expliciet aan dat werkplekken minimaal 7 m² respectievelijk 8 m² groot moeten zijn. Toch moet ook hier de invloed van wetgeving niet overschat worden. In Zweden en Italië is het vierkante-metergebruik relatief hoog, terwijl de wetgeving op dit gebied net zo minimaal is als in Groot-Brittannië.

Belangrijker dan wetgeving is de cultuur van een land. Het eerste cultuuraspect dat van invloed is op het ontwerp van werkplekken is hiërarchie. In de Zweedse egalitaire cultuur krijgt iedere werknemer zijn eigen kamer. In de meer hiërarchische Britse cultuur worden zulke kamerkantoren beschouwd als privileges voor de hogere echelons. In Nederland, Duitsland en Italië wordt hiërarchie tot uiting gebracht in de grootte van kamers en het aantal personen per kamer.

Een tweede aspect van cultuur dat van invloed is op het ontwerp van de werkplek, is de mate van individualisme. De populariteit van kamerkantoren in Duitsland kan goed worden verklaard uit het belang dat men daar hecht aan privacy en persoonlijke ruimte. Op dezelfde wijze kunnen Zweedse kantoren gezien worden als een reflectie van Zwedens 'sociaal individualisme'. Het individuele aspect wordt weerspiegeld in individuele kantoorruimten, het sociale aspect in gemeenschappelijke ruimten. Het is dan ook niet verwonderlijk dat het combikantoor, een combinatie van individuele en gemeenschappelijke ruimten, een Zweedse uitvinding is.

Alleen in Groot-Brittannië is de relatie tussen individualisme en werkpleklayouts niet duidelijk. Volgens de cultuurstudies zijn Britten zeer individualistisch. Toch zijn de Britten gehuisvest in *open plans* waarin ze een minimum aan privacy en territorium hebben. Zoals eerder uitgelegd is, heeft deze tegenstelling te maken met kosten en hiërarchie. Net zo belangrijk is het feit dat Britse werknemers relatief weinig inbreng hebben in het ontwerp en bij het opstellen van het programma van eisen.

Een derde aspect van cultuur dat van invloed is op het ontwerp van de werkplek, is de wijze waarop mensen met elkaar omgaan. De meeste landen in deze studie zijn zogenaamde neutrale culturen. Dit houdt in dat mensen op een vrij gereserveerde manier met elkaar omgaan. Italië is een uitzondering. Italië heeft een zogenaamde affectieve cultuur. Dit houdt in dat de interactie tussen mensen relatief emotioneel is. Dit verschil kan verklaren waarom werkplekinnovaties zoals telewerken in Italië minder populair zijn dan in de rest van Europa. De Italiaanse expressieve manier van interactie is waarschijnlijk moeilijker te vervangen door e-mail of video conferencing dan meer 'neutrale' manieren van interactie. Een belangrijkere verklaring ligt echter toch in het hiërarchische karakter van de Italiaanse cultuur. Door de sterke hiërarchie zijn Italiaanse managers minder snel geneigd hun werknemers te laten werken 'waar en wanneer ze maar willen' dan Noordelijke managers.

Conclusies

Op basis van de bevindingen kan geconcludeerd worden dat er een sterke relatie bestaat tussen het ontwerp van kantoorgebouwen en hun nationale context. De toepassing en interpretatie van kantoorconcepten worden sterk beïnvloed door de stedenbouwkundige context, marktcondities, arbeidsverhoudingen, cultuur en wetgeving in een land. Dergelijke verschillen maken duidelijk dat het kantoorgebouw niet alleen een vertaling is van functionele behoeften of technologische mogelijkheden, maar ook een reflectie van de sociale, economische en culturele context waarin het ontwerp tot stand komt.

 Rest de vraag hoe het komt dat nationale context een dergelijke sterke invloed op het ontwerp kan hebben. Zoals in de introductie gesteld is, wordt over het algemeen functie als de meest bepalende factor gezien bij het ontwerp van kantoorgebouwen. Kantoren zijn in de eerste plaats productiefactoren. Daarom zou het ontwerp moeten voortvloeien uit het primaire proces van de gebruiker. Het is echter duidelijk dat soortgelijke organisaties gehuisvest zijn in sterk verschillende gebouwen.

Grofweg zijn er drie redenen waarom nationale context een grotere invloed kan hebben op het ontwerp dan de functionele eisen van een organisatie. Ten eerste zijn functionele eisen niet zo duidelijk of objectief als wordt voorgesteld. De term efficiëntie bijvoorbeeld heeft een andere betekenis in Amsterdam dan in Londen waar huren twee keer zo hoog zijn. Hetzelfde geldt voor andere ogenschijnlijk objectieve eisen ten aanzien van flexibiliteit, kosten en gebruiksvriendelijkheid.

De tweede reden is dat het relatieve belang van functionele eisen per land kan verschillen. Gebouwen moeten altijd voldoen aan diverse eisen. Welke eisen het belangrijkst zijn, hangt af van de machtsverhoudingen tussen de betrokken partijen (werknemers, vakbonden, management, projectontwikkelaar, etc.). Het is bijvoorbeeld duidelijk dat in een markt die traditioneel beheerst wordt door projectontwikkelaars, de wensen van eindgebruikers een geringere rol spelen dan in een markt waarin eigenaar-gebruikers overheersen.

De derde en belangrijkste reden waarom nationale context een grote impact kan hebben op het ontwerp van kantoren is, dat de relatie tussen functie en vorm niet zo sterk is als vaak wordt gedacht. In handboeken voor het ontwerpen van kantoren wordt vaak gesteld dat elke type activiteit of functie vraagt om zijn eigen type ruimte. De internationale verschillen laten echter duidelijk zien dat soortgelijke activiteiten kunnen plaatsvinden in sterk verschillende gebouwen. Deze observatie ondersteunt het idee dat voor elk ontwerpprobleem een diversiteit aan oplossingen is. Welke oplossing wordt gekozen hangt sterk af van de nationale context.

In de loop van de tijd hebben de sociale, culturele en economische omstandigheden ontwerpoplossingen gecreëerd die algemeen geaccepteerd zijn. Deze oplossingen zijn geïnstitutionaliseerd in standaardprogramma's van eisen, ontwerphandleidingen en zelfs regelgeving. De oplossingen maken eveneens deel uit van de 'impliciete' kennis van ontwerpers en opdrachtgevers, gevormd door wat ze gewend zijn en om zich heen zien. Deze oplossingen zijn niet noodzakelijkerwijs de juiste, maar in de loop der tijd zijn ze onderdeel geworden van een nationale ontwerpcultuur die zeer moeilijk te veranderen is.

Implicaties voor de praktijk

De beschreven internationale verschillen maken duidelijk dat opdrachtgevers en ontwerpers rekening moeten houden met de nationale context.

Een praktisch probleem zijn verschillen in wetgeving. Het is bijvoorbeeld niet mogelijk een Brits werkplektype van 6 m² toe te passen in Nederland of Duitsland. In deze landen moet een werkplek minimaal 7 m² respectievelijk 8 m² groot zijn.

Meer fundamentele problemen hebben te maken met het verwachtingspatroon van werknemers. Het oordeel van werknemers over hun kantoor wordt sterk bepaald door wat ze gewend zijn. Zeker in Duitsland, Zweden en Nederland kan het toepassen van buitenlandse concepten op bezwaren stuiten omdat het vaak een achteruitgang in ruimte en privacy betekent. Dit kan problemen geven omdat Continentaal Europese werknemers relatief veel zeggenschap hebben.

De praktische boodschap voor internationaal opererende architecten en opdrachtgevers is, dat ze zich bewust moeten zijn van de context waarin ze opereren. Ze moeten zich ervan bewust zijn dat de fysieke eigenschappen van kantoren verbonden zijn met dieper gelegen en moeilijk te veranderen karakteristieken van een land, zoals stedelijke structuren, marktomstandigheden, arbeidsverhoudingen, cultuur en wetgeving. Dit betekent echter niet ze klakkeloos de locale ontwerpcultuur hoeven over te nemen. Juist het ter discussie stellen van de impliciete veronderstellingen in een ontwerp leidt tot een aanscherping en verbetering van de bouwopgave.

ACKNOWLEDGEMENTS

University is said to be an ivory tower. Researchers are believed to work in isolation behind their computers. No such thing is true. Especially when you are writing a book like this, you work together with a great number of people. I want to thank all of them for their contribution.

First of all, I would like to thank Hans de Jonge and Geert Dewulf. After my graduation, Hans offered me the opportunity to start this project. He has always been confident that I could bring it to a good end. I have a great respect for the way he has created a successful and dynamic research group. Geert has been my supervisor on a day-to-day basis. In his own humorous (Belgian?) way, he has guided my staggering steps into science. I want to thank him for his ever critical, but always constructive comments on my work.

I would also like to thank all the people I have interviewed during my research (see List of interviewees). Without their inside knowledge of local markets and cultures I could not have written this book. In particular I would like to thank Adrian Leaman, who has been visiting professor at our department. He taught me a lot about science and British humour. The same holds for Frank Duffy. It has been a great experience to work with him during his visits to Delft.

I owe a lot to my colleagues at the Department of Real Estate and Project Management. In particular, I am grateful to my room-mates Peter Krumm and Paul 'Dog' Vos. Both have always been loyal, cheerful companions (thanks mates). I want to thank Gert-Joost Peek and Theo van der Voort for their valuable comments on my work. I am also very grateful to my Norwegian colleagues Siri Blakstad and Mathias Harang: takk så mye! I want to thank Jeroen Gerrissen for helping me to become a 'healthy' computer worker.

Finally, I am very grateful to my friends from my home town, Dordrecht, (including Esther) for accepting the fact that I have spent too many nights behind my computer instead of being with them in the pub. In particular I would like to thank Fred Lohman, with whom I have worked too many weekends in Delft. In addition, I owe a lot to my friends from Iria (including Geert): Σασ ευχαριστῶ πολυ!

Last but not least I want to thank my parents, Henk and Lotti van Meel, for their unconditional support (it's a cliché, but in this case 100% true) and for reading every letter of my work. The same holds for my brother, Jeroen van Meel. Without his help I would not have been able to finish this work (thanks, big brother).